Politics of Recuperation

This book opens a fascinating window into the meaning of personal and collective resilience in Europe today. The crisis came, it ravaged a whole generation, but did it stop it? No! This is a book about rebuilding after the hurricane of financial oppression. But it is also a reflexion about the limits and margins of contemporary democracy. The Portuguese response to externally enforced 'austerity' is surely a prime illustration of the creative forces that lurk within Europe's internal margins.

JOÃO DE PINA CABRAL, *University of Kent, UK*

This book offers hope and resources to dwell in a world that seems to be heading to a permanent state of crisis. Here, recuperation is proposed as a theoretical figure that unveils how modest activities of mending, engagement and care entail a power of reparation of the political sphere. These insights offer us an alternative narrative to the one condemning people in Southern Europe to the role of passive subjects of dispossessions. Despite the dramatic period, the diverse ethnographic accounts describe how citizen inventiveness have coped with the collapse of their social worlds.

ADOLFO ESTALELLA, *Madrid Complutense University, Spain*

Transcending the analytical divide between European city contexts and those located in the Global South, the different contributions in this timely book offer a richly detailed tapestry and in-depth exploration of the 'resonant micropolitics' of crisis and its immediate aftermaths across Portugal. In doing so, this broad range of scholars open up anthropological vistas of recuperation and repair, thereby enlarging our understanding of the possibilities for regenerating *living together* in today's broken worlds.

FILIP DE BOECK, *University of Leuven, Belgium*

I really like the ethnographic sensibility that the contributors bring to the material and the way the collection approaches socially embedded practices of repair and recuperation. Since the experience of living under difficult conditions is so widespread in the world today, the themes of recuperation and repair make this book useful for a broad range of scholars who are interested in how people manage their lives under constrained circumstances. At the same time, the grounded ethnographic approach makes the book essential reading for anyone working in the field of Portugal studies.

MATT ROSEN, *Ohio University, USA*

LONDON SCHOOL OF ECONOMICS MONOGRAPHS ON SOCIAL ANTHROPOLOGY

Managing Editor: Laura Bear

The Monographs on Social Anthropology were established in 1940 and aim to publish results of modern anthropological research of primary interest to specialists. The continuation of the series was made possible by a grant-in-aid from the Wenner-Gren Foundation for Anthropological Research, and more recently by a further grant from the Governors of the London School of Economics and Political Science. Income from sales is returned to a revolving fund to assist further publications. The Monographs are under the direction of an Editorial Board associated with the Department of Anthropology of the London School of Economics and Political Science.

Politics of Recuperation

Repair and Recovery in Post-Crisis Portugal

EDITED BY FRANCISCO MARTÍNEZ

BLOOMSBURY ACADEMIC
LONDON • NEW YORK • OXFORD • NEW DELHI • SYDNEY

BLOOMSBURY ACADEMIC
Bloomsbury Publishing Plc
50 Bedford Square, London, WC1B 3DP, UK
1385 Broadway, New York, NY 10018, USA

BLOOMSBURY, BLOOMSBURY ACADEMIC and the Diana logo are trademarks of Bloomsbury Publishing Plc

First published in Great Britain 2020

Copyright © Francisco Martínez and Contributors, 2020

Francisco Martínez has asserted his right under the Copyright, Designs and Patents Act, 1988, to be identified as Editor of this work.

This work is published subject to a Creative Commons Attribution Non-commercial No Derivatives Licence. You may share this work for non-commercial purposes only, provided you give attribution to the copyright holder and the publisher.

Cover design: Ben Anslow
Photography by Nuno Marques, Barcelos, 2016

All rights reserved. No part of this publication may be reproduced or transmitted in any form or by any means, electronic or mechanical, including photocopying, recording, or any information storage or retrieval system, without prior permission in writing from the publishers.

Bloomsbury Publishing Plc does not have any control over, or responsibility for, any third-party websites referred to or in this book. All internet addresses given in this book were correct at the time of going to press. The author and publisher regret any inconvenience caused if addresses have changed or sites have ceased to exist, but can accept no responsibility for any such changes.

A catalogue record for this book is available from the British Library.

A catalog record for this book is available from the Library of Congress.

ISBN: HB: 978-1-3501-3305-1
ePDF: 978-1-3501-3306-8
eBook: 978-1-3501-3307-5

Typeset by RefineCatch Limited, Bungay, Suffolk
Printed and bound in Great Britain

To find out more about our authors and books visit www.bloomsbury.com and sign up for our newsletters.

Contents

List of Figures and Table ix
Notes on Contributors xi

Introduction: The material culture of recuperation 1
Francisco Martínez

1 Recuperative modes of action: Reciprocity, dependence and resistance to austerity policies in Rural Portugal 37
Ema Pires

2 'Beautiful people eat ugly fruit': Ugliness and the cracks in the system 55
André Nóvoa

3 If buildings could talk: Makeshift urbanity on the outskirts of Lisbon 75
Giacomo Pozzi

4 Geographies of public art and urban regeneration in Lisbon 101
Chiara Pussetti and Vitor Barros

5 The compost of recuperation: Fabricating social ties in the interstices 119
Marcos Farias Ferreira and Francisco Martínez

6 The place of recuperation: Limits and challenges of urban recovery in post-austerity Portugal 139
Luís Mendes and André Carmo

7 Secondary agents of recuperation within the Hindu community in Lisbon 155
Inês Lourenço

8 Recuperation and vice versa in Portuguese folk art 171
Maria Manuela Restivo and Luciano Moreira with photos by Nuno Marques

9 Recuperative dances: Reconnecting through *kizomba* in a crisis context 181
Livia Jiménez Sedano

Conclusion: Repair as repopulating the devastated desert of our political and social imaginations 207
Tomás Sánchez Criado

Afterword: Micro-spaces of resilience and resistance – coping with the multiple crises in Portugal 221
Isabel David

Index 227

Figures and Table

Figures

Intro.1	Feira da Ladra. Francisco Martínez, 2014.	9
Intro.2	The material culture of recuperation. Francisco Martínez, 2014.	9
Inro.3	Manel, capture of a video. Francisco Martínez, 2014.	11
Intro.4	José García. Francisco Martínez, 2016.	12
Intro.5	Entrance to the repair house Boa Ideia. Francisco Martínez, 2016.	13
Intro.6	Antonio García. Francisco Martínez, 2016.	14
Intro.7	Antonio García in his workshop. Francisco Martínez, 2016.	15
Intro.8	Joaquim. Francisco Martínez, 2016.	17
Intro.9	Joaquim's repair workshop. Francisco Martínez, 2016.	17
Intro.10	Antonio's working tools. Francisco Martínez, 2016.	20
1.1	Shrinking Sweet Breads on the move: Bread-seller David, mobile worker for Padaria Zé do Moinho, Gáfete, Crato. Ema Pires.	44
2.1	A member choosing their basket at Parede, delivery point near Lisbon. André Nóvoa.	57
2.2	An example of a mixed basket. André Nóvoa.	58
2.3	Ugly Fruit's van, used for picking up the fruit and relocating it to the delivery points. André Nóvoa.	61
2.4	An 'ugly' apple – too small, according to normal standards. André Nóvoa.	69
4.1	Political graffiti in Mouraria. EBANOCollective.	102
4.2–4.3	Ghetto 6. EBANOCollective.	106

LIST OF FIGURES AND TABLE

4.4–4.5	*Sin Street*. EBANOCollective.	110–11
4.6–4.7	*Sophia & Florbela*. EBANOCollective.	113
5.1–5.10	Fabrica de Alternativas of Algés. Marcos Farias Ferreira.	122, 124, 127, 131
7.1	Current Shiva Temple building, Santo António dos Cavaleiros. Inês Lourenço.	158
7.2	*Vrat katha* book carried to Portugal in 1993 by Bina Achoca from Salamanga, Mozambique. Inês Lourenço.	166
8.1	Adão de Castro Almeida's workshop and his masks in Lazarim. Nuno Marques.	174
8.2	Daniel Silva, a young apprentice, making a mask in Lazarim. Nuno Marques.	174
8.3	Lazarim masks at the Iberian Mask Interpretative Centre (CIMI). Nuno Marques.	175
8.4	Carnival of Lazarim, where the masks are publicly used. Nuno Marques.	175
8.5	Querubim Rocha's workshop in Bisalhães. Nuno Marques.	176
8.6	Querubim Rocha's workshop in Bisalhães. Nuno Marques.	176
8.7	Júlia and António Ramalho's workspace in Barcelos. Nuno Marques.	178
8.8	Júlia Côta's work and dining space in Barcelos. Nuno Marques.	178
9.1	*Kizomba* dancing at *Ondeando disco*, Almada, 2014. Livia Jiménez Sedano.	189
Conc.1	Feira da Ladra. Tomás Sánchez Criado, 2018.	208

Table

1.1	Employees in Crato and Monte da Pedra, by place of residence and activity, as of National Census, 2011.	39

Notes on Contributors

Vitor Barros has conducted research, published and managed projects in the fields of migration, health, cultural heritage and public art. A photographer and cinematographer, Vitor is also a founding member of EBANOCollective, designing and producing ethnography-based cultural events, projects and installations. He currently holds a Science and Technology Management Fellowship in the H2020 project ROCK at the Institute of Social Sciences, University of Lisbon, Portugal.

André Carmo is Assistant Professor of Geography at the School of Sciences and Technology, University of Évora, and Associate Researcher at the Centre of Geographical Studies, University of Lisbon. His research interests include issues related to urban studies, social and cultural geographies as well as geographical thinking and geographical education.

Tomás Sánchez Criado is Senior Researcher at the Chair of Urban Anthropology, Department of European Ethnology, Humboldt-University of Berlin, Germany. In the last years, he has been developing an anthropological engagement with of inclusive design and urbanism, paying special attention to do-it-yourself (DIY), free culture and open-design activist initiatives. He has co-edited the volumen, *Experimental Collaborations: Ethnography through Fieldwork Devices* (Berghahn, 2018), and co-convenes the Collaboratory for Ethnographic Experimentation network.

Isabel David is Assistant Professor at the Institute of Social and Political Sciences, and a Research Fellow at the Centre for Public Administration and Public Policies at the Orient Institute at Universidade de Lisboa (University of Lisbon), Portugal. She is a member of the editorial board of *Research and Policy on Turkey* and co-editor of "Culture, Society and Political Economy in Turkey" book series with Peter Lang.

Marcos Farias Ferreira has a PhD in Social Sciences from the University of Lisbon, Portugal, and an MSc Economics in International Politics from Aberystwyth University, UK. He is Assistant Professor at the School of Social and Political Sciences, University of Lisbon.

Livia Jiménez Sedano is Lecturer in the Department of Social Anthropology at the National Distance Education University (UNED), Madrid, Spain. As Postdoctoral Fellow during 2013–18, she worked on her project, 'Dancing Ethnicities in a Transnational Social World'. She has done fieldwork in dancing contexts in Madrid and Lisbon, including African discos, dance schools, dancing associations and public celebrations. Also, she has worked on several research projects about issues related to ethnicity, children, gender, immigration and social exclusion, including the coordination of an Observatory of exclusion processes in urban areas of South Spain.

Inês Lourenço has a PhD in Anthropology (ISCTE/IUL, University Institute of Lisbon), and works at Centre for Research in Anthropology of the University Institute of Lisbon. Her research focuses on the Hindu/Indian diaspora in Portugal, dealing with topics such as consumption and heritage among communities of Indian origin in Portugal.

Francisco Martínez is Lecturer at the School of Museum Studies, University of Leicester, UK. In 2018, he was awarded the Early Career Prize of the European Association of Social Anthropologists. Francisco has been a postdoctoral researcher at the University of Helsinki and at Aalto University, Finland. Currently, he is also the editor of the new Berghahn book series, 'Politics of Repair', and a member of the editorial boards of the *Anthropological Journal of European Cultures* and *HAU: Journal of Ethnographic Theory*. Francisco has edited several books, including *Repair, Brokenness, Breakthrough* (Berghahn, 2019), and is the author of *Remains of the Soviet Past in Estonia* (UCL Press, 2018). He has also curated a number of exhibitions, including

Objects of Attention (Estonian Museum of Applied Art & Design, Tallinn, 2019).

Luís Mendes is Lecturer at the Institute of Geography and Spatial Planning of the Universidade de Lisboa (IGOT-UL), Lisbon, Portugal, and, since 2003, has been Researcher at the Centre for Geographical Studies of the Universidade de Lisboa (CEG/UL), focusing on the study of gentrification and urban regeneration. Luís also won the Amilcar Patrício Award 2005 from the Portuguese Association of Geographers.

Luciano Moreira has an MSc in Psychology from the University of Porto (UP), Portugal. He is a PhD candidate in Digital Media at the University of Porto, with a Foundation for Science and Technology (FCT) grant. Luciano also teaches at the Faculty of Engineering of the University of Porto. His areas of interest include representations and practices around digital media and science, as well as scientific research methods. He is a member of the alhures studio, dedicated to the promotion and problematisation of ethnographic heritage.

André Nóvoa is a team-member of ERC Colour of Labour project, based at the Institute of Social Sciences, University of Lisboa. André has a PhD in geography from Royal Holloway, University of London (2014), and was previously trained as a historian (BA) and an anthropologist (MA). He has been conducting research within the mobility studies field. He was a researcher at Northeastern University, Boston, USA, developing work on public mobility policies, and was assistant editor of HAU: Journal of Ethnographic Theory, based at the School of Oriental and African Studies (SOAS), University of London, UK.

Ema Pires is Assistant Professor at the School of Social Sciences, University of Évora, Portugal. Having done prolonged anthropological fieldwork in Portugal and West Malaysia, her research interests deal with social appropriations of built form, tourism, heritagisation processes and the politics of identity and space in Asian and European contexts. She is a researcher at the Institute of Contemporary History, Lisbon, Portugal, and a visiting scholar in National University of Brasília, Brazil.

Giacomo Pozzi is Post-Doctoral Fellow in Cultural Anthropology at the Department of Human Sciences 'Riccardo Massa', University of Milano-Bicocca, Milan, Italy. In 2018, he gained his PhD in Cultural and Social Anthropology at the University of Milano-Bicocca in co-tutorship with the ISCTE-Instituto Universitário de Lisboa, Lisbon, Portugal. He is editor of the international journal *Antropologia*, and author of different articles focusing on resettlement policies in Lisbon in Portugal and evictions in Milan in Italy.

Chiara Pussetti has a PhD in Cultural Anthropology from the University of Turin (2003), Italy, and has published extensively on anthropology of body and emotions, medical anthropology, visual anthropology and migration studies. Chiara is presently Postdoctoral Researcher of the Institute of Social Sciences of the University of Lisbon (SFRH/BPD/95998/2013), Portugal, and is a member of the EBANOCollective. From 2007, as anthropologist, artist and curator, she has coordinated a dozen projects. Currently, she coordinates as Principal Investigator the project ROCK (Horizon 2020 Innovative Action SC5-21 Cultural Heritage as a Driver for Sustainable Growth, 2017–19). She is also Principal Investigator of the Project 'EXCEL: The Pursuit of Excellence: Biotechnologies, Enhancement and Body Capital in Portugal' (PTDC/SOC-ANT/30572/2017).

Maria Manuela Restivo studied Anthropology at the University of Coimbra and Museology at the University of Porto, Portugal. She is currently a PhD candidate at the University of Porto with an FCT grant. She researches and curates exhibitions focused mainly on the popular and vernacular arts, but also on the intersection between artistic practices and the social and human sciences. She is the founder of alhures studio, dedicated to the promotion and problematisation of ethnographic heritage.

Introduction

The material culture of recuperation

Francisco Martínez

This anthology is a way of beginning a conversation about the experience of recuperation and how societies make themselves durable. The research assesses recuperation both analytically and conceptually by looking into the local notions of recovery and taking this term as a theoretical operator, applied to ethnographic data. A key aim of these theoretically informed ethnographies is to contribute to anthropological and political debates by paying attention to practices of reconstitution, resilience and value allocation and how they can produce an unpredictable patchwork of services, provisions, networks or even infrastructures (Simone, 2004). In this light, we intend to find more adequate analytical tools for understanding the stakes of recuperation and its infrastructural qualities (self-maintenance, self-building, self-repair), as suggestive acts of resilience and also as potent political possibilities. The collection looks at recuperative practices as having significance beyond the causes and context of crisis and austerity policies precisely because recuperation is a multidimensional and reflexive process and not simply an outcome of vulnerability. Indeed, the term 'recuperation' has a double meaning – an active transitive sense, loosely synonymous with *reviving* something, but also an intransitive sense, which does not have a direct object and refers to regaining a former state or condition.

Any conversation about how societies rebuild themselves calls for empirical detail and the examination of both the embodied experience of reception and the materiality of recuperation (Guyer, 2017). The different essays present multiple registers of social sustainability that move from transformative actions to the material and the organisational, rendering the actual suffering of people understandable, knowable and actionable (Tironi and Rodríguez-Giralt, 2017). Also, the concept of recuperation is used in reference to a process of recovery, even if this experience might lack a clear design and exceed original intentions, or else agents do not necessarily share the same set of goals. The concept of recuperation is, therefore, proposed to contribute to creating new relational qualities and alternative constellations of meaning, reframing how we think about the consequences of financial crisis and instantiating politics in different spaces and registers.

The studies demonstrate, however, that recuperation is not always an active choice; at the same time, neither is it a direct outcome of austerity policies, nor a choice made with a specific end in mind. In this light, we prefer to speak of a crisis-induced new regime of patchwork provision in relation to the changing role of the state, the punitive nature of austerity measures (David, 2018), and a new, economised governmentality (Collier, 2011). By reflecting on the limits and potentialities of the concept of 'recuperation', this book highlights a number of coping mechanisms within the context of the multiple crises experienced in Portugal over the last decade, while also compensating for an important theoretical lack in prior research by testing the applicability of the concept of recuperation and refining its comparative potential. Hence, the emphasis is no longer on the management of abundance, but on how to enhance social sustainability and epistemic repair through the reuse of disqualified resources.

Originally, we wanted to include the word 'austerity' in the title of this volume, but this term has been rather co-opted by current political and economic interpretations, making use of its positive meanings (i.e. self-discipline, frugality) to euphemistically hide poverty, privatisation and a shrinking state.[1] Hence, we opted for the term 'post-crisis', thinking of how the effects of calling something a 'crisis' go beyond a specific historic period and geography (as happened with other 'posts', such as 'postcolonialism' and 'postsocialism'). As Janet Roitman points out (2013), crisis forecloses our range of thought about what is taking place and how to respond to it, making it difficult to think outside of a non-crisis narration. Still, in its 'post' condition, crisis remains as a lived reality and classificatory label, having consequences in the varied domains of people's everyday lives and shaping social change because of the cognitive order that crisis generates (Shevchenko, 2009).

Concerned with continuity and change in a post-crisis context, ours is also an exercise of conceptual repair, when the available theory has little to say about how the crisis experience has affected the subsistence of certain practices, values and meanings. As Susana Narotzky and Niko Besnier (2014) observe, crises reconfigure values and sentiments regarding moral obligations, forcing change in traditional modes of livelihood and, in some cases, entailing unexpected processes of deskilling and dematerialisation of links, too. In Portugal, the financial crisis that brought with it a devaluation of people as individuals has paradoxically generated a revaluation of past things and of people as a collective, producing, in turn, a new regime of thingness, alternative modes of living and more sustainable ways of inhabiting a place. Accordingly, our study of recuperations stresses the importance of reconstituting initiatives in a relational and political sense, while it also entails the systemic questioning of human security and social participation.

A crisis entails multiple processes of disqualification, breaking chains of cultural transmission, linkages and synergies. These are processes beyond individual control which provoke the vanishing of in-between tools of social organisation, a general mood of pessimism about the future and, in many cases, a self-reflexive fatigue.[1] In such a context, the contributions examine both urban and rural lives in conversation with anthropological scholarship on kinship, religion, dance, housing, food, heritage and the engagement with humble discarded objects, in forms ranging from straightforward ethnographic reporting to more self-reflexive and visual essays. The authors examine how people are involved in reparative efforts through different registers of engagement, asking what kind of social ties are generated, in what ways recuperation is related to practices of political openings, and which processes of social sustainability are reactivated in austerity regimes. Specifically, recuperation is studied here in terms of reciprocity (Pires), place-making (Pozzi), negotiating intersections (Farias Ferreira and Martínez), urban commonality (Mendes and Carmo), reuse (Nóvoa), resources of hope (Pussetti and Barros), reconnection of different bodies and histories (Jiménez Sedano), generational interweaving through the transmission of legacies (Lourenço) and emancipation through discourses of cultural heritage (Restivo, Moreira and Marques).

Furthermore, they show that language is not sufficient as a resource for thinking about recuperation – we also need to study public arrangements and bodily engagements with other people and with things, paying attention to the affects involved, too. The research appears as deeply contemporary, as it has accompanied actual social changes in a proactive way while also demonstrating a transversal appeal. The focus on recuperation allows us to consider the sociocultural resources that people rely upon in the margins of what has been traditionally assumed to be the themes of politics, economics and infrastructure; namely, reciprocity, revaluation of past things and ecologies of care. But how is recuperation made political? And, how do ordinary things come to matter politically? Any recuperation is a performed valuation and valorisation, meant to affirm a collective idea through daily engagement with practices of care and through rituals that embody cultural continuity. Also, recuperation can be understood as a state of awareness, one which indicates not simply a mode of engaging with problems but also a way of 'feeling together' about them (Estalella and Corsín Jiménez, 2016). For us, therefore, it has been important to connect seemingly individual acts of repair and recovery to macro-level politics and crises, theorising also about how recuperation can be part of what constitutes societies and public policy by enabling vulnerable segments of society to advance their interest.

Recuperation publics and micropolitics

Recuperation is presented as an alternative type of focal point for gazing at politics and updating and upgrading the conditions that sustain social relationships. We put the focus on how recuperations help recover the living bygone skills and connections and coagulate an assemblage of everyday actions that make possible what the state cannot do. Even if they are not necessarily politically conscious actions as such (at least in traditional terms), recuperative practices can act as drivers of assemblage and transformation, having consequences for how we think about social relations across the political landscape. In the anthology, we propose examining recuperative practices as a suturing intersection, one which connects people and has significance as public feelings, engendering revaluations, positive effects and forms of reciprocity that might endure longer than the crisis experience. Also, this collection reconsiders conceptualisations generated through or derived from people's unequal experience of crises. It treats politics as a struggle to define the world in terms of what is important, meaningful and valuable, paying particular attention to the manner in which certain ways of seeing, acting, speaking and being in public are legitimised and shifted (Rancière, 2006). In this light, we can talk of micropolitics, referring to the relationship between formal politics (i.e. winning elections, passing legislation and so forth) and the set of cultural practices that prime subjects to act in particular ways, turning everyday life into a site of politicised self-making. But recuperation is also a form of infrapolitics, lying beneath the threshold of politics, passing politically unnoticed, addressing social problems via politically disqualified means (Scott, 1990; Marche, 2012).

The anthology approaches recuperation from the perspective of relational bonds, which operate in a society's interstices and become intermingled political, economic and cultural modes of valuation. The politics of recuperation are grounded in lives and practical experiences, enacting a rupture from current politics, not in the name of the political, but rather oriented toward the relationship between people (Moreiras, 2010). We can notice emerging alternatives at the edge of the market economy that exemplify this idea, such as kid-to-kid shops selling second-hand stuff for children, or the 'garbage coin' promoted by the neighbourhood authorities of Campolide, a district in the heart of Lisbon. Specifically, this initiative is meant to prompt recycling within the local neighbourhood and boost the local economy by giving garbage bills (equivalent to €2 per kilo of recycled rubbish) to be spent exclusively in local shops (pharmacies, cafés, restaurants, hairdressers, optics, grocery stores, etc.).

In the process of recovery, people return to the tools and relations they already know and reconstruct them according to the current situation (Strathern, 2014). Recuperation concerns, however, shifting the 'orders of worth' (Boltanski and Thévenot, 2006), and refers to a rather selective process, one 'which can include many heterogeneous elements, chosen by a variety of actors' (Guyer, 2017: 82). Recuperative actions propose to go back, in order to go forward, reassess from where we came and what has been cast aside, reconsidering why and for whom things matter. As such, these actions play a central role in the large-scale patterns of social change, linking recuperative experiences with the possibility of enacting political transformation through them.

The concept of recuperation is thus relevant to understanding the negotiations of economic hardships, the reinforcement of ties within communities, and endeavours to suture the cracks in the system (De Boeck and Baloji, 2016), helping to enable spaces for doing things otherwise by combining a recuperation of one's self and one's world. An example of this is the repair café Regueirão dos Anjos (RDA), a cultural garage that first appeared in Lisbon in 2009 and went hand in hand with the economic hardships faced by Portugal. This is a free meeting place for people to repair items and recuperate together, generating empathy for an amateurish approach to fixing. Everyone is welcome to participate within a cultural programme that includes ping-pong, yoga, film sessions, music concerts, workshops on contemporary art, cooking and making musical instruments, as well as parties and discussions about pataphysics, transhumanism and feminist theory. Probably, the most popular activities at the RDA are the cycling workshop and the cooperative kitchen, which offers a daily menu and special dinners. Another example of the relevance of the theme of this volume is that it has been chosen for the 2017 Bienal de Arte Contemporânea de Coimbra ('Curar e Reparar', *Healing and Repairing*), as explained by the organisers in the following quote:

> Healing refers to care, to the possibility of practising the kind of care that restores; it necessarily implies a condition of fragility,

one's own or another's. There is disease implicit in the word heal, but mostly restorative practice, the exercise of restoration, or the restitution of an organism to its rightful condition.

Repairing, on the other hand, has myriad possible connotations; in Portuguese, it means to mend, improve and recompose. It also means to use, compensate and restore all economical procedures which imply a certain conservation.

However, the Portuguese word for repair has yet another set of meanings which imply paying attention, watching with acuity, observing, focusing; ultimately, the availability towards the world which arises from the chance to focus on what is before us, slowing down time and not imposing our views.

The organisers of the event draw not on the assumption that art itself heals, but that it can help identify healing processes. Accordingly, they have included the artist Kader Attia within the programme, who is known for making works of art that incarnate repairing the effects of colonialism. Attia (2014) insists that the act of repair has to be acknowledged as ethical and political, addressing damage, occultation, loss or weakness. In similar terms, the local art group EBANOCollective has traced care-seeking itineraries in Lisbon related to migration and marginality, treating public spaces and bodies as vehicles of communication that can also have a repairing effect (Pussetti, 2013). In her new project, which runs parallel to the work being done by the EBANOCollective, anthropologist Chiara Pussetti (2019) continues with the study of body repairs and wounded storytellers. Specifically, she puts the ethnographic focus on marginalised individuals who undergo cosmetic interventions as a way of minimising those physical signs that mark them as migrants. As Pussetti explains, the self-optimisation aspiration of body manipulation is meant to facilitate social inclusion and professional opportunities, reproducing colonial, racial hierarchies in turn, as well as assuming personal responsibility via the shape of their body or the colour of their skin.

In short, each crisis creates the necessity for a recuperation, but not the know-how. In this book, we discuss the reshaping of value in a vegan co-op initiative, refurbishment projects correlated to the maintenance of traditions and intergenerational ties, the daily making-do of precariously positioned individuals, the reframing of *kizomba* dancing, and the creative preservation of heritage as sustained activities offering solace, all of which contribute to creating transcendental narratives of reconstitution through the remaking of relationships – drawing attention to the political dimension of recuperation.

A repairer's tale

Repair helps to contextualise things in people's lives and to understand the way objects become loaded with particular significance. In an ethnographic study of practices of object maintenance in England, Nicky Gregson, Alan Metcalfe and Louise Crewe (2009) observed that repair activities can rekindle an owner's relationship with an item. Specifically, they examined the restorative acts surrounding three objects (a dining-room table, a TV cabinet and a leather suite), noting how such acts tell about specific conjunctures of people, materials and activities within households. The researchers concluded that repair practices are a way through which social relations are performed and worked out. This practice acquires special relevance in a context of crisis that breaks the continuity between the different senses and definitions of life. The reparative efforts then become a declaration of necessity and a condition of existence for those involved, thereby producing particular infrastructures and environments of everyday life (Oroza, 2009; Larkin, 2016). In repairing, you can mobilise resources and provide the conditions for constituting an alternative order. We can thus talk of a crafting existence, of building ourselves back up. Repairing then becomes a para-infrastructure of everyday living, a response that does not run against, counter to or after a crisis, but rather through and beside it, generating a particular material culture and infrastructural forms (see the Feira da Ladra, Figures Intro.1–2).

In critical times, repair work appears as a key competence that sustains what is possible and feasible. It provides a stabilising network that secures an epistemological and practical continuation, in many cases a complex one. For instance, in my fieldwork in Estonia, repair appeared as a temporal practice related to the modalities of experiencing and assessing the Soviet past (Martínez, 2018b). In Georgia, I noticed

INTRODUCTION: THE MATERIAL CULTURE OF RECUPERATION 9

FIGURE INTRO.1 *Feira da Ladra. Francisco Martínez, 2014.*

FIGURE INTRO.2 *The material culture of recuperation. Francisco Martínez, 2014.*

how brokenness has a number of specific political uses and the way local efforts at patching things up do not produce durable forms of repair (Martínez and Agu, 2016; Martínez 2019), and in some cases, repairing is just a way of keeping people busy (Ssorin-Chaikov, 2003). Also, in Berlin, the recovery of analogue photo booths could be understood as a form of place-making and an answer to social acceleration (Martínez, 2018a). In all of these cases, the analysis of repair practices helped me to understand people's ideas about their society, drawing attention to the links between the social and the subjective.

In Lisbon, I visited the city's repair *houses*, where the owners have been fixing shoes, clothes, furniture, cutlery and watches throughout different generations; also, I met with 'rolling' repairers, such as knife-grinders, who sharpen dull knives and scissors on a bike or motorcycle. By observing the way people rescue past objects and extend the life of things, local values and orders of worth came to the forefront. They demonstrate, for instance, that kinship relationships are key to understanding mending activities in Portugal. Hence, I invite you to follow me on a tour around Lisbon in order to encounter many of the issues that are addressed in this book.

In the streets of the Telheiras neighbourhood, I met Manel, one of these rolling knife-grinders, who walks dozens of kilometres each day with a sharpening device on a bike (Figure Intro.3). I discovered the presence of the *amolador* in the neighbourhood because of the particular knife-grinder's tune, already recorded in Galicia by Alan Lomax sixty years ago and recovered by Miles Davis in the track 'The Pan Piper' from the album *Sketches from Spain*. During our meeting, Manel stated that the number of clients had increased since the financial crisis had started. However, he was quite reluctant to talk about his professional activity, as evidenced in my field notes:

> When I try to talk to him, Manel reacts evasively and tries to avoid communicating. The more I insist, the more suspicious he is of me. We cross a courtyard, turn left at the corner, enter into a new *rua*, and only after several minutes of persistence does Manel give up and answer a few of my questions: he has been doing this job since he was a child and says that he walks 12 hours per day, seven days a week (he looked at me as if I were a Martian when I mentioned the word 'holiday' and 'taxes'). Manel shares that he

survives mostly by grinding knives for restaurants at €1.5 each (€2.5 for the scissors, and €5 for the umbrellas). I am not familiar with some of the words he uses, which sound archaic to me, as for instance *arrebitar*, which means to rivet the holes of a pan; or *esmoril*, the emery grinder. Before Manel left, he asked for '€5 for the talking.'

Field notes, 19 April 2015[2]

When discussing how austerity is materialised in biographies, my informants noted that the 'life expectancy' of items within Portuguese society was changing, explaining that this is not only due to economic shortage, but also because of a moral reappraisal and a reactivated sense of affection.[3] In this sense, repair practices do not directly correlate with inefficiency and shortage, but rather with social sustainability and moral sentiments. Such a correlation of value and values made me think about the connection between repair and emerging forms of political collectivity, ideas that gave impulse to this book. In the city, I visited different repair shops, especially those of knife-grinders. In Rua Acácio de Paiva 10, I found the repair house 'Good Idea' (Loja da Boa Ideia), managed by José García and María Míguez (Figures Intro.4–5). As they stated, since the crisis, people have been repairing more items:

FIGURE INTRO.3 *Manel, captured on video. Francisco Martínez, 2014.*

There was the time when people got rid of everything. Since 2008, we have around 25 per cent more demand, which does not imply a corresponding benefit, as we work more but cannot raise our prices . . . the explanation being that people bring in more products for repair of a lower quality, and that means more work for me and less benefit . . . But that does not mean that only poor people or marginals come here for repairs. Also, those driving Mercedes visit the shop . . . A new phenomenon is that people went to their lumber and tried to find and recover old stuff there, repurposing things that were stored in warehouses, sometimes from their parents or grandparents. For instance, a few days ago a person came here with an umbrella, saying that it had been bought in 1951 by her grandparents when they went to Paris on a honeymoon. So, at times there is also an affective side to the demands we receive. Another example is this umbrella from the eighteenth century; a relic that used to belong to a bishop. Or these clippers. They represent a challenge for me, as these kinds of repair jobs require meticulous research.

Interview, 6 November 2016

FIGURE INTRO.4 *José García. Francisco Martínez, 2016.*

INTRODUCTION: THE MATERIAL CULTURE OF RECUPERATION 13

FIGURE INTRO.5 *Entrance to the repair house Boa Ideia. Francisco Martínez, 2016.*

For José, the work of rolling knife-grinders is of a lower quality since they have worse tools and are new to the business, not learning the job from their parents as he did. As José puts it, family ties are important for passing down knowledge, and the *métier* of the knife-grinder is first and foremost characterised by being transmitted from generation to generation. Traditionally, repair workshops, or *casas*, have been places of autonomy and self-sufficient work, which also had a strong pedagogical dimension (see Sennett, 2008). However, José laments the fact that repair work seems to have no future, since it is barely profitable nowadays:

> We are bound to go extinct. It is sad, because it means that skills will be lost, and in our case, part of the identity of my family as well . . . For us, this is a business, of course, but we don't do it just because of the money. As these have traditionally been family businesses, even home-shops, our relationship with the clients is very close, based on solidarity and confidence, being an active

part of the life of the neighbourhood. Still, there are lonely people who come here just to talk.

Interview, 6 November 2016

José and María have been married for forty-two years. He has worked as a knife-grinder for fifty-three years (since 1964). 'The secret of this profession is patience,' confesses José, who remarks that the quality of things in Europe after the Second World War is the best he has ever encountered. His brother, Antonio García, has another knife-grinding shop at Avenida Almirante Reis 173 (Figures Intro.6–7). For Antonio, it is surprising that people come to his repair shop to have things fixed up, especially items with little value, such as umbrellas, and they pay €10 for the service, when they can buy a new one produced in China for €7. Decisions to rehabilitate or repair things are also informed via a retrospective exercise, and not simply by the cost of time, money or effort required. In this sense, their work encompasses much more than a technique of material repair. Mending practices might well work as 'anchoring rituals' (Shevchenko,

FIGURE INTRO.6 *Antonio García. Francisco Martínez, 2016.*

FIGURE INTRO.7 *Antonio García in his workshop. Francisco Martínez, 2016.*

2009) and a form of 'preservation without permission' (Brand, 2012), one involving people repair, too (Henke, 2000).

One of the things Antonio likes about his job is that clients often provide personal details to make him understand the *value* of the object, approaching personal possessions as implicit life stories (Hoskins, 1998). Repairability is not simply limited by the materiality of the device or by economic calculations, but also by emotional notions of value, intergenerational ties and projections towards the future. In a way, Antonio's statement confirms what Arjun Appadurai asserted decades ago (1986) – that value is a circumstantial assessment made by subjects in a given context based on economic efficiency, but also on cultural representations, symbolic boundaries, personal emotions and moral discourses. Value, rather than being intrinsic to goods, is ingrained within social relations and shaped by how people perceive and use things (Gregson and Crewe, 2003). Nonetheless, it would be overly simplistic to assume that repair work is what results once people sort things out, placing too much emphasis and responsibility on individuals and ignoring the socioeconomic aspects of the practice (i.e. a lack of choice). In this light, it is convenient to echo the question initially posed by Zsuzsa Gille (2007: 21): When a product is thrown away after three months of use, is the consideration of waste or zero value decided by the manufacturer or the consumer?

> Most of my clients are elderly people. Young people do not come into this shop . . . In this epoch of accelerated rhythm, my profession has no place. Nowadays, nobody has the patience to learn how to repair things . . . and at times, it is no longer possible to find the right material.
>
> Interview with ANTONIO, 6 November 2016

In less than a year from now, Antonio will close down the shop, as his children will not continue the business. 'They do not like it,' Antonio confides. He does not recommend it either; it is unhealthy. Household and kinship have been crucial to repair work in Portugal, appearing just as much socially significant as mechanisation and the division of labour. When his father died, Antonio left school and joined the family business. In the beginning, he helped out, before then working as a mobile *amolador* for seven years, grinding knives while travelling around Lisbon on a bike. Finally, he took over Casa García (García's repair shop).

I wanted to visit other repair shops, such as the one on Rua dos Anjos, however neighbours told me it had closed down a couple of years ago when the *amolador* had died and nobody wanted to take over the shop. On the internet, I found that there were only five repair shops left in Lisbon, whereas a few decades ago there had been twenty-one (at least one per neighbourhood). Finally, I managed to find another repair shop that was open, albeit one that restores old furniture. 'Since 1962, it comes in old and goes out new,' says the advertising on the shop Laire e Nunes (Avenida Elias García, 155). It feels like stepping back in time there. Joaquim, the owner, is proud to repair things without using any electronic devices, yet he feels as if he is living out of sync with contemporary society (Figures Intro.8–9). 'This is like a museum . . . the best time for me and the shop has already passed,' he sadly notes (interview, 7 November 2016).

INTRODUCTION: THE MATERIAL CULTURE OF RECUPERATION 17

FIGURE INTRO.8 *Joaquim. Francisco Martínez, 2016.*

FIGURE INTRO.9 *Joaquim's repair shop. Francisco Martínez, 2016.*

Why is repair work so nostalgic today?

Repair is a form of knowledge in motion, being transmitted between people as well as learned through objects. In the field, I learnt that the engagement of people with their possessions gives them an opportunity to anchor their personal biographies and narratives (Marcoux, 2001). Further, repair work can be considered simultaneously an act of exteriorisation and of interiorisation (Tisseron, 1999), combining collective and personal resonance (Martínez, 2017), and recovering thoughts and ideas that remained unacknowledged for a long time by rescuing neglected objects (Grossman, 2015). Nonetheless, it is a paradox that academic interest in, and celebration of, repair work have increased over the last decade (Laviolette, 2006; Graham and Thrift, 2007; Gregson, Metcalfe and Crewe, 2009; Dant, 2009; DeSilvey, Bond and Ryan, 2013; König, 2013; Denis and Pontille, 2013; Jackson, 2014; Anstett and Ortar, 2015; Houston, 2017; Martínez and Laviolette, 2019), including the offering of a tax rebate in Sweden for citizens who repair rather than replace goods. Yet, even still, traditional repair shops are about to disappear because of a lack of generational replacement and cultural protection. Indeed, professionals engaged in repair work are not situated on the receiving end of globalisation. Despite a demand for repair work, professionals hardly make profits.

Even if domestic mending skills seem to be in decline because of the availability of cheap, mass-produced products (König, 2013), repair work still plays an important social role – the main purpose of repair interventions might be to set other things in motion, not simply to fix something, but also the relations and associations around it or the society at large. However, no one fixes the repairers – they also require maintenance and recuperative care. Repair cafés such as RDA, despite their good will, do not engage enough with the transmission of old professional knowledge and intergenerational reconnection. Why are the repair professions languishing at the margins of recuperation? And why are discourses about the disappearance of this profession so bitter in contrast to the vanishing of other jobs, such as postal-service mail sorters, sewing-machine operators or news vendors? What makes repair workers different from others is that they engage in practices of endurance, creating a web of connections implicated in the experience of community and shaping identities that reflect back onto the community.

In this time of 'accelerated archaeology' (Stallabrass, 1996), it is increasingly hard to establish genealogies and a sense of continuity. With the vanishing of repair shops such as the ones owned by Antonio, Joaquim and José and Maria, particular skills that cannot be transmitted digitally will also disappear, as will traditional forms of negotiating value through the process of fixing. Overall, efforts that cannot be quantified seem to be under threat. In different blogs, people refer to repair shops as a 'relic' in danger of vanishing, which they might eventually visit just for nostalgic reasons (*matar as saudades*), or to see the *amolador*, who is always willing to chat (*dar dois dedos de conversa*) while working. In some cases, bloggers make a claim for changing the way we see and value our repair workers, elevating this type of under-appreciated labour to a higher social status, for instance as an element of urban kindness, sustaining neighbourhood relations. Also, repair workers respond to the demands for tradition and community as if they were artisans. The value of their work, despite having a price, is rather indeterminate, and their home-based economies intertwine labour with kin-like ties. In these cases, repair work and recuperation go hand in hand, since the work and skills of such workers help restore value to objects and resources that have been wasted or neglected, demonstrating care and reconnecting personal biographies with public materiality.

The hands of recuperation

As this research shows, repair has consequences for how we think for social relations through the transmissions occurring between material objects and social actors, multiplying the forms of political engagement. This gesture is intrinsically relational, grounded in specific contexts and structures, generating positive affects, contributing to how we organise our everyday experiences, and helping to recover identities, histories, ideas and relations. Repair is thus not a minor but a major knowledge. It involves a range of situated imaginations and reflections, being practiced as a process of exchange between the material qualities of the thing and the problem-solving capacity of the repairer – manifested in the ability to transform or fix objects through tools and skills (Figure Intro.10; and Sennett, 2008). Reparative knowing is always built upon material practices and honed skills, which produce a pragmatic way of looking at the world, a temporal perspective and an awareness of what one has and what one needs. Reparative practices have thus to do with the body, material perception and sensual experiences within the world, as well as to choices about what to attend to and how. Likewise, knowledge and value emerge with repair, revealing the dynamic relationship between praxis and material sensitivity, and between the subject and its society.

Repair is part of a wider process of social learning and cultural transmission, as well as a mechanism of adaptation to changing circumstances. Sociomaterial disruptions are pervasive; people react to them through the rework of things, extending the life of relations while answering to failure and breakdown. And yet, in the practice of repair, it is hard to establish a clear distinction between beginnings and endings. It is, rather, a vernacular ordering in flux, organising,

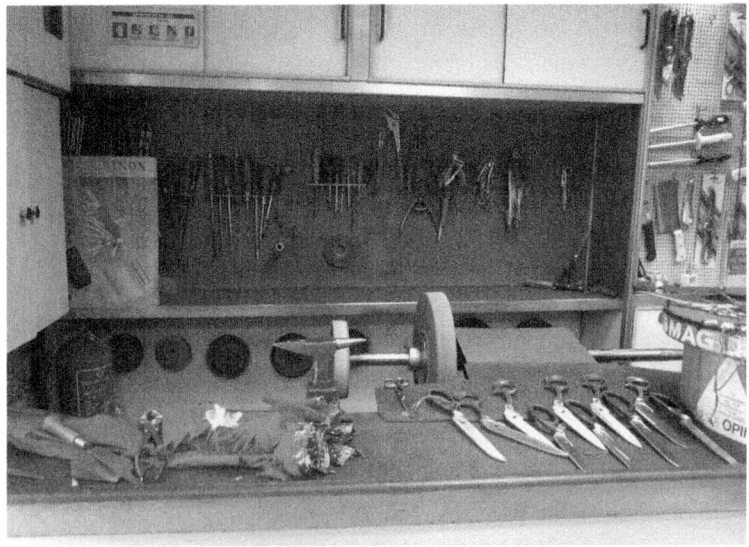

FIGURE INTRO.10 *Antonio's working tools. Francisco Martínez, 2016.*

reformulating, experimenting, juxtaposing and overall extending the notion of care towards things (Puig de la Bellacasa, 2011). We repair because things break but also because we are affected by their breakage and we care about them (Spelman, 2002). We can talk of 'affective transmissions' occurring at the intersections of subjectivity, materialities and representations (Stewart, 2007). As Yael Navaro-Yashin explains (2012), 'affect' is a relational phenomenon generated in our encounter with objects and built forms, one which can be passed on.

Indeed, to repair is, first of all, a form of passing through and carrying out. But how could we describe the connection between repair and the transmission of knowledge and culture? In her study of apprenticeship with coppersmith masters of Michoacán, Mexico, Michelle Feder-Nadoff (2019) foregrounds that skills can be practiced but not acquired, as it is only emergent in-relation-to, found in the action itself. A skill is thus an intangible quality gained, paradoxically, through tangible experiences, gradual accumulation and multifarious interactions (Ingold, 2013; Tonkinwise, 2008). We can argue that repairing activates varied interactions, connections and material dynamics – with different people and things. Also, that these gestures are part of wider processes of recuperation and cultural transmission.

Even if the unfolding of repair remains invisible or illegible, and often goes without saying, this practice adds a human dimension to the public sphere. Repair is a secular form of informal transmission of knowledge, emotions and practices. Moreover, cultural transmission is not always where we think it is; it also happens in ordinary places and activities. Knowledge is passed down generationally in the repair workshops, disseminating positive affects within the neighbourhood, safeguarding cultural items and establishing continuity in the social order.

From repair to recuperation

Crises are situations in which repairing and recuperative care coincide with the whole human project. Repair work engages with signs of use and the traces of what is left behind, helping to connect generations and ensure stability in the material world. Fixing is thus a sign of material trust and an enactment of respect, being aware that others have been here before us and will come after us, too. Both terms – repair and recuperation – refer to a process that starts by going back, assessing something from the past and favouring the continuation of an active life practice; this is manifested in the Latinate prefix 're'. However, while repair work is an organic part of everyday life that makes the cycle of iteration begin once again, recuperation correlates with recovering the self through our relations to others and the world surrounding us, referring to a holistic process of reconstitution and renewal (Guyer, 2017).

As Maria Puig de la Bellacasa notes (2011), we can all feel a sense of concern, but 'to care' directs us to a notion of material doing. In this respect, repair work can be considered a form of material participation – a quotidian practice of public-making that entails the engagement of people with the sociomaterial conditions of their everyday lives (Marres, 2012). Material possessions are part of both social and personal recuperation, despite their transience. In this light, recuperation appears as not simply being extended to things or to other people, but rather co-produced with them. Also, the act of throwing away demonstrates a relationship between things and human security and highlights how recuperation entails leaving the storage mode of participation to enter into the mobilisation mode (Cherrier and Ponner, 2010; Guyer, 2017).

This study argues that the struggle with the effects of crisis is also a struggle over meanings and values. Through this process, the recovery of past things and skills appears as one of the symbolic instruments used in negotiating changes, but also as a personal quest for comprehension. Repair work is remarkably widespread and attached to concrete problems. In a time of crisis and of mass production, destruction and abandonment, the impetus to repair is worthy of admiration, to perpetuate the life of things a little longer, to be concerned and pay attention to the scarcity of resources, to reuse and to sustainability. Indeed, the act of repairing can be considered a barometer of social interactions, a contact zone between different powers, one located at the intersection that links the state to society (Gerasimova and Chuikina, 2009). This practice reflects back on the everyday forms of state formation from below, embedding micro-scale realities into the system. Also, repair work helps sustain the commonality of urban dwelling, and its disappearance might hinder the experience of recuperation. These practices foster increases in the self-worth of individuals which has also an echo in collective political agency.

But let us not romanticise repair work, since this practice can also be arranged as a series of 'small mutinies' (Berglund, 2019), or with little regard for nuanced moral and economic implications. Repair also has a flip side that runs counter to the healing process – namely, the potentially unhealthy aspects of hoarding and holding onto broken things. Accordingly, throwing things away might in some cases be felt as liberating and generative of positive feelings, too. Likewise, all repairs are vulnerable to larger forces and need to be maintained (or defended). Furthermore, the very acts of resilience suggested by repair work could be re-appropriated by the system under question as a means of political stability. Hence, repair work can be simply restorative or rather transformative, static or dynamic, defensive or generative. This project is mostly concerned with the generative aspects of repair work – with how one set of values and relations displaces another.

As we see in the cases of Manel, José, María, Antonio and Joaquim, fixing can be a part of different new beginnings but also of decay (see also, Leavitt Cohn, 2016). In other words, there can be repair work without recuperation; things can be fixed and refurbished without social sustainability or without generating further political changes. A relevant question, accordingly, is whether there can be recuperation without repair work. This practice not only produces relationships and narratives that can be systemically co-opted, but repair work itself is intrinsically experimental and done through multiple interactions that draw upon different traditions – hence, repairing is not always easy to homogenise or incorporate.

A right to recuperation

Could broken instruments and wasted things work as an allegory for contemporary Portuguese society – being in a state of disrepair and in need of recuperation? As sociologist Antonio Barreto has pointed out (2002), Portuguese society has been organised for many decades through asymmetries, polarisation and dyssynchrony, all of which point to a durable state of exception. This time, afflicted by mounting fiscal imbalances, the Portuguese government was forced to ask for a bailout from the European Central Bank (ECB), European Commission (EC) and the International Monetary Fund (IMF), the so-called 'Troika', which ushered in a series of austerity measures with deep fiscal cuts in all sectors of an already fragile welfare state. The imperative of debt repayment came to dominate policy, drawing citizens into its mechanisms and rhythms of repayment (Bear, 2015), and thereby implying a fall from the previous heights of wealth, security, sanity, career progress and retirement expectations that have characterised welfare societies (Knight, 2015).

In certain respects, such as how welfare infrastructures were being undone and state-provided services being commodified, with care being increasingly accessed through personal connections, with exacerbated social inequality that determines life chances and with radical changes in the forms of material provision, we could draw parallels between Portugal and other European societies, not only of the south but also of the east (Bockman and Eyal, 2002; Stenning and Hörschelmann, 2008; Martínez, 2014). One of the outcomes of austerity policies is an increasing blurring of the lines between state and society. Another outcome has been to extend ambiguity and shame into new domains (de Abreu, 2018). To a great extent, these effects are produced through crisis narratives, which establish the conditions for specific sociotechnical interventions and histories of failure. Crises cause contradictions to become visible everywhere in society (Koselleck, 2006), implying not only suffering but also assessment as well as a productive epistemological challenge (Roitman, 2013).

In Portugal, people became poorer and fewer in number, while the population increased in age and enjoyed fewer social rights than a decade ago.[4] Precarity also generates mental borders: in the case of Portugal, losing one's standard of living and facing a reduction in citizenship rights and failed expectations affect people's bodies and minds along with the encompassing environment, too. A crisis condition implies a change in public moods, with consequences in political participation and the severing of some bonds. It is felt as a lack of self-worth and as a sense of being robbed of a future, affecting self-understanding and community life (Pina Cabral, 2018).[5]

Austerity policies are characterised by multiple devaluations and a simultaneous hyper-presence and hyper-absence of the state. Hence, we can consider the study of recuperating efforts as a vantage point for understanding how structures of meaning and the integrity of societies have been eroded by the effects of the financial crisis and austerity measures; however, it is also important to be aware of the fact that recuperation does not necessarily connote a well-designed type of doing and that both the motivations and range of effects attributed to recuperation might also predate or occur outside the austerity regime. For instance, communal dinners, urban gardens, anti-food-waste initiatives, street markets, time banks or neighbourhood associations have all previously existed and their reinvigoration might not simply be due to ideological motivations or responding to the suffering brought on by austerity measures; they may also be tied to wider social and ecological interests, or conversely, to factors that are not economic and political in their origin. This does not mean, however, that we ignore civic attempts to mobilise citizens and reclaim the public space on behalf of a radical conception of politics (Harper and Afonso, 2016; Farias Ferreira and Terrenas, 2017), but rather point out that recuperation is practiced at the intersection of three dimensions: crisis (intensifying precarious conditions while at the same time doing away with processes of revaluation and assessment), people (in a state of repair as a collective) and the state (characterised by neoliberal retreat and austerity policies).

Broken, yet not defeated

The volume gathers together insights into recuperating activities with special attention paid to the social resources mobilised in these processes, how people organise themselves by relying on traditional cultures and infrastructures, and the new idioms of social participation derived from the crisis experience. As services crack and gaps appear in the relations between state and society, alternative modalities of relating to each other and to our surroundings come to the fore.

These might include anticipatory elements that assemble the future in the present while being based on traditional uses that are resuscitated, reconfigured and updated (Rakopoulos, 2016) through the application of principles of self-organisation, repair and reciprocity (Dalakoglou, 2016). Hence, the relevance of asking what kind of relationships have been activated through the crisis experience and the context of uncertainty, how and by whom, and what types of knowledge have either emerged or been acquired during the process of recuperation.

Crises are inscribed in material forms and also in voids between the state and society. In these cracks, we find the elements of perseverance, resilience and recovery, all of which are under study in this volume. Within the unsettling configurations of crises, suturing activities emerge to patch over the gaps and cracks in the system following very mixed intentions (Ortner, 1995). In turn, everyday micropowers generate new types of performing care, novel ways of thinking about individual and collective selves, and diverse notions of the public itself and its association with political life (Thrift, 2005; Gray, 2016; Theodossopoulos, 2016). As exposed by the selected contributions herein, practices of recuperation help people to develop alternative life projects and to mobilise others and the resources for it, which together constitute social transformations and resonant micropolitics. The revalorisation and recuperation of things and people are themselves complex and constitutive aspects of a new kind of social dynamics, providing alternatives to crisis logics and ordering. We can see it, for instance, in André Nóvoa's chapter about the politics of ugliness and how the classifications we use can be counterproductive for recuperation. The author presents a study of the new Ugly Fruit cooperative, which sells non-standardised fruits and veggies at low cost, thereby preventing the discarding of food and offering new sources of revenue to local producers.

Another key point of this volume is to show how any recuperative action is intimately integrated within the existing regimes of knowledge and relatedness, i.e. socially embedded and culturally informed, finding nuances rooted within local history, material culture and relations of kinship, but also existing within spaces of economic normativity and power hierarchies. By examining everyday struggles in a rural area, Ema Pires demonstrates how recuperation has intersected with the structural forms of vulnerability in the life trajectories of three women. The author pays attention to the socioeconomic constraints and a sense of brokenness generated by the financial crisis, arguing that, in rural areas, recuperation is grounded in everyday strategies and metaphors of reciprocity. Furthermore, Pires shows that clientelism might not only be voluntary, but also the best option for mitigating precarity and a sense of uncertainty, in which people need to make use of every resource they have at their disposal to resolve their problems. As pointed out by Čarna Brković in the case of Bosnia and Herzegovina (2017), favours are a systemic response to social realities, not simply related to the crisis experience but also to the changing aspects of the neoliberal state.

Crises usually entail a personal relocation on the map of social relations. By studying the values that can be retrieved from engaging with the past legacies of the Hindu community in Lisbon as a counter-crisis effort, Inês Lourenço's essay contributes to developing an anthropology of cultural and social retrieval as part of a worldview of conforming relations, aesthetics, affects and internal pacification. Ethnographically, she examines the retrieval of generational bonds through the material culture of the community and points out how building and care are correlated and serve to reinvigorate relations between the private and the public. In her chapter, Livia Jiménez Sedano focuses on the *kizomba* phenomenon and how recuperation becomes embodied, changing the way people interpret and experience everyday life. As the author foregrounds, the dance floor helped people, first to alleviate stress and uncertainty, and second to repair postcolonial relations through a specific form of dance attunement and togetherness.

Recuperation builds on the craftsmanship of everyday life and unfolds within multiple interactions and spatial practices. This is demonstrated, for instance, by Giacomo Pozzi, Chiara Pussetti and Vitor Barros, who present recuperation as a mode of 'dwelling' that is generative of other processes that transform collective narratives and entail direct sociospatial implications, such as new imaginaries of the economic and the political. Through qualitative experiences, such as sharing, exchanging, displaying, discussing or handmaking, skills of crafting and repairing can shape political questions, especially in terms of public participation and the production of values. In recovering value, people generate and extend 'intersubjective spacetimes' (Munn, 1986), transforming the quality of social relations. It is thus not surprising that repair practices are taking on a new centrality, becoming a matter of concern for both policy and anthropological research, as noted by Isabel David in her contribution.

Luís Mendes, André Carmo, Marcos Farias Ferreira and Francisco Martínez locate the political and its pragmatics by taking Lisbon as the main locus for both the praxis of and contention with neoliberal policies. They reconsider different neighbourhood initiatives as agents of recuperative activism that work compost-like, preparing the emergent and making politics perceptible. Their study of how forms of community action fill in the gaps left by the state's abandonment foreground, first of all, the need to enlarge the number and quality of spaces that constitute the political. Also, it shows how recuperating efforts are vested in existing value systems and grounded structures, and that the very relations recovered in a time of crisis can be commodified or transformed into goods or services to be consumed. Hence, it is relevant to put the emphasis on the ways in which repair practices contribute to assembling networks and platforms for different forms of life, care, reciprocity and political anticipation instead of becoming another element of social engineering. In this vein, Maria Restivo, Luciano Moreira and Nuno Marques expose how official strategies of recuperation might serve to deepen marginalisation instead of resolve it.

Similarly, Tomás Sánchez Criado puts an emphasis on the social aspects of recuperation to criticise moralising stereotypes about economic irresponsibility and fiscal incontinence and suggestions of penitence and constraint in Southern European societies (Raudon and Shore, 2018). Drawing on Bonaventura de Sousa Santos' distinction between welfare state and welfare society (1995), Criado argues for the need to acknowledge the relevance of do-it-yourself (DIY) ecologies of support in the form of systems of mutual aid based on kinship and neighbourhood ties. Such a coagulation of caring modes constitutes forms of social infrastructure in a non-commoditised manner and with a logic of reciprocity, raising the question of the public of recuperation. Indeed, Portugal has traditionally relied on households as a profuse network mobilised to restore or maintain social order.

In Portugal, ecologies of knowledge transmission and support have often reproduced a household-centred logic, situating houses as prominent institutions for solidifying processes of continuity and inclusion (Lévi-Strauss, 1982). However, this might be changing and different forms of relatedness and degrees of *house-ness* are appearing in post-crisis Portuguese society. As the reader will see with a wide range of ethnographic cases, this change in relatedness reflects both a disintegration of social bonds and the attempt to repair them. In short, we can conclude by arguing that recuperation does not appear *de novo*, but rather builds on the legacy of previous social forms, welfare systems, infrastructural connections and historical entanglements. In this process, recuperation generates positive affects and expands our conception of what constitutes the political, thus broadening the considerations for the social and public.[6]

Notes

1 The word 'austerity' derives from an ancient Greek term describing a 'dryness of the tongue'. In Latin, *austeritatem* refers to self-discipline, rigour and gravity, while in Old French, *austerité* meant harshness and cruelty.

2 Words quoted in this introduction are from the author's ethnographic research, which was done with the consent of the subject and an awareness that these words could end up in print.

3 Overall, recycling increased by 9 per cent in Portugal in 2014, together with upcycling practices – which give new life to an item considered obsolete; see: http://expresso.sapo.pt/ponto-verde-aumenta-reciclagem-em-9=f909224 (accessed 3 August 2019).

4 About 200,000 people left the country between 2011 and 2013, more because of the austerity measures than because of the crisis itself. Another important piece of data shows that the number of medical diagnoses and exams fell by 26.5 per cent (due to the worsening of the service in public hospitals). There also appeared to have been a decline in health and a 50 per cent decrease in highway traffic as well as in the speed of the cars driving on those highways. Likewise, we can notice the effects of the financial crisis and austerity policies in terms of an increase in the number of homeless people in Lisbon

(over 2,000 according to official statistics); the shutting-off of the water supply service to 32,000 families in the country between 2011 and 2013 for not paying the corresponding invoice; and how the middle class has now been downgraded to an 'embarrassed poor' and precariats, thereby changing the traditional understanding of urban inequality and establishing a new multidimensionality of poverty. Furthermore, austerity measures have provoked an extensive demand for social kitchens.

5 Family and kinship relations at large remain as the hidden hand that sustains today's working poor in Southern Europe. Yet, as pointed out by João Pina Cabral, the working poor know that 'they rely on their families and local communities to survive, but they do not know how they will contribute towards ensuring the future sustainability of those very same families and local communities' (2018: 387).

6 The contributions in this volume were presented in Lisbon (27 April 2018) at an international seminar supported by the research project 'H2020 ROCK Regeneration and Optimisation of Cultural Heritage in Creative and Knowledge Cities' (Societal Challenge 5), grant agreement NUMBER – 730280; see: www.rockproject.eu (accessed 3 August 2019).

References

Alexander, C. and J. Reno (2012) 'Introduction', in C. Alexander and J. Reno (eds), *Economies of Recycling*, London: Zed, pp. 1–33.

Anstett, É. and N. Ortar (eds) (2015) *La deuxième vie des objets. Recyclage et récupération dans les sociétés contemporaines*, Paris: Pétra.

Appadurai, A. (ed.) (1986) *The Social Life of Things*, Cambridge: Cambridge University Press.

Attia, K. (2014) *The Repair from Occident to Extra-Occidental Cultures*, Berlin: Green Box.

Barreto, A. (2002) *O Tempo de Incerteza*, Lisbon: Relógio d'Água.

Bear, L. (2015) *Navigating Austerity: Currents of Debt Along a South Asian River*, Palo Alto, CA: Stanford University Press.

Berglund, E. (2019) 'Small mutinies in the comfortable slot: The new environmentalism as repair', in F. Martínez and P. Laviolette (eds), *Repair, Brokenness, Breakthrough: Ethnographic Responses*, Oxford: Berghahn, pp. 228–44.

Bockman, J. and G. Eyal (2002) 'Eastern Europe as a laboratory for economic knowledge: The transnational roots of neoliberalism', *American Journal of Sociology*, 108 (2): 310–52.

Boltanski, L. and L. Thévenot (2006) *On Justification: The Economies of Worth*, Princeton, NJ: Princeton University Press.

Brand, S. (2012) 'Preservation without permission: The Paris urban eXperiment', *Introduction to the Long Now Seminar*, Seminars about Long-Term Thinking, 13 November.

Brković, Č. (2017) *Managing Ambiguity: How Clientelism, Citizenship, and Power Shape Personhood in Bosnia and Herzegovina*, Oxford: Berghahn.

Cherrier, H. and T. Ponnor (2010) 'A study of hoarding behavior and attachment to material possessions', *Qualitative Market Research: An International Journal*, 13 (1): 8–23.

Collier, S. J. (2011) *Post-Soviet Social: Neoliberalism, Social Modernity, Biopolitics*, Princeton, NJ: Princeton University Press.

Dalakoglou, D. (2016) 'Infrastructural gap: Commons, state and anthropology', *City*, 20 (6): 822–31.

Dant, T. (2009) *The Work of Repair: Gesture, Emotion and Sensual Knowledge*, Lancaster: Lancaster University Press.

David, I. (ed.) (2018) *Crisis, Austerity, and Transformation: How Disciplinary Neoliberalism is Changing Portugal*, Lanham, MD: Lexington.

De Abreu, M. J. A. (2018) 'May day supermarket: Crisis, impasse, medium', *Critical Inquiry*, 44 (4): 745–65.

De Boeck, F. and S. Baloji (2016) *Suturing the City. Living Together in Congo's Urban Worlds*, London: Autograph.

Denis, J. and D. Pontille (2013) 'Material ordering and the care of things', *CSI Papers*, 34: 1–25.

DeSilvey, C., S. Bond and J. R. Ryan (2013) *Visible Mending*, Axminster: Uniform.

Estalella, A. and Corsín Jiménez, A. (2016) 'Matters of sense: Preoccupation in Madrid's popular assemblies movement', in A. Blok and I. Farías (eds), *Urban Cosmopolitics*, New York: Routledge, pp. 147–63.

Farias Ferreira, M. F. and J. Terrenas (2017) 'The people's assembly of Algés: Heterotopia and radical democracy in crisis-stricken Portugal', in I. David (ed.), *Crisis, Austerity, and Transformation: How Disciplinary Neoliberalism is Changing Portugal*, Lanham, MD: Lexington, pp. 81–100.

Feder-Nadoff, M. (2019) 'Bodies of knowledge: Towards an anthropology of making', *Entanglements*, 2 (1): 59–75.

Gerasimova, E. and S. Chuikina (2009) 'The repair society', *Russian Studies in History*, 48 (1): 58–74.

Gille, Z. (2007) *From the Cult of Waste to the Trash Heap of History: The Politics of Waste in Socialist and Post-Socialist Hungary*, Bloomington, IN: Indiana University Press.

Graham, S. and N. Thrift (2007) 'Out of order: Understanding repair and maintenance', *Theory, Culture & Society*, 24 (3): 1–25.

Gray, L. E. (2016) 'Registering protest: Voice, precarity, and return in crisis Portugal', *History and Anthropology*, 27: 60–73.
Gregson, N. and L. Crewe (2003) *Second-Hand Cultures*, Oxford: Berg.
Gregson, N., A. Metcalfe and L. Crewe (2009) 'Practices of object maintenance and repair: How consumers attend to consumer objects within the home', *Journal of Consumer Culture*, 9 (2): 248–72.
Grossman, A. (2015) 'Forgotten domestic objects: Capturing involuntary memories in post-Communist Bucharest', *Home Cultures*, 12 (3): 291–310.
Guyer, J. I. (2017) 'Aftermaths and recuperation in Anthropology', *Hau: Journal of Ethnographic Theory*, 7 (1): 81–103.
Harper, K. and A. I. Afonso (2016) 'Cultivating civic ecology: A photovoice study with urban gardeners in Lisbon, Portugal', *Anthropology in Action*, 23 (1): 6–13.
Henke, C. (2000) 'The mechanics of workplace order: Toward a sociology of repair', *Berkeley Journal of Sociology*, 44: 55–81.
Hoskins, J. (1998) *Biographical Objects: How Things Tell the Stories of People's Lives*, London: Routledge.
Houston, L. (2017) 'The timeliness of repair', *Continent*, 6 (1): 51–5.
Ingold, T. (2013) *Making: Anthropology, Archaeology, Art and Architecture*, London: Routledge.
Jackson, S. J. (2014) 'Rethinking repair', in T. Gillespie, P. J. Boczkowski and K. A. Foot (eds), *Media Technologies: Essays on Technology, Materiality, and Society*, Cambridge: MIT Press, pp. 221–39.
Knight, D. M. (2015) *History, Time, and Economic Crisis in Central Greece*, New York: Palgrave Macmillan.
Knight, D. M. and C. Stewart (2016) 'Ethnographies of austerity: Temporality, crisis and affect in Southern Europe', *History and Anthropology*, 27: 1–18.
König, A. (2013) 'A stitch in time: Changing cultural constructions of craft and mending', *Culture Unbound*, 5 (33): 569–85.
Koselleck, R. (2006) 'Crisis', *Journal of the History of Ideas*, 67: 357–400.
Larkin, B. (2016) 'Ambient infrastructures: Generator life in Nigeria', *Technosphere Magazine*, 15 November. Available at: https://technosphere-magazine.hkw.de/p/Ambient-Infrastructures-Generator-Life-in-Nigeria-fCgtKng7vpt7otmky9vnFw (accessed 11 August 2019).
Laviolette, P. (2006) 'Ships of relations: Navigating through local Cornish maritime art', *International Journal of Heritage Studies*, 12 (1): 69–92.
Leavitt Cohn, M. (2016) 'Convivial decay: Entangled lifetimes in a geriatric infrastructure', *Proceedings of the 19th ACM Conference on Computer-Supported Cooperative Work & Social Computing*, 1511–23.
Lévi-Strauss, C. (1982) *The Way of the Masks*, London: Jonathan Cape.

Marche, G. (2012) 'Introduction: Why infrapolitics matters', *Revue française d'études américaines*, 131: 3–18.
Marcoux, J.-S. (2001) 'The "Casser Maison" ritual: Constructing the self by emptying the home', *Journal of Material Culture*, 6 (2): 213–35.
Marres, N. (2012) *Material Participation: Technology, the Environment and Everyday Publics*, Basingstoke: Palgrave Macmillan.
Martínez, F. (2014) 'Post-socialist modernity . . .', in F. Martínez and K. Slabina (eds), *Playgrounds and Battlefields*, Tallinn: Tallinn University Press, pp. 139–78.
Martínez, F. (2017) 'Waste is not the end: For an anthropology of care, maintenance and repair', *Social Anthropology*, 25 (3): 346–50.
Martínez, F. (2018a) 'Analogue photo booths in Berlin: A stage, a trap, a condenser and four shots for kissing the person you love', *Anthropology and Photography*, 10: 1–25.
Martínez, F. (2018b) *Remains of the Soviet Past in Estonia: An Anthropology of Forgetting, Repair and Urban Traces*, London: UCL Press.
Martínez, F. (2019) 'What's in a hole? Voids out of place and politics below the state in Georgia', in F. Martínez and P. Laviolette (eds), *Repair, Brokenness, Breakthrough: Ethnographic Responses*. Oxford: Berghahn, pp. 121–44.
Martínez, F. and M. Agu (2016) *Aesthetics of Repair in Contemporary Georgia*, Tartu: Tartu Art Museum.
Martínez, F. and P. Laviolette (eds) (2019) *Repair, Breakages, Breakthroughs: Ethnographic Responses*, Oxford: Berghahn.
Moreiras, A. (2010) 'Infrapolitical literature: Hispanism and the border', *New Centennial Review*, 10 (2): 183–204.
Munn N. (1986) *The Fame of Gawa: A Symbolic Study of Value Transformation in a Massim Society (Papua New Guinea)*, Durham, NC: Duke University Press.
Narotzky, S. and N. Besnier (2014) 'Crisis, value, and hope: Rethinking the economy: An introduction', *Current Anthropology*, 55 (S9): 4–16.
Navaro-Yashin, Y. (2012) *The Make-Believe Space*, Durham, NC: Duke University Press.
Oroza, E. (2009) *NIKIMDILI. Une étude sur la désobéissance technologique et quelques formes de reinvention*, Cité du design: Université de Saint-Étienne.
Ortner, S. (1995) 'Resistance and the problem of ethnographic refusal', *Comparative Studies in Society and History*, 37 (1): 173–93.
Pina Cabral, J. (2018) 'Familiar persons in dark times', *Social Anthropology*, 26 (3): 376–90.
Puig de la Bellacasa, M. (2011) 'Matters of care in technoscience: Assembling neglected things', *Social Studies of Science*, 41 (1): 85–106.

Pussetti, C. (2013) '"Woundscapes": Suffering, creativity and bare life – Practices and processes of an ethnography-based art exhibition', *Critical Arts*, 27 (5): 569–86.
Pussetti, C. (2019) 'From ebony to ivory: 'Cosmetic' investments in the body', *Anthropological Journal of European Cultures*, 28 (1): 64–72.
Rakopoulos, T. (2016) 'The other side of the crisis: Solidarity networks in Greece', *Social Anthropology*, 24 (2): 142–51.
Rancière, J. (2006) *Politics and Aesthetics*. London: Continuum.
Raudon, S. and C. Shore (2018) 'The Eurozone crisis, Greece and European integration: Anthropological perspectives on austerity in the EU', *Anthropological Journal of European Cultures*, 27: 64–83.
Roitman, J. (2013) *Anti-Crisis*, Durham, NC: Duke University Press.
Santos, B. de S. (1995) 'Sociedade-providência ou autoritarismo social?', *Revista Crítica de Ciências Sociais*, 42: i–vii.
Scott, J. (1990) *Domination and the Arts of Resistance*, New Haven, CT: Yale University Press.
Sennett, Ri. (2008) *The Craftsman*, London: Penguin.
Shevchenko, O. (2009) *Crisis and the Everyday in Postsocialist Moscow*, Bloomington, IN: Indiana University Press.
Simone, A.-M. (2004) 'People as infrastructure: Intersecting fragments in Johannesburg', *Public Culture*, 16 (3): 407–29.
Spelman, E. (2002) *Repair: The Impulse to Restore in a Fragile World*, Boston, MA: Beacon Press.
Ssorin-Chaikov, N. (2003) *The Social Life of the State in Subarctic Siberia*, Stanford, CA: Stanford University Press.
Stallabrass, J. (1996) *Gargantua: Manufactured Mass Culture*, London: Verso.
Stenning, A. and K. Hörschelmann (2008) 'History, geography and difference in the post-socialist world: Or, do we still need post-socialism?', *Antipode*, 40: 312–35.
Stewart, K. (2007) *Ordinary Affects*, Durham, NC: Duke University Press.
Strathern, M. (2014) 'Anthropological reasoning: Some threads of thought', *HAU Journal of Ethnographic Theory*, 4 (3): 23–37.
The Coimbra Biennial of Contemporary Art (2017) 'Curar e Reparar Healing and Repairing'. Available at: http://2017.anozero-bienaldecoimbra.pt/en/about/ (accessed 3 August 2019)
Theodossopoulos, D. (2016) 'Philanthropy or solidarity? Ethical dilemmas about humanitarianism in crisis-afflicted Greece', *Social Anthropology*, 24 (2): 167–84.
Thrift, N. (2005) 'But malice aforethought: Cities and the natural history of hatred', *Transactions of the Institute of British Geographers*, 30 (2): 133–50.
Tironi, M. and I. Rodríguez-Giralt (2017) 'Healing, knowing, enduring: care and politics in damaged worlds', *Sociological Review Monographs*, 65 (2): 89–109.

Tisseron, S. (1999) *Comment l'esprit vient aux objets*, Paris: Aubier.
Tonkinwise, C. (2008) 'Visualisation as a method for knowledge discovery', *Studies in Material Thinking* 1. Available at: https://www.materialthinking.org/sites/default/files/papers/Cameron.pdf (accessed April 2019).

1

Recuperative modes of action

Reciprocity, dependence and resistance to austerity policies in Rural Portugal

Ema Pires

In recent years, Portugal has experienced austerity policies – a reconfiguration of both society and state that started in 2011 after a loan was made by the Troika (the European Central Bank, EU Commission and International Monetary Fund) to the country to balance its financial accounts after the economic crisis.[1] This chapter studies how residents of a Portuguese village deal precariously with this context of crisis and how the austerity measures have affected their ordinary compromises and relations. An intense period of ethnographic research was carried out between May 2012 and June 2013, which has continued into the present. Based on this research, I argue that the residents of Monte da Pedra have dealt with the effects of austerity by engaging in various types of recuperative practices in order to cope with the crisis condition. Namely, people recuperated skills from past times and solidarity and reciprocity bonds among friends and relatives to manage the lack of resources.

Older informants, in particular, able to recall past times of scarcity, adjusted their daily lives to crisis in a smoother way by reconnecting with their previous knowledge of reciprocal relations – either in the exchange of food, services, dubious favours or money.

Monte da Pedra

This chapter explores the day-to-day negotiations of precarity and reactions to 'austerity' in Monte da Pedra, a small village in southern Portugal. Taking insights from the daily life of my informants as the focal point of my research, I gathered several voices to describe the effects of the financial crisis and the resulting austerity policies in rural areas. As the collected data shows, practices of reciprocity emerged and were reinvigorated to cope with economic constraints and unexpected vulnerabilities. During the Troika years, the social strategies residents engaged in to fix their lives and their budgets increased reciprocal practices, and hence, reconfigured local relational dynamics in multiple ways, for instance by intensifying the circulation and exchange of some items – money, food and favours.

Monte da Pedra (Stone Hill) is one of the rural parishes (freguesias) of the municipality of Crato, located in the district of Portalegre in Portugal. The sociodemographic structure of the village follows the pattern of depopulation that characterises other rural areas of Southern Europe. The village has a public cultural centre, which has a library, a community centre (where older people spend their days and have their meals), a club for hunting and fishing, a local association of women doing crafts, a pharmacy, a closed school that now operates as a medical centre once a week, one grocery store and, finally, two cafés, where most of the social life takes place. In November 2015, the village had 260 residents (70 per cent of whom were retired and over 65 years old);[2] among the residents, 12 people gained subsidies from the European Union (EU) as farmers and cattle owners; 1 person got a monthly subsidy from the social services (Rendimento Social de Inserção); and finally, two family houses got daily meals from social services. Since February 2017, the social services started providing daily meals to 4 more residents, who were living alone and were unemployed or retired from work due to health issues.[3]

Around Monte da Pedra, there is a major plantation of eucalyptus that is owned by a paper company, which has given some seasonal work to villagers. Agriculture is another activity practised by some residents, mainly small-scale agriculture for private consumption and cattle (cows and sheep). Indeed, agriculture is no longer the main way of living in the village (see Table 1.1). The main employer is the Community Centre (Centro Comunitário), a local branch of Crato's Charity (Misericórdia),[4] which employs nine people, mostly women, who care for the elderly and transport them to their houses at the end of the day. The Junta de Freguesia, the local administrative power of the state, gives work to three people in services. The annual budget of the Freguesia was €56,000 before the crisis and has dropped down to €44,000 since then. This local context of expense cuts has followed a general pattern, as shown in the following section.

The rural area under analysis is an example of parts of Europe that were largely unknown and unaccounted for (either by the media, governments or academia) during the Troika years. Through the practice of prolonged ethnographic research, one is able to grasp the subtle modes of action of people when dealing with constraints of austerity. By employing subtle modes of action, I refer to a vast array of recuperative practices. This is illustrated in the case under empirical analysis that depicts the transitional (in)visibilities over several years at the cemetery during Dia de Finados (All Souls' Day) celebrations.

TABLE 1.1 Employees in Crato and Monte da Pedra, by place of residence and activity, as of National Census, 2011.

Activity	Crato	Monte da Pedra
Primary sector	51	6
Secondary sector	183	14
Third sector (social)	516	20
Third sector (economics)	242	12
Total	992	52

Source: Instituto Nacional de Estatística (INE, 2011, author's translation).

Before the crisis, one could note the presence of luxuriant natural flowers as reminders marking and beautifying beloved ones' graves; however, since then, a plastic floral landscape has been established as the scenic stage for material cultures at the social space dedicated to the dead. What would be the 'recuperative practice' in this case – the economising effort or the continuous beautification of family graves?

Several social scientists have recently studied the effects of the 'crisis' in Portugal. An example is the anthropologist, Antónia Pedroso de Lima (2016), who studied the theme of interpersonal care in times of crisis, based on in-depth interviews conducted in several Portuguese cities. Another anthropologist, Paulo Raposo (2015), edited a special issue on artistic movements and contestations to austerity. He has also been an activist member of one of the many civic movements that emerged in Portugal in reaction to the crisis. Yet another anthropologist, Ricardo Campos, also involved in examining art practices, has reflected on the relation between *graffiti* and the crisis, in a visual essay published in 2014. Within the field of sociology, researchers of the Laboratory of Crisis and Alternatives and Centro de Estudos Sociais of University of Coimbra, have articulated general frameworks for the analysis of the country (de Sousa Santos, 2011), while others have focused on producing critical knowledge from a macro-sociological reading of the challenges unveiled by official statistics (Joaquim, 2015). However, all of these studies rely on urban dimensions of resistance to austerity. Indeed, Portuguese rural territories have been in the shadow of public discussions for years and social scientists have given very little attention to the crisis in rural areas. The current chapter responds to this omission by looking into the social effects of austerity policies from the empirical perspective of a rural context, one of a low-density population.

The Troika years

Between 2011 and 2014, Portugal's financial autonomy and sovereignty were dependent upon the regulation by three international institutions, commonly known as the 'Troika' – the ECB, the EC and the IMF. The loan that the Portuguese state contracted from them was in the field of national governmental measures of major cuts in expenses. These had various impacts on peoples' lives. For example, family incomes were reduced (due to cuts in pensions and salaries), public services had shrinking budgets, there was a major rise in taxes (namely, the ones applied to consumption goods and services), and, in order to get extended revenues, the Portuguese state rulers sold and/or privatised many assets (buildings and companies), such as the Postal Services (CTT), the Electricity Distribution Company (EDP) and even the National Electricity Network (the material assets that make the circulation of electric power in the country possible). The sense of precocity and vulnerability is not new to Portuguese history but was more acute in these Troika years: poverty levels were rising at a rapid pace, thus causing an erosion of the people's horizon of expectations (and a lack of confidence in the state as a welfare provider). During the crisis, the national government made agreements to cooperate with private institutions (IPSS) for funding for social action and supporting the most fragile populations and groups. For instance, in 2013, about 19.5 per cent of the Portuguese population was at risk of poverty, which might lead us to question to what extent public spending to mitigate social vulnerability and precarity contributes to the reduction of the risk of poverty (Joaquim, 2015).

In order to cut expenses, the national government adopted measures to reorganise the territory with the purpose of reducing costs. This reorganisation was made from a viewpoint of Lisbon urban realities. Many public services in rural areas of the country were extinguished or decreased: railway circulation lines were closed as well as civil courts, health services, schools and local government units (freguesias). The network of highways in the interior of the country, which had previously been freely accessible, became accessible only on payment of a toll, thus bringing another rise in costs to residents in rural areas, either directly or indirectly (such as in the rise of the price of goods consumed after transportation through those roads). Also, neoliberalising welfare arrangements, in the form of a selective reconfiguration of different aspects of social protection, led, in turn, to the proliferation of ambiguities.

The context described above gives us a broad framework of the situation in the region where Monte da Pedra is located. In the next section, I will illustrate the effects of the crisis through the daily struggles of three women: Josefina, Alberta and Margarida, and their life stories, which are punctuated by uncertainty and vulnerability. I will then expand on the discussion of the concepts of reciprocity, vulnerability and dependence, and how they can be part of social repair and a recuperative mode of action. Crisis studies need to be anchored in dense ethnographic data 'to capture the actual decisions or non-decisions that people make' (Knight and Stewart, 2016: 11). More nuanced terms are also needed to illuminate these makeshift solutions that are neither designed to last forever nor imply restoring a previously good state of affairs that is now broken. In what follows, I use concepts of repair (Martínez, this volume) and recuperation (Guyer, 2017) to make sense of the ethnographic material I collected from Josefina, Alberta and Margarida, explaining how these concepts apply specifically to the accounts of the three women's practices.

Saving into a plastic bottle

Josefina is 71 years old and was born and bred in Monte da Pedra. She is the mother of two unmarried sons, who live with her. All her life she worked in the fields and in farm works, until a work accident made her homebound owing to irreversible problems with her shoulder. With the compensation she received from the insurance company, Josefina, who was used to saving, began saving even more money. This woman had been proficient in managing scarcity since childhood because her family was one of the poorest in the village. For years, she has been used to storing her savings in a plastic bottle, even before the crisis started.

The savings scheme is collaborative: together with other people, Josefina agrees to put a fixed amount of money each week (a coin of €1 or €2) in an empty 5 litre water bottle (jug). The savings are divided and redistributed among savers when the jug is full. On that day, Josefina opens the jug, pours it on top of her bed and, in the presence of other savers, collects and divides all the money. Josefina has one savings scheme with her children and another with her neighbours. In case any of the savers needs money, the jug may be opened before it is full, and so, the money is redistributed among everyone, in advance. The secret seems to be discipline, frugality and contention. Josefina does not drink coffee outside of her own home and has few conspicuous consumption habits. After years of saving, she managed to complete the payment of her house. Afonso, her oldest son, also bought a small car; and Vasco, the youngest, bought a computer.

For Josefina, the real crisis was before. Evoking the temporality of her youth, she remembers when there was nothing to eat and how women in the village had sexual intercourse with men in exchange for a piece of bread for their children. The boom times of consumption today, she says, brought the crisis now. But the real crisis, according to Josefina, was then. Would Josefina have a different reading of the Troika years if both her sons were unemployed? Vasco has a regular salary as a craftsman of Portuguese traditional street pavements (calceteiro) in the municipality. Afonso worked as a bricklayer before the crisis, but has now been unemployed for years. He cultivates a vegetable garden that provides part of the food needs of the family. Josefina's family still redistributes food among family, friends and neighbours. She also sells eggs in an informal way. Her savings practice is known in the village and, as a consequence, her neighbours occasionally borrow small amounts of money from her. Josefina's current life gives her more power to redistribute money and other items among family and neighbours. Also, she is now able to do things that in the past she could never imagine, such as going on day trips to Fátima, a religious shrine in central Portugal. Even so, her lifestyle and consumption practices are so self-constrained that she only had her first birthday cake when she turned 71 (personal communication, 11 March 2017).

In the post-austerity times, Josefina and her sons are still saving for the jug (€2 per week each). Vasco still works as a *calceteiro* for the town hall. Afonso keeps himself busy doing odd jobs in the village as a servant and painter in construction works or in agricultural activities. Despite being in a situation of underemployment, Afonso managed to save enough money to become a shepherd and he now owns eighteen sheep. It is also worth mentioning that Afonso, who is in his mid-40s, is among the few residents aged under 50 who still practice agriculture for subsistence on a daily basis. His vegetable garden also extends his family's budget. The social construction of Josefina in the local context now makes her a 'Lady' (senhora), a social distinction that, in the past, was only given to women who either did not work in the fields or belonged to the most privileged socioeconomic groups.

As we see in Josefina's case, the materiality of the water bottle is the tangible aspect of a network of economic and social relations that increased during the crisis. This scheme unveils otherwise invisible aspects of how people are engaging in initiatives meant to reinvigorate the social fabric beyond the logics of the market through saving schemes that increase reciprocity and dependence; in turn, also enhancing intergenerational bonds between family and community members, a process comparable to the one described by Lourenço (this volume). Some aspects of my case study are also comparable to Nóvoa's analysis (this volume) of how the circulation of the 'ugly' and small-sized fruits instead contributes to reshaping values, cultural meanings and social relations at large. In the village of Monte da Pedra, practices of recuperation were also extended towards adjustments to the types and sizes of food items that circulated. Indeed, along with exchanging food and things through neighbours' reciprocity, families started to economise by reducing the amount of bread purchased. As a consequence of this, one of the local bread suppliers fixed his own production and adjusted it to the consumers' recession by redimensioning the size of his food items in the form of miniaturised breads, sold at more affordable prices (Figure 1.1).

FIGURE 1.1 *Shrinking Sweet Breads on the move: Bread-seller David, mobile worker for Padaria Zé do Moinho, Gáfete, Crato. Ema Pires.*

Alberta and the privatisation of health services

Alberta, who is 84 years old, was born in a nearby town and has lived in Monte da Pedra since her marriage. She is a widow and has three daughters, all of whom migrated to urban areas. She has worked in the fields all her life. During the Troika years, she lived alone on a pension of €300. She usually spent a monthly amount of €40 to pay firefighters for transportation. Other monthly costs, besides paying for food and heating, are medicines. Alberta buys the medicines in the local pharmacy, which has been in the village for decades. This post competes with the pharmacy of the Misericórdia of Crato, which holds the oligopoly for the redistribution of drugs in Crato town. Crato's pharmacy has been managed by descendants of the head man (Provedor) of Crato's Misericórdia. Most users of the Community Centre care are advised by the workers of the Centre to acquire the drugs through the Crato's Misericórdia pharmacy.

In November 2015, Alberta was preparing for eye surgery. During his time, her doctor, who worked at the public hospital, located in Portalegre, gave her a prescription that required her to have a number of blood tests before the operation. As the blood-collection station was already closed that day at the hospital, she brought the form home. The following morning, she went to the village Community Centre (the local branch of Crato's Misericórdia) for a blood check. There, she was informed that she had to pay €20 for the service. Alberta, who can neither read nor write, refused to pay and went home without doing the blood tests. She did not give up. After calling one of her grandchildren, who works as health technician, she waited another day and went to see the nurse (nursing services visit once a week in the village). The nurse then told her that, in the case of doing the blood test in any of the public places, she would not have to pay for anything. The nearest public collecting points were in Crato (14 km) or Portalegre (35 km). She then found out that the village's Misericórdia had a protocol with a private laboratory for the collection of blood samples in Monte da Pedra. Since that was a private place, she was asked to pay that amount of money. Alberta, accompanied by her neighbour, then decided to go to the nearby town (Crato) for the blood test. Her transport to Crato was facilitated by the neighbours;

otherwise, she would have had to pay a taxi or ambulance to take her there. (Field notes, 8 October 2015.)

Margarida, the faithful gardener

Margarida, who is 55 years old, was brought up in Monte da Pedra. Her father used to work in the railways and her mother worked as a rural worker. Unlike her mother, she has never worked in the fields for a living. She studied and did some short courses, which were funded by the EU. During her professional life, she became used to being underemployed. However, in recent years, due to the crisis, she became permanently unemployed. Margarida has earned a subsidy (given by the state) for taking care of Aloísio, her 41-year-old handicapped younger brother. Margarida has an unmarried son and is married to a man who works in the quarries of a nearby town. During the crisis, when the quarry stopped operating, her husband was forced to go five months without receiving any salary. Then, Margarida had to struggle even more to fix the holes in the family budget. First, she stopped going to the café to save money. Then, later on, she decided to go to the Town Hall of Crato and ask for a job from the mayor. Margarida's family has been, since her youth, a supporter of the political party that rules the municipality. In the face of the current constraints of Troika policies and the impact it has had on her house, she became a client in a patronage relationship with the mayor. Margarida's agency enabled her to balance her family's budget, even though her position is not free from the social sanctions placed on her by other residents. In the local elections of 2013, Monte da Pedra was the only parish where the elected mayor's party of Crato's Town Hall did not win. In exchange for her loyalty, the mayor gave her a non-permanent post as a gardener in a private gardening company that works for the Town Hall. She now earns about €500 per month.

Political reciprocities

From my personal observations, I have come to realise that patronage, which was studied by José Cutileiro (2004 [1977]) in southern Portugal in the 1960s, has remained recurrent and vivid in the village of Monte da Pedra. This is notwithstanding the major differences in the two contexts: democracy now, and dictatorship then, with the persistence of the institution of patronage having now been displaced by other actors who replaced the former landowners as employers. Margarida's case is a clear example of this. The absence of resources drove her into recalling and reconnecting to these traditional forms of patron–client relationships. The mayor (ruler of Town Hall) and the head man (Provedor) of Crato's Misericórdia (Charity) are the main redistributors of resources (and therefore favours) among residents. For instance, they have been the main (and nearly the only) job providers in the region of Crato. Hence, access to a paying job usually means working under the structure of obedience of those two leaders.

Sometimes, as a means to gain the consideration of the gatekeepers of jobs, especially in the Town Hall, one needs to embark on a political relationship of patronage and become a client of the mayor. I have been observing this since 2013 to the present. Several residents have had their jobs taken away or given back, depending on who was the political leader. I have an in-depth experience and knowledge of the patron–client network in the village due to my personal participation in the local elections of 2013 as a member of one of the lists of candidates. During the election campaign, I was approached by some residents, who clearly asked me what I had to offer them in case they voted for the party I was enlisted in. Locally, patronage is, indeed, a model for making politics. In particular, one political leader has been known for making promises of future benefits and even for giving amounts of money (tips? of €20) to residents to motivate their vote.

As Daniel Knight and Charles Stewart explain, austerity 'differs from endemic underdevelopment and poverty, in that it applies to situations where societies or individuals that formerly enjoyed a higher standard of consumption must now make do with less' (2016: 2). It is in this sense that we can explain the 'in a state of repair' understanding of my informants' struggles to imagine alternative futures in present times of precarity and uncertainty. In this context, the future itself is placed on hold, waiting to be recuperated – even if through favour, clientelistic relationships.

Once we ethnographically consider the effects of 'crisis' in the daily lives of the residents, we find, however, some heterogeneity in people's perceptions; a diversity that often varies, depending on the age group and lifestyle of each informant. Among the older informants (those over 65 years of age), the memory of other times of crisis makes them evoke past times of scarcity. According to these older residents, the crisis 'comes and goes', and relationships stay. But for younger residents in the parish (in the absence of a broader timescale, and with stronger consumption practices), the crisis is not simply about managing ambiguity and scarcity, but it has suspended their future plans or even destroyed their lives in various modes. For instance, unemployment and the rising cost of living are the two major impacts identified by them. Both factors have had a direct impact on their family budgets, a situation that has been mitigated by migration and loans (and/or gifts, money and favours) between members of the extended family and friendship networks.

As we can see in Margarida's case, the times of austerity also bring Monte da Pedra's social space and other forms of reciprocity to the surface: namely, the reinforcement of traditional patron–client bonds. The ties between patrons and clients are an old social institution in the Mediterranean region. Recalling James C. Scott, this relationship is:

> a special case of dyadic . . . ties involving a largely instrumental friendship in which an individual of higher socio-economic status (patron) uses his own influence and resources to provide protection or benefits, or both, for a person of lower status (client) who, for his part, reciprocates by offering general support and assistance, including personal services, to the patron.
>
> 1972: 92

The recovery of patronage ties is, indeed, one of the visible dimensions of austerity times in Monte da Pedra. The relationship is constructed between citizens and the providers of employment, as Margarida's case clearly shows. More detailed analysis of this process is beyond the scope of this chapter, and will require a deeper focus on how 'useful friendships' cannot be understood simply in terms of the 'corruption' or 'patronage' for personal profit. For instance, in her study of *veze* and *štele* relations in Bosnia and Herzegovina (2017), Čarna Brković argues that neoliberalism converged and merged with these particular forms of clientelism in the last years, in which ambiguity became not a temporary status but the norm. Also, Andreas Diekmann depicts reciprocity as a 'dimensional', non-categorical, 'variable', which may be 'conditional and unconditional', but also 'positive or negative', as well as 'altruistic and egoistic' (2004: 489). Framing reciprocity comes into context here. As Lauren Berlant has shown, 'exchange value is not identical to the price of things, but marks a determination of what else a thing can get exchanged *for*, as though money were not involved, exactly, in the mediations' (2010: 109). As she describes, value is related to optimism and attachment, thus referring to the subject's sense of what is needed to keep on living, and hence, to what is expected yet absent, believing that the act of exchange can provide some recognition or at least a precarious compromise.

A necessary evil?

The reflection emerging from my ethnographic data is inspired by recent works engaging in anthropological studies of crisis in Southern Europe (Knight and Stewart, 2016; Papataxiarchis, 2016). In contrast to the research mentioned above, Leonard Seabrooke and Rune Thomsen (2016) have analysed online comments about austerity from internet users located in Britain and Denmark. The opinions of these users present austerity as 'a necessary evil' for the 'lazy' Southern European countries. Writing an ethnographic work from the perspective of people living in the south of Europe, one is compelled to recall that the categorisations collected by Seabrooke and Thomsen also reached rural southern Portugal. Indeed, the perception of austerity as *necessary evil* entered the village houses mimetically reproduced by some Portuguese politicians, such as (former) President of the Republic Aníbal Cavaco Silva, who gave public support to the government that ruled the country during the Troika years. In an interview on national TV, he informed the viewers that his pension was also cut, like many other pensions in the country, owing to the austerity measures. The president's mediatised comment gave rise to the residents' immediate reactions in the village. In Café Boavista, one of Monte da Pedra's leisure spaces, a group of clients promptly came out with the idea to start a public collection to help the politician: symbolically, one coin of one cent would be given by each subscriber. This anecdotal example reminds us that humour and irony may be pervasive *weapons* used by the *weak* (evoking the title of James Scott's book) as subtle movements, collective actions of symbolic resistance in times of precarity and vulnerability. Therefore, in the context under analysis, the villagers did not accept austerity as a necessary evil but rather made an ironic gesture towards the president. This ironic gesture unveils, also, the subtle modes of action that people living in precarious conditions have towards their rulers.

Precarity is most often a relationally and existentially shared condition, distributed in hierarchical relations of inequality. Furthermore, the distribution of precariousness is a process that produces not only subjects, but also insecurity and order, as well as different political, social and legal compensations (Lorey, 2015). Precarisation means being vulnerable, contingent and with a very reduced number of alternatives. In this co-relation of weaknesses, voluntary dependence and repair appear as emancipatory practices of self-empowerment, paradoxically. We are reminded by Kathleen Stewart that, 'Precarity's forms are compositional and decompositional' (2012: 524), entailing also a promise of potentiality.

In this case study, ambiguity appears as a key attribute of power, useful to reinforce the position of those who manage to dominate the social world of favours. These forms of political reciprocity are one of the outcomes of the uncertainty generated, hence not simply the result of a 'flawed' statehood but an intrinsic part of the system, blurring the lines between public and private, and reproducing an unequal distribution of resources based on socially existing positions (Brković, 2017). To negotiate uncertainty and vulnerability, people locate themselves on the map of social relations and reproduce existing power relations and hierarchies, linking the state to society in particular ways (Alexander, 2002; Brković, 2017).

This calls for a final word on framing the linkages and intersections between the ambiguity of power and reciprocity. In a fascinating study, James Ferguson (2013) demonstrates that dependence is not only a condition of shameful passivity, but in some contexts of shared vulnerability, it can also be practiced as a cultural 'mode of action', helping to enhance human potential rather than obliterate it. Based on detailed research in the context of South Africa, his analysis aptly dismantles the liberal thought and common-sense notion of dependence as opposed to freedom. Following the transition from a labour-scarce economy to today's era of labour surplus, Ferguson infers that: 'it is not dependence, but its absence that is really terrifying' (ibid.: 232). This cultural mode of action is also present, as we have seen in some of my informants' agencies as part of their survival strategies during the Troika years. This relational dimension of dependency and favours thus helps us to understand the precarious repairs and political reciprocities in which my informants immerse themselves.

Concluding considerations

My ethnography has explored the effects of austerity in a rural village in Portugal by following the daily lives of three women in order to understand their recuperative practices in times of financial crisis and uncertainty about the present and the future. The collected data infer that the residents' strategies have reinvigorated practices of political reciprocity as well as the exchange of things, services and dubious favours. During the Troika years, the rural area under analysis experienced the partial dismantling of the state welfare system, such as the closing down or privatisation of public transport and services. This gave rise to an increase in the prices of essential goods and services such as heating, gas or food items, while it also brought further inequality to the population in their access to services and mobility. My informants objected to the idea of austerity 'as a necessary evil', by engaging in recuperative modes of action that include the use of irony (as shown in the public collection of coins for the President of the Republic) and practices of reciprocity that create alternatives to the eroding state welfare protection of citizens.

In post-austerity times, Margarida, the faithful gardener, is still working for the private company paid by the mayor to clean and beautify the village. Her son is currently also working for the mayor's office. She hopes the mayor, their patron, will keep on protecting them in exchange for her political loyalty. Alberta's subtle acts of resistance to the privatisation of health services have been enduring.

In 2016, she had a minor stroke and went to stay with her daughters, who live near Lisbon. Since then, Alberta has gradually recovered from health issues and occasionally visits her house on weekend family trips. She would like to return to her house, but her siblings try to convince her that she is safer to stay with her daughters than being on her own. Alberta's plans, however, were devoted to going back to Monte da Pedra in spring 2017 and spending a couple of months at her home (personal communication, 12 March 2017). Following her plans, Alberta returned to Monte da Pedra in May 2017. Since then, she has been using the facilities of the elderly at the Community Centre. She lives an independent life. Her children visit her regularly but her return reintegrated her into the local network of neighbours' solidarity and reciprocity.

Josefina's case of upward social mobility makes her an example of the skills a person needs to manage the present (and resist austerity): to convene its knowledge of the past and her habits, which she has always adapted to scarcity to cope with the new context. This is not, however, the perception of other, younger, residents. For them, the Troika years dismantled at a fast pace the peoples' confidence in present institutions and the state, as well as in the future, generating a sense of brokenness. My informants coped with this vulnerable condition by engaging in precarious modes of action to mend their daily lives: either by saving their coins in plastic bottles, increasing food-item redistribution or by recycling old forms of political reciprocities to defend themselves against the vulnerabilities of the present.

The insights of this research suggest that, in the rural area under analysis, people dealt with the broken social condition and a shrinking welfare state in various recuperative ways. In particular, people answered their new uncertainty and vulnerability by increasing reciprocity, by reinvigorating communal bonds and by the recovery of old practices and relations from the past. However, these subtle modes of repair generated ambivalent outcomes. Some residents, such as Margarida, recuperated old practices of patronage and became clients in the network of relationships of dependence with political leaders. Others, such as Josefina, resorted to expanding previous practices of reciprocity and solidarity at the margins of the capitalist system. The concept of recuperation enables us to read about the complexities and grey tones of dependent modes of action in Monte da Pedra in a greater light, thus bringing the practice of political reciprocity further into the core of our broken social worlds.

Notes

1 Words quoted in this chapter are from the author's ethnographic research, which was done with the consent of the subject and an awareness that these words could end up in print. Earlier versions of this research were presented at research seminars held in El Barco de Ávila, Spain, and Lisbon University Institute, Portugal. I am thankful for the comments of colleagues present at those meetings, namely, María Cátedra, José Sobral, Antónia P. Lima and Brian J. O'Neill. I also thank Francisco Martínez (for his generous feedback on subsequent versions of this chapter) and Daniel Rodrigues (for his collaboration in the production of Table 1.1). Last, but not least, acknowledgements are due to the residents of Monte da Pedra (particularly, the informants, whose daily lives are presented here under fictional names, for extending their reciprocity towards me); and to my father, Júlio Pires (1943–2016), for his insights into political reciprocities and the subtle movements of people, things and life.
2 Personal communication, November 2015. Interview with the local treasurer of the parish (tesoureira da Junta de Freguesia).
3 Interview with Justina, one of the residents getting daily meals.
4 Santa Casa da Misericórdia do Crato is a local charity, designated by the state as Private Institution of Social Solidarity (Instituição Particular de Solidariedade Social, IPSS).

References

Alexander, C. (2002) *Personal States: Making Connections between People and Bureaucracy in Turkey*, Oxford: Oxford University Press.

Berlant, L. (2010) 'Cruel optimism', in M. Gregg and G. Seighworth (eds), *The Affect Theory Reader*, Durham, NC: Duke University Press, pp. 93–116.

Brković, Č. (2017) *Managing Ambiguity: How Clientelism, Citizenship, and Power Shape Personhood in Bosnia and Herzegovina*, Oxford: Berghahn.

Campos, R. (2014) 'A luta voltou ao muro (ensaio visual)', *Análise Social* 212, XLIX (3º). Available at: http://analisesocial.ics.ul.pt/documentos/AS_212_EV.pdf. (accessed 3 August 2019).

Cutileiro, J. (2004 [1977]) *Ricos e Pobres no Alentejo: Uma Sociedade Rural Portuguesa*, Lisbon: Horizonte.

de Sousa Santos, B. (2011) *Portugal – Ensaio Contra a Auto-flagelação*, Coimbra: Almedina.

Diekmann, A. (2004) 'The power of reciprocity: Fairness, reciprocity, and stakes in variants of the dictator game', *Journal of Conflict Resolution*, 48 (4): 487–505.

Ferguson, J. (2013) 'Declarations of dependence: Labour, personhood, and welfare in southern Africa', *Journal of the Royal Anthropological Institute*, 19: 223–42.

Gregg, M. and G. J. Seighworth (eds) (2010) *The Affect Theory Reader*, Durham, NC: Duke University Press.

Guyer, J. (2017) 'Aftermaths and recuperations in anthropology', *HAU: Journal of Ethnographic Theory*, 7 (1): 81–103.

Instituto Nacional de Estatística (INE) (2011) *Censos 2011*, Lisbon: INE.

Joaquim, C. (2015) 'Proteção social, terceiro setor e equipamentos sociais: que modelo para Portugal?', *Cadernos do Observatório #3*, Centro de Estudos Sociais/Universidade de Coimbra. Available at: www.ces.uc.pt/observatorios/crisalt. (accessed 3 August 2019).

Knight, D. and C. Stewart (2016) 'Ethnographies of austerity: Temporality crisis and affect in Southern Europe', *History and Anthropology*, 27 (1): 1–18.

Lorey, I. (2015) *State of Insecurity: Government of the Precarious*, London: Verso.

Papataxiarchis, E. (2016) 'Unwrapping solidarity? Society reborn in austerity', *Social Anthropology*, 24 (2): 205–10.

Pedroso de Lima, A. (2016) 'O cuidado como elemento de sustentabilidade em situações de crise. Portugal entre o Estado providência e as relações interpessoais', *Cadernos Pagu*, (46): 79–105.

Raposo, P. (2015) '"Artivismo": articulando dissidências, criando insurgências', *Cadernos de Arte e Antropologia*, 4 (2). Available at: http://cadernosaa.revues.org/909 (accessed 3 August 2019).

Scott, J. C. (1972) 'Patron–client politics and political change in South-East Asia', *Annual Review of Political Science*, 66 (1): 91–113.

Seabrooke, L. and R. R. Thomsen (2016) 'Making sense of austerity: Everyday narratives in Denmark and United Kingdom', *Politics*, 36 (3): 250–611–12.

Stewart, K. (2012) 'Precarity's forms', *Cultural Anthropology*, 27 (3): 518–25.

2

'Beautiful people eat ugly fruit'

Ugliness and the cracks in the system

André Nóvoa

I hate slick and pretty things. I prefer mistakes and accidents. Which is why I like things like cuts and bruises – they're like little flowers.
DAVID LYNCH (1998)

Introduction

Let us leave the words on ugliness from filmmaker David Lynch for now. I shall return to them in the conclusions; hopefully, they will be more self-explanatory by then. The title of this essay is a quote from Ugly Fruit's slogan[1]. Ugly Fruit is a Portuguese cooperative that promotes zero-waste practices by restocking and selling non-standardised fruit, as per EU legislation, at a low cost and without profit. Ugly Fruit creates non-profit bridges between producers and consumers, thus preventing the discard of food and offering new sources of revenue to local producers. The project started in Lisbon in 2013, during the peak of the crisis of the Troika bailout, which ran during 2011–14, and rapidly spread to other parts of the city, as well as Porto, the second-largest city in Portugal, reaching a total of seven delivery points. The case of Ugly Fruit appears to be relevant for two main reasons. First, it emerges as a creative endeavour in granting not only low-cost healthy food solutions during a socioeconomic crisis, but also in the endorsement of zero-waste cultures, the reduction of greenhouse gas (GHG) emissions and ecological activism. This alone could bear the potential to be seen as a form of recuperation. However, and perhaps more importantly, Ugly Fruit is further implicitly stating that 'ugly is okay', which may phenomenologically position the non-normative, the non-standard or the *outsider* at the heart of social transformation. Ugliness becomes a means to counter the crisis. In this way, by pushing the individual towards the ugly, Ugly Fruit may be challenging and broadening out our very own understandings of consumption, social norms and culture. This could be seen as *recuperation*.

Ugly Fruit: The project

Ugly Fruit began in 2013 in Intendente, a small district in the heart of Lisbon, which used to be seen by the public as a 'problematic' quarter, but has benefited from a series of actions and policies in urban renewal in the last decade, claiming a new centrality within the city. Right from the start, the aims of the project were clear and simple: contribute to putting a halt to food waste by picking up non-standardised fruit, as per EU legislation, that local producers were unable to sell to mainstream retailers and chains before trading them in mixed baskets directly to the public. Ugly Fruit was an instant hit. In less than two years, the project saw six more delivery points installed in both Lisbon and Porto, including on the outskirts of both cities. Today, all of them have waiting lists, except for the delivery point in Vila Nova de Gaia – a city that sits across the Douro River from Porto. New delivery points are currently being envisioned and planned.

Ugly Fruit functions as a cooperative of associated consumers. There are two main legal figures here: first, the cooperative members,

UGLINESS AND THE CRACKS IN THE SYSTEM 57

who are the ones who take part in the cooperative's daily works (currently, 11 people); second, the associated consumers, all of those who have the right to pick up the fruit, weekly, at the delivery point of their choosing (currently, about 3,000 people; see Figures 2.1–2.2). In any case, the project's manifesto positions the consumer at its heart by stating that: 'the preference for aesthetically perfect products is a logic that has been imposed, largely, by consumers, who consistently opted for products with a more standardised appearance'.[2] Because of this, it is the consumer who needs to be catered for: 'we consider that it is the consumers who must unite now to reclaim ugly fruit and vegetables as a viable option of consumption'.[3] This was reiterated by Isabel Soares, one of the cooperative members, who verbalised that: 'our goal is to build direct bridges between the producer and the consumer, but it is the consumer that lies in the heart of our project – it is them that we need to cater for'.[4]

FIGURE 2.1 *A member choosing their basket at Parede, delivery point near Lisbon. André Nóvoa.*

FIGURE 2.2 *An example of a mixed basket. André Nóvoa.*

Thus, Ugly Fruit is repositioning the consumer as the strong link between food waste and new consumerist ethics by staging it as the axial legal figure of the project. In other words, instead of uniting producers and granting them a platform to sell their (neglected) products, Ugly Fruit is legally binding consumers with the same institution and bestowing upon them an ethical and social responsibility. As per the institution's regulation, everyone needs to be preregistered in the cooperative and pay an annual fee of €5 to become an associated consumer, after which they are free to sign up at a delivery point of their choosing to collect their weekly mixed baskets. The sale to the public happens at a predetermined, fixed location, the so-called Ugly Fruit delivery points, once a week. Members come in the late afternoon and leave with the baskets of their choice, paying for these separately upon collection: the small basket costs €3.5 (about 4 kg and comes with a variety of seven different types of fruits and veggies) and the bigger one goes for €7 (about 8 kg and has an assortment of eight species).

Contextualising Ugly Fruit

Ugly Fruit both appropriates and sponsors a green discourse that is a combination of new ecological movements, zero-waste cultures, mobility transitions and low-carbon activism. First and foremost, the cooperative's goal is the prevention of food discard. Some scholars have started to pay attention to this phenomenon even though it is a relatively new topic in academia (Evans, Campbell and Murcott, 2013). Some argue that food waste has become normal in modern societies as a consequence of households negotiating the complex demands of everyday life (Evens, 2014), whilst others prefer to focus on the mischiefs of contemporary consumerism models, whereby surplus has become mainstream and an often used metaphor for well-being and healthy societies (Campbell, 2012). Ugly Fruit knits these two visions by promoting a critique of the contemporary consumer, whilst at the same time disapproving of mainstream chains that have been unable to reclaim non-standardised fruit as a viable product. Thus, they engage in present-day social movements that attempt to prevent food waste and to promote zero-waste cultures.

One emanation of such cultures, which could be considered more radicalised, is dumpster-diving or, as some like to call it, 'freeganism'. To some extent, this is the modern-day, urban version of yesteryear's gleaning – the practice of collecting leftover crops in rural contexts (King, 1989). Dumpster-diving involves salvaging objects, commodities or even food that has been thrown away despite being in a good condition. It most certainly began as a practice amongst the poor, who were left with no choice but to look for free food in the waste of others. More recently, dumpster-diving has developed into an urban subculture, chiefly amongst the youth, who wish to make a stand against capitalism and high levels of consumerism (Lotman, 2015). At least this is what Dylan Clark seems to imply with his notion of 'punk cuisine' (2004) or Victoria Moré through her explorations of a freegan community in Illinois (2011). Dumpster-diving goes beyond industrial recycling because it cuts out the middleman – no one stands in between the waste and the consumer any more. In a way, Ugly Fruit embodies these new emerging practices of zero waste, found in various youth cultures, recycling movements and ecological activism.

But Ugly Fruit goes far beyond this. The cooperative is not only focused on preventing the waste of edible food but also incorporates a green discourse on energy saving and GHG emissions cuts. By channelling locally produced food to local consumers, the cooperative replicates the models of sustainability found in mobility transition theories. These theories assume that, in a world characterised by the constant flux of goods and people across boundless distances, humanity must engage with different forms of movement and travel, ones that cut back the high levels of pollution and GHG emissions. Scholars operate under this premise to develop a critical analysis of how this *transitioning* might spur. One way to reinvent current mobility regimes is through technological development, such as those preconised by the analytical models of the so-called 'multilevel perspective' (Geels, 2002; Geels and Kemp, 2012). However, others still exist. We can also move less, or we can confer new meanings to particular forms of mobility so they become more convincing or socially acceptable (Temenos et al., 2017).

One of these is the transition towns' movement, established in 2006 through the foundation of the Transition Network (Aiken, 2012). The network has been created to empower a number of grassroots responses to climate change that seek to increase the self-sufficiency of towns around the globe to counter the effects of peak oil. The equation is simple: if commodities and goods move less than they currently do, a significant percentage of GHG emissions is automatically cut down in transport and freight. Ugly Fruit takes on this premise by working with local producers and local consumers, regardless of the fact that it would be very challenging for a small Portuguese cooperative to do otherwise because of logistics. Indeed, on their website, Ugly Fruit expresses that this is done due to the 'environmentally responsible trait' of the project.[5] Once more, this was reinforced by Isabel Soares during our interview, in which she stated that: 'we never pick up fruit and veggies beyond a 70 km radius of the delivery points; also, we don't offer home deliveries – both have to do with the necessity of cutting down GHG emissions and pollution' (Figure 2.3).[6]

In her latest book (2015), Anna Tsing explores the possibility of life in the ruins of capitalism. She sets about to examine the afterlife of things and people beyond the vicious cycle of production-

FIGURE 2.3 *Ugly Fruit's van, used for picking up the fruit and relocating it to the delivery points. André Nóvoa.*

turned-destruction that we came to call 'progress'. According to Tsing, progress became a metonym for a recalcitrant, never-ending expansion that only comes to a halt when landscapes become redundant and depleted – it is then time for progress to go somewhere else, leaving behind inhospitable sites of unruly encounters and indeterminacy, a concept that she uses to describe the taxonomy of social encounters that eludes modern reasoning, centred on a 'progressist' view of history. Tsing explores what happens *next*, at the margins of capitalism and progress. When everything seems in ruin, only rubble is left and life appears to fold (Gordillo, 2014). What happens next are unexpected patchworks of collaboration between and across species (both human and non-human) that Tsing calls 'contaminated diversity'. She examines these issues through an analysis of mushroom-picking and its supply chains, primarily due to the fact that the Matsutake mushroom (a Japanese delicacy) was the first life form that blossomed in Hiroshima after the bombings.

Tsing comes to the conclusion that, even in the most devoid sites, such as logged forests or nuclear barrens, new forms of trade, commerce and multispecies collaborations appear, many of which have the potential to carve out new understandings of freedom and social relations. Moreover, many have the potential to explain what humanity will probably look like after climate change hits the fan or some other human-provoked disaster takes place. An analogy can be drawn between Tsing's mushrooms and Ugly Fruit. It is clear that the cooperative did not surface in or within desolate geographies. On the contrary, Ugly Fruit was given birth to and thrived in the densely populated urban context of a European capital. Furthermore, it is in a 'pericapitalist' condition, to use Tsing's terms once again, which means that both inside and outside of capitalism, the cooperative is a non-profit enterprise that cuts out the middleman, thus disrupting the regular commodity chains of capitalism (where most profits are made); however, it still relies on those producers who crop and harvest for a capitalist system. Even when taking this into account, the fruit still come from a wasteland of sorts: it is collected, packed and sold when 'progress' is no longer interested in the soils from where it came. The fruit of the cooperative are to be found in the leftovers of the global market economy, unfit for the standards of consumerism, rescued from the wreckages of a capitalist engine and withdrawn from circulation as if it were matter out of place (Douglas, 1966).

In so doing, Ugly Fruit could be manufacturing a particular kind of recuperation, turning a heterogeneously contaminated diversity into a reconstituted entity (Guyer, 2017). By salvaging (another concept used by Tsing) the unwanted crops of capitalism, the cooperative is potentially creating an original *interspecies* collaboration between the consumer and the producer and with the fruit themselves. This contaminated diversity goes two ways: not only is the fruit redefined as edible (not mere waste any more), but also the consumers themselves embrace new identities through the appropriation of the latter. Fruits gain agency. As Bruno Latour (2005) would put it, an agency which might fabricate new consumer profiles – linked with responsible behaviour, ecological conducts and so forth. A consumer holding an ugly fruit is, perhaps, no longer a mere consumer; just as a man holding a hammer becomes something else – a worker, for instance (Latour and Venn, 2002). Fruit and humans become an 'assemblage' at the edges of capitalism, carved out from the waste of regular market functioning.

It may be the case that biological products and/or local foods provide a steadier route towards an 'ecological citizenship' (Dobson, 2003), or a better shortcut to 'shopping for sustainability' (Seyfang, 2005) than Ugly Fruit is able to offer. It is more efficient to put on ecological 'masks' by picking up healthy food in a mainstream supermarket or by entering a local grocery shop than by attending a small venue to pick up mixed baskets of fruit, wherein everyone is pretty much doing the same thing. Ugly Fruit may not allow for a socially plentiful exhibition of identities. However, in a way, it may be more substantial than the latter since it bears the potential to disrupt capitalism to further extents: biological products are often produced and procured along the normal routes of capitalism; that is, if 'following the thing' (Marcus, 1995), we see the customary producer-intermediaries-consumer chain, with the distributor retaining large profits, whereas Ugly Fruit cuts off the middleman by not claiming any intermediary revenues.

To some degree, this can be seen as recuperation as conceptualised throughout the various contributions of this volume. Ugly Fruit represents a recuperative endeavour in the sense that it pays attention and readies something that has been neglected, thus entailing an assessment of how the actual society and market economy are organised. Ugly Fruit not only works towards *recuperating* our social reality because it is endorsing less waste and healthy food solutions at low costs,[7] but perhaps more boldly because it has the potential to introduce transcendental narratives of reconstitution as well as recuperative infrastructures (Martínez, this volume), weaving new practices and understandings of consumerism through original assemblages of human-fruits. Is this not the transmission of affect in a relational way (Navaro-Yashin, 2012)? Is this not the attribution of new values to old or abject things, to yesterday's waste? Is this not the creation of new identities, emerging out of creative responses to the socioeconomic crisis? Is this not *recuperation*?

Less is more?

One of the aspects that I would like to highlight in Ugly Fruit's practical dimension[8] is the fact that the cooperative's actions do not seem to embody an uncritical representation of *less* as the new awesome, in contrast (most of the time) with a broader network of social and ecological movements in which the cooperative is framed upon. We often see a number of new environmentally engaged institutions, non-governmental organisations (NGOs) or governmental actors take on a conceptualisation of recuperation that envisions less waste, less production, less consumerism and less movement as positive. If not explicitly, or at least implicitly, many of these embody and countersign a *weltanschauung*, where things would ideally move less (as prescribed by transition-town movements, local-foods advocates or mobility transition theorists) and, perhaps, with a reduced production. The broader arena of social movements and activist geographies that Ugly Fruit is based on seems to engage with the modernist dictum of 'less is more'.

It is possible to find such a predicament in recent academic works. Astrid Matthey, for instance, thinks that actions towards a sustainable economic de-growth come with sensations or feelings of loss, owing to the current high levels of consumption, which have become conventional. In her study, 'the results suggest that the acceptance of economic de-growth would be facilitated if people's material aspirations were moderated, and the extent to which material achievements are emphasised in our daily environment were reduced' (2010: 567). This reasoning is also to be found outside of academia's walls. A recent initiative at Washington University in St. Louis, Missouri, precisely entitled 'less is more', recommends students and faculty to 'turn off lights, take shorter showers, buy fewer (disposable) products' and so forth.[9] These types of initiatives are spread out across various quadrants of society. And it must be said that they do have their merits – unquestionably. But, it is also necessary to address them from a critical perspective.

Taken uncritically, this kind of reasoning can prove itself dangerous. Architect Pier Vittorio Aureli reveals how a romanticisation of the notion of *less* is counterproductive. At the very least, when less is imposed upon us (through a number of social discourses, in a Foucaultian manner, through top-down programmes or through several other techniques), and not a conscious exercise of our own doing. Instead of pushing us towards a new progressist condition, a romanticisation of *less* may be doing the very opposite: it may be further secularising and legitimising an ascetic way of life that is one of the groundworks of capitalism itself, rather than challenging the status quo – this genealogy is traceable. Asceticism loomed as a religious practice that commended a rejection of worldly pleasures through reclusion and self-control. According to Aureli, capitalism picked up on this notion and gave it a simple, yet truly transformative, twist: it merged asceticism with entrepreneurial idealism. The advent of capitalism happened alongside the rise of social housing (deprived of all luxury, with very small spaces, void of everything but the *essential*), forcing the working class not only to lead a monk-type way of life, but also to become the micro-entrepreneurs of their own minimal economies.

First, individuals were stimulated to tolerate inferior standards of living. Then, they had to become the micro-entrepreneurs of their own small economies: their houses. The adaptation of asceticism into a 'potential for development is a betrayal of its core principles' (Aureli, 2013: 33). Instead of rallying individuals to an independence from the centres of power, allowing for the crafting of new ways of life that challenge hegemonic modes of governance, asceticism from the vantage point of capitalism is 'appropriated as a moral imperative directing the subject to work harder, produce, accumulate and finally consume more' (ibid.). This perversion, which is foundational to the idea of private property, fabricated the notion that less is more. Indeed, workers are optimised under regimes of austerity, where rhythms, time and space converge to ultimately do more with less: more work in fewer hours, more production with fewer resources and more investment with less capital. 'Just as scarcity of resources represents one of the fundamental tropes of capitalism – an exhortation to perform productively by competition and abnegation – asceticism becomes the moral legitimation of the status quo' (ibid.).

In a way, this is the same reflexive exercise that Slavoj Žižek (2012) demands of us when buying a Starbucks coffee: one is not only purchasing a drink but also an ideology. Starbucks vividly displays posters and advertisements across its stores, exhibiting messages of fair trade, awareness raising, charity work and the like. In Žižek's perspective, this makes it that the consumer is not only buying a coffee but also offloading their own guilt for consuming. It is a postmodern confessionary of sorts. Just like the monk and his cell became the blueprint for the working class, social housing and private property, so is fair trade, to some extent, a secularisation of the confessionary. Naturally, fair trade does have its merits and many people worldwide have seen their lives improved due to it, but it simultaneously bolsters the status quo rather than countering it. It is like Tsing's 'pericapitalist' condition: it is both here and there, outside and inside, both doing this and that.

Aureli, too, alerts us to this perversion: yes, it may be good to save resources, to consume less, to produce less or to move less, but this is also a perversion in the sense that it tends to naturalise and legitimise what remains truly to be challenged: the idea of private property, (predatory) capitalism, reiterations of accumulation and possession. The contemporary aestheticisation of an austere society naturalises frugality in a dangerous way. Recent emanations of such aestheticisation include a return to the 'austerity chic' as incarnated by the likes of Steve Jobs (who was always wearing blue jeans and a black sweater, and was constantly photographed in an emptiness of material life, except for the technology that he had built by himself) and Apple (minimalist design, with all-white stores, containing nothing but the *essential*). Being austere has been branded as a new contemporary expression for the rejection of hegemonic values. Yet, when taken uncritically, it is precisely reinforcing those values as opposed to countering them. Although imagining a new regime of worldwide consumerism as of paramount importance, it seems that a *fetishisation* of austere asceticism is at odds with a deconstruction of . . . austerity. If things are to change, we must reformulate a notion that is *less* centred on the individual and individual possession, which is almost never the case. And we must also say that less is not more; indeed, 'less is just enough' (Aureli, 2013).

What I would emphasise in Ugly Fruit is that the cooperative does not seem to be interested in engaging with an uncritical perspective of less as more. Ugly Fruit is not advocating that things should be less consumed or less produced or less moved about. This contrasts with a broader field of ecological activism, mobility transitions movements and environmental awareness that Ugly Fruit fits into. Here, less is many times celebrated as the new cool, too often with uncritical perspectives – which is the most pernicious part. Instead, Ugly Fruit is redirecting leftovers to consumers. Therefore, they are not about less consumerism or less movement or less production. In my interview with Isabel Soares, she stressed that: 'I think that producing and consuming less is something that we should be thinking about, but we do not take these ideas and use them as slogans for our cooperative; we don't tell anyone to move less, or consume less – we have one main struggle only, which is to prevent food from being thrown away.'[10] In other words, they are about salvaging the discards of capitalism. All they want less of is waste, which seems to me a strong premise. It must be said that the cooperative is not also moving against ideas of less. They do not take a particular critical stand against it; they simply do what they do. But what they do is interesting because they may be able to challenge capitalist logics, to counter austerity and promote a new consumerist behaviour without uncritically appealing to the austere-less as the new chic.

But Ugly Fruit's importance may go even beyond this. The value of Ugly Fruit does not end with its practical dimension – the cooperative's actions and deeds also harbour a symbolical importance. There is a deeper layer of *recuperation* to be found, which I will now explain further.

Ugliness as recuperation

Anthropologist Mary Douglas made a compelling analysis of cultural margins through the lenses of *dirt*. In *Purity and Danger* (1966), she argued that dirt is matter out of place. Take a shoe, for instance. Shoes are not considered dirty when worn on a stroll down the street, but using them inside the house in some cultural contexts (e.g. in Nordic countries) can cause discomfort; or, in a more caricatured way, shoes are certainly to be perceived as being dirty when on top of a table or inside a refrigerator. We laugh at such images because they make no *sense*; they disrupt the normal order of things, their natural place, their expected belongings. Douglas concludes that dirt reflects our very own cultural anxieties and needs to be disposed of, stashed away, preferably remaining invisible. Hence, dirt can also be used as a tool for activism: a recurring theme of activist imaginings is a scene of protesters throwing tomatoes at politicians.

Can we not see ugliness as a form of metaphysical dirt? Just as dirt can be arrayed in a more bodily way to unbalance social order, so, too, can ugliness, which has been used to metaphysically upset certain social structures. Throughout several historical periods, ugliness has been hailed as a tool for social and cultural transformation, most notably perhaps, as Umberto Eco explains in *On Ugliness*, during the modernist period of the early twentieth century. Here, ugliness was used to thwart cultural norms, aesthetic canons and, from there, broader hegemonic structures. Eco states that the ugliness of Futurism was deliberately provocative, and 'that of German Expressionism was to be an ugliness that sprang from the denunciation of social ills' (Eco, 2007: 368). Lesley Higgins reinforces this notion by claiming that ugliness, for many modernist writers, was elevated to an artistic heyday that was meant to provoke, shock or awe the public. The objective was to 'displace the misogyny and homophobia which governed individual and artistic responses and utterances' (Higgins, 2002: 1).

Ugliness thus contains an intrinsic politics and can be mobilised in a political way. By political, I mean the distribution of power and the relations formed in the process: who and what gets to be called ugly? And by whom? And to what extent? And with what purpose? The 'politics of ugliness', taking Ela Przybylo's expression (2010), can be particularly enlightening to show how ugliness is often deployed to ascertain power over someone (calling someone ugly in public, for instance), to shatter the barriers of social convention (by doing something ugly in non-inviting social contexts), to disturb certain social norms and so forth. Przybylo herself discusses the possibility of mobilising ugliness as a feminist weapon. She claims that women can purposefully exhibit themselves in an ugly style to break established cultural margins and social binaries. Similarly, Karina Eileraas (1997) has analysed how ugliness is used by a number of female rock bands to challenge vernacular assumptions of femininity: those who take women as clean subjects, preferably immobile (see, Cresswell and Uteng, 2008) and compounded.

Let us go back to our case study. Ugly Fruit is self-evidently based on the fruit being *ugly* (Figure 2.4). Naturally, this ugliness is transformed into *cuteness* quite rapidly. The fruit is reinvented to appeal to the public as a charming and adorable object. But this is a transformation itself fashioned by the cooperative: ugly fruit is not, in essence, cute, it is rather phenomenologically so – ugliness was transformed into cuteness through a *process* (one that involved awareness raising, marketing, advertisement, and so forth). Particularly interesting is how this process can become a metaphor for how the most effective responses to the crisis come from the strangeness or uncanniness of things, people and ideas. Ugliness here may stand as a metonym for the non-standard, the irregular (the fruit is inclusively codified in law as such)[11] or the *outsider*. To think outside of the box, to appropriate culturally what was once at the margins or to see value in the ugliness of objects suddenly becomes a spur for change. A spur for *recuperation*. In the meantime, Ugly Fruit may be broadening our understanding, not simply of consumerism but also of politics and culture themselves, serving as an inspiration for upcoming responses and *recuperative* efforts.

FIGURE 2.4 *An 'ugly' apple – too small, according to normal standards.* André Nóvoa.

To conclude

Now is the time to return to David Lynch's epigraph: 'I hate slick and pretty things. I prefer mistakes and accidents. Which is why I like things like cuts and bruises – they're like little flowers.' Here, Lynch seems to be emphasising the creative force of ugliness. According to him, mistakes, accidents, cuts and bruises – all potentially described as ugly (or other similar adjectives) – are like little flowers: they contain the potential for life, for different forms of life, for divergent existences. In a word, they contain the potential for *recuperation*. Accidents, negligence and mistakes, such as a socioeconomic crisis, sometimes harbour creative responses, which endure the life cycle of the crisis itself and come to change certain values, norms and attitudes. I do not wish to adhere to the neoliberal dictum that sees 'creative destruction' and crisis as an 'opportunity' as there are no opportunities here. Instead, there are responses – and, sometimes, enduring ones. I believe this to be an interesting metaphor for the case of Ugly Fruit.

Ugly Fruit may have a very practical *recuperative* dimension. The cooperative is saving wasted food, redirecting it towards the public at very low cost, making no profit as the middleman and potentially catering for the emergence of new identities and eco-ethical behaviours. Human and fruit thus become an assemblage that may not only disrupt the normal mobilities of commodities (from the producer to the distributor to the supplier to the consumer), but also, more importantly, one that can edge the market economy by salvaging what was once viewed as waste. In doing so, food is saved, local producers get to sell more and people get to buy good fruit at low prices. This may be seen as recuperation, with a presumable bricolage between individuals (in the form of a cooperative, which is interesting in itself) and things (in the form of irregular fruit) sponsoring a creative response in time of crisis.

But Ugly Fruit may also have a symbolical dimension. Because it is *ugly*. As stated in the last section of the essay, ugliness contains a political potential for challenging structures and norms, developing alternative visions of society with the potential to recuperate *us*, and not simply the market economy. From the artistic movements of the early twentieth century to the works of anthropologists like Douglas, ugliness appears as a form to upset social order, artistic canons, societal conventions and cultural beliefs. Ugliness has been used by modernists to expose social ills, by feminists to criticise misogyny or by others to render the cruelties of our time. The ugliness of Ugly Fruit bears a potential for challenging how we feel about consumerism and, perhaps in a deeper way, about culture in a more abstract way. Here, the non-standard, the irregular, the *outsider* may become recuperative. This process, or movement, may be presented as an interesting metonym for how to act in times of crisis: it is necessary to think beyond our own imaginary borders, to push the margins afar, to stretch them, and then to look closer and address the cracks in the system. Only then can *recuperation* appear in its finest form.

Notes

1 Ugly Fruit is a personal translation of the Portuguese 'Fruta Feia', which is the official name of the project. The pages that follow should be read as a reflexive essay, penned after a first approach to the field. A couple of interviews have been conducted with the directors of Ugly Fruit, and some time was spent wandering in and around two of the cooperative's delivery points. This is thus an explorative piece, wherein a number of theoretical points are raised after having made initial contact with the site. The idea is to use the experiences (and successes) of Ugly Fruit as an illustration to kindle unexpected dialogues between authors from different fields.

2 Quote taken from Ugly Fruit's website (December 2016), available at: http://frutafeia.pt/pt/perguntas-frequentes/perguntas-frequentes (accessed 3 August 2019).

3 Ibid.
4 Interview conducted by the author, Isabel Soares, 16 January 2017.
5 Ibid.
6 Ibid.
7 Thereby challenging the pillars that hold together the 'rubbish society' (O'Brien, 2008).
8 By practical dimension, I mean the actual saving of food, via its redirection, the opening of new channels of healthier consumerism and the catering for new ecological identities, as opposed to a symbolic dimension, which I will deal with later on.

9 Washington University's campaign 'Less is More' website (December 2016), available at: https://sustainability.wustl.edu/get-involved/less-is-more/ (accessed 3 August 2019).
10 Interview conducted by the author, Isabel Soares, 16 January 2017.
11 See EU marketing standards for fruit and vegetables here (December 2016), available at: https://ec.europa.eu/agriculture/fruit-and-vegetables/marketing-standards_en (accessed 3 August 2019).

References

Aiken, G. (2012) 'Community transitions to low carbon futures in the Transition Towns Network', *Geography Compass*, 6 (2): 89–99.
Aureli, P. V. (2013) *Less is Enough: On Architecture and Asceticism*, Moscow: Strelka.
Campbell, H. (2012) 'Let us eat cake? Historically reframing the problem of world hunger and its purported solutions', in C. Rosin et al. (eds), *Food Systems Failure: The Global Food Crisis and the Future of Agriculture*, London: Earthscan, pp. 30–45.
Clark, D. (2004) 'The raw and the rotten: Punk cuisine', *Ethnology*, 43 (1): 19–31.
Cresswell, T. and T. P. Uteng (2008) *Gendered Mobilities*, New York: Ashgate.
Dobson, A. (2003) *Citizenship and the Environment*, Oxford: Oxford University Press.
Douglas, M. (1966) *Purity and Danger: An Analysis of Concepts of Pollution and Taboo*, New York: Routledge and Keegan Paul.
Eco, U. (2007) *On Ugliness*, London: Harvill Secker.
Eileraas, K. (1997) 'Witches, bitches and fluids: Girl bands performing ugliness as resistance', *TDR: The Drama Review*, 41 (3): 122–39.
Evans, D. (2014) *Food Waste*, London: Bloomsbury.
Evans, D., H. Campbell and A. Murcott (2013) 'A brief pre-history of food waste and the social sciences', *Sociological Review*, 60 (S2): 5–26.
Geels, F. W. (2002) 'Technological transitions as evolutionary reconfiguration processes: A multi-level perspective and a case-study', *Research Policy*, 31: 1257–74.
Geels, F. and R. Kemp (2012) 'The multi-level perspective as a new perspective for studying socio-technical transitions', in F. W. Geels, R. Kemp, G. Dudley and G. Lyons (eds), *Automobility in Transition? A Socio-Technical Analysis of Sustainable Transport*, New York: Routledge, pp. 49–79.
Gordillo, G. (2014) *Rubble: The Afterlife of Destruction*, Durham, NC: Duke University Press.

Guyer, J. I. (2017) 'Aftermaths and recuperation in anthropology', *Hau: Journal of Ethnographic Theory* 7 (1): 81–103.

Higgins, L. (2002) *The Modernist Cult of Ugliness*, New York: Palgrave McMillan.

King, P. (1989) 'Gleaners, farmers and the failure of legal sanctions in England 1750–1850', *Past & Present*, 125: 116–50.

Latour, B. (2005) *Reassembling the Social: An Introduction to Actor-Network-Theory*, Oxford: Oxford University Press.

Latour, B. and C. Venn (2002) 'Morality and technology: The end of the means', *Theory, Culture & Society*, 19 (5–6): 247–60.

Lotman, A. (2015) 'No bins for the prissy: Dumpster divers and disgust', in F. Martínez and P. Runnel (eds), *Hopeless Youth!* Tartu: Estonian National Museum, pp. 68–70.

Lynch, D. (1998) 'Lynch night', Exhibition catalogue. Available at: http://www.thecityofabsurdity.com/events/lynchnight2.html (accessed 3 August 2019).

Marcus, G. (1995) 'Ethnography in/of the world system: The emergence of multi-sited ethnography', *Annual Review of Anthropology*, 24: 95–117.

Matthey, A. (2010) 'Less is more: The influence of aspirations and priming on well-being', *Journal of Cleaner Production*, 18: 567–70.

Moré, V. (2011) 'Dumpster dinners: An ethnographic study of freeganism', *Journal for Undergraduate Ethnography*, 1: 43–55.

Navaro-Yashin, Y. (2012) *The Make-Believe Space: Affective Geography in a Postway Polity*, Durham, NC: Duke University Press.

O'Brien, M. (2008) *A Crisis of Waste? Understanding the Rubbish Society*, London: Routledge.

Przybylo, E. (2010) 'The politics of ugliness', *eSharp*, 16: 1–26.

Seyfang, G. (2005) 'Hopping for sustainability: Can sustainable consumption promote ecological citizenship?', *Environmental Politics*, 14 (2): 290–306.

Temenos, C., A. Nikolaeva, T. Schwanen, T. Cresswell, F. Sengers, M. Watson and M. Sheller (2017) 'Theorizing mobility transitions: An interdisciplinary conversation', *Transfers*, 7 (1): 113–29.

Tsing, A. (2015) *The Mushroom at the End of the World*, Princeton, NJ: Princeton University Press.

Žižek, S. (2012) *The Pervert's Guide to Ideology*, Director: Sophie Fiennes, Zeitgeist Films.

3

If buildings could talk
Makeshift urbanity on the outskirts of Lisbon

Giacomo Pozzi

This chapter is based on the study of recuperative dwelling practices in an informal settlement located in the Lisbon Metropolitan Area. Drawing on ethnographic material, it discusses how operations of repair and re-appropriation of dwellings evolve as world-making practices that create a different degree of production of space and belonging to Santa Filomena. In this neighbourhood, recuperation occurs through the act of 'mending' materials that would otherwise be treated as waste, as well as by 'fixing up' things in absence of formal protocols and in an ethnographically observed context of vulnerability and permanent crisis. From this perspective, acts of repair and re-appropriation can be considered, not only as analytical concepts but also as gestures generative of positive affects and communal participation. An interesting paradox here is that, once the makeshift urbanity is deemed legitimated and made to look formal, the immediate intervention – initially considered as temporary – sets the terms of what happens later and acquires a durable condition.

'If these houses could talk...'

'If these houses could talk and the institutions were able to listen, this would not happen.' This comment was made by Zezinha, a 62-year-old Cape Verdean migrant residing in the Santa Filomena neighbourhood of Amadora on the outskirts of Lisbon, while we sat together watching her home being demolished. Zezinha spoke to me perched atop of a mountain of clothes she had kept there in the small two-storey house, her home from 2007 to that moment in 2014. She supported herself by trading clothing and goods with Cape Verde. Given the high costs of shipping by sea, Zezinha accumulated as large a store of goods as possible before sending them on to Praia, on the Island of Santiago, for her cousin to sell. Not far from us, a bulldozer obliterated every shard of Zezinha's life and work with methodical and mechanical violence. The scene was presided over by police officers in riot gear, while some neighbours paused for a moment to watch the grim spectacle, captivated by the aesthetic of the destruction (Harms, 2013) which the entire neighbourhood was fated to undergo.

At the beginning of the 1960s, the Santa Filomena neighbourhood rose as the result of land occupations situated near the railway line that connects Lisbon to the city of Sintra. The squatters were primarily Portuguese families migrating from rural areas in the south of the country. Following the wars of independence of the Portuguese colonies, which ended between 1973 and 1975, and the intense sub-urbanisation process (Nunes, 2013), the *bairro* (neighbourhood in Portuguese) became the destination and refuge to migrants from West Africa and *retornados* (Góis, 2006; Grassi, 2006; Batalha and Carling, 2008; Pardue, 2013).[1] Initially, according to the narratives of the inhabitants I met during the fieldwork, the houses were built using waste, scraps and ragpicked versatile material, such as cardboard or wood; later, in coincidence with a deeper material and symbolical rooting of the migrants in the area, constructions were built with bricks, some of them of remarkable dimension and quality. Those houses were built by the male population of the area, occupied as manpower in the construction industry (Cachado, 2013; Alves, 2013).[2]

This chapter is grounded on the study of a peculiar form of dwelling which emerged in an informal settlement located in the Lisbon

Metropolitan Area. The research proposes an ethnographic analysis of recuperative place-making practices (and memories) – intended as operations of repair and re-appropriation – acted between the construction of the settlement, started in the 1960s and a government rehousing programme that, in 2015, provoked its extinction (Pozzi, 2017a–b). The ethnographic fieldwork, conducted between December 2013 and May 2014, was mainly carried out in the Santa Filomena *bairro*, located in Amadora. At the time of my fieldwork research, this area was characterised by an elevated spatial, ethnic and socioeconomic segregation of the inhabitants, mainly migrants native of the former Portuguese colonies, in particular Cape Verde.[3] On the one hand, I intend to focus on a long-term historical perspective as a way of illustrating the contingency of local housing informality. On the other hand, in keeping with the analytical perspective of this book, I privilege the interpretation of the key role played by recovery and repair practices in constructing living spaces in an urban context. In light of this role, then, official planning does not appear as the sole or even primary maker of housing and building policies on the outskirts of Lisbon.

The research involved a heterogeneous range of data-collection tools, mainly participant observation and observing participation. The data was recorded by hand notes in notebooks or on the computer once I arrived back at the place where I was staying. I maintained a daily, constant presence in the neighbourhood. I spent most of my time in two parts of the district occupied primarily by adults, most of them women, and children. Beyond the Cape Verdean family structure, which is matrifocal (Giuffrè, 2007), I believe I was overwhelmingly welcomed by women because I was interested in housing issues. The houses in the neighbourhood are run by women and, although they were built by men, it is the women who are in charge of managing them and worrying about future accommodations. I was invited to many lunches, a privileged moment of sharing. I helped hoe vegetable gardens, clear land, cook and hang up the laundry. Playing cards and hanging out at the bar helped me make contact with adult men. I had more difficulty interacting with young people, hindered by their daily pursuit of forms of informal income production and initial suspicion towards me. Towards the end of the research, I established ties with some young people, thanks, above all, to the fact that we protested side by side against local institutions, such as a demonstration held in the city hall and an act of squatting. I never made audio-recordings of these moments of 'everyday' research, but in some cases I used a camera. I then conducted unstructured interviews with some privileged informants, all in Portuguese, except for one conducted in Cape Verde Creole (which I understand, but speak with great difficulty).[4]

'If these houses could talk . . .,' I reflected at length on Zezinha's words, which seemed to represent a warning and methodological approach at one and the same time. After all, the ethnographic research I had been conducting in the *bairro* of Santa Filomena for several months aspired to do precisely this: to enable the houses to speak or, at least, to help them resonate in the words of the people who still lived there, in the narrated memories of those who had already been forcibly evicted. Janet Carsten recently argued that anthropology should be more engaged in listening to homes. Not so much to dialogue with them as objects in and of themselves, but because houses 'embody the interconnections between individual trajectories, kinship and the state' (Carsten, 2018: 103). Responding to Carsten's call, in this chapter I maintain that the poetics and poietics of dwelling (Herzfeld, 2016) represent a privileged standpoint for uncovering both 'the politics and practice of small incursions in material spaces, the possibilities these open up, and the forms of sociality they might entail' (Tonkiss, 2013: 315).

I intend to analyse the historical and sociopolitical processes of the production of the Santa Filomena neighbourhood as the result of efforts of public re-appropriation and recuperation in a context conditioned by insecurity, indeterminacy and imperfection. This long-term perspective has the potential to help us understand the situation of contemporary, post-crisis[5] Portugal and shed light on forms of communal recuperation and makeshift urbanism. The innovative character of this chapter lies in the fact that it approaches practices of makeshift urbanism not exclusively as object or process, but also as a strategy of recovering and re-appropriating something that has been thrown out or neglected.[6] As a result, positive affects of care, responsibility and social participation (Martínez, 2017) are made to circulate in the public sphere and critical world-making is enacted. This 'modest ontology of mending and repair' can be interpreted as a makeshift urbanism: a practice characterised by collective world-making, an improvised materialism and a specific political imaginary (Vasuvedan, 2015).

Building on ethnographic observation of the *permanent crisis* of the habitants of Santa Filomena, I seek to demonstrate how informal practices of re-appropriation, repair and reinterpretation were enacted to deal with the constant experience of vulnerability, coming to represent 'micropolitics' of recuperating (Martínez in this volume). I therefore propose to address makeshift interventions as a restorative and anthropo-poietic praxis (Remotti, 2002): anthropo-poietic because it is intimately caught up with sociocultural tactics, rituals and community values that produce specific forms of humanity (both as hegemonic or subaltern process); and restorative because of its capacity to recuperate – through ordinary experiences of care and building – the fragmentation of social, familial and community networks that can be caused by crisis, such as migration, social, political and economic exclusion, and forced removal. As I will show, these interventions produced new forms of communal participation in a regime of vulnerability and precariousness, building a future for those who were viewed as people without a future.

In the first part of the chapter, I outline the theoretical background and analytical concepts and instruments that constitute the interpretative foundations of my research hypothesis. In the second part, I describe the social history of the city of Amadora and the rise of the neighbourhood of Santa Filomena. I move between oral and written sources: the voices of the inhabitants occupy a privileged position in the hierarchy of sources, representing valuable insights into the larger flow of history. In the third section, I present the cultural biography of a specific building, relating the past and present local mending practices enacted in the production of livable spaces. These sections directly highlight the complex and ambiguous dynamics triggered when dwelling informality meets institutional normativity.

Informal dwelling as transgressive re-appropriation

It is not the goal of this chapter to engage comparatively with the vast body of anthropological literature on informality and 'do-it-yourself-urbanism' (Iveson, 2013),[7] which has already shown that housing vulnerability constitutes a structural phenomenon of capitalist-type economic policies characterising the living conditions of a vast swathe of the world's population. This fact would seem to confirm (with the due historical-geographical differences) the argument put forward by Friedrich Engels almost a century and a half ago, of the central place of housing in the reproduction of the mechanisms that reproduce capitalist marginality, exploitation and production. In this case, I make use of the term 'autoconstruction' to refer to the global phenomenon of marginal workers, who become 'home owners through a radicalizing process called autoconstruction (autoconstrução), in which they build their own houses in the urban hinterland under precarious material and legal circumstance' (Holston, 1991: 447). According to Colin Ward (2002), autoconstruction and subaltern urbanism play a significant role in the history and contemporary life of housing (Holston, 1991; Roy, 2011; Iveson, 2013) and this seems to be true in the Portuguese context as well (Cachado and Baia, 2012). In general, as the Santa Filomena case confirms, squatters occupy buildings or land with the intention of relatively long-term use (Pruijt, 2013). In this sense, squatting, and dwelling informality more generally, could represent an expression of widespread housing precarity and a radical form of living and producing the city.

Italian urban planners Carlo Cellamare and Francesca Cognetti recently asserted that processes and practices of re-appropriation:

> are able to strengthen other 'indirect' dimensions: the experimentation of alternative economies, the value of diversity, the caring dimension, the rationalities of the re-use and a richer and more complex way of inhabiting. These experiences invite also to reflect on the opportunity (or not) to have mechanisms of reinforcing some social capabilities gotten started: organisation and self-regulatory capabilities, capability of 'returning' some of the urban parts to the city, triggering care processes and skills focused on the handling of public issues.
>
> 2014: 7

According to this perspective, it could even be argued that informal practices of re-appropriation are not simply 'returning some of the urban parts of the city', but are actually contributing to the recovery of these areas by disseminating interstitial processes of (material, symbolical and theoretical) 'centralization of the margins' (Malighetti, 2012).

Likewise, and echoing Keith Hart (1973), I suggest that informality can be interpreted as a political reparative poetic and example of communal recuperation, in my case study constituting specific ways of transgressing the ideology of the neoliberal city. The verb *to transgress* comes from the Latin *transgredior* and means literally *to go through*. The term 'transgression' may include a great variety of forms of adaptation, reaction and resistance, in the cases examined enacted by residents in a Portuguese context. According to Michel Foucault, transgression is an action that 'involves the limit, that narrow zone of a line where it displays the flash of its passage, but perhaps also its entire trajectory, even its origin; it is likely that transgression has its entire space in the line it crosses' (1977: 33–4). It is precisely the fact that these actions are enacted inside the limits that gives them the power to overcome these limits, that is, to transgress them. The concept of transgression can thus represent a useful interpretative tool for analysing the effects of austerity. In this sense, repair itself can be considered an act of recuperative transgression, a symbolic and social strategy for overcoming scarcity through the transformative excess of ordinary materiality.

Home and world-making

Amadora, once called Porcalhota, was established in 1885–6 when it ceded from the ancient community of Benfica. In the nineteenth century, the village was characterised by a rural economy and high incidence of farmers and shepherds. On 17 April 1916, it was elevated to the status of an administrative fraction (*Freguesia*) of the Municipality of Oeiras. It was then promoted to *vila* (town) on 24 June 1937 under the dictatorship of António de Oliveira Salazar (1932–68). It was not until 11 September 1979, a few years after the end of the totalitarian regime, that the Municipality of Amadora was created. In the mid-1950s, the city underwent 'a sharp increase of the population', to quote a municipal officer responsible for implementing the rehousing programme in the area (interview, 27 February 2014),[8] together with an intense process of urbanisation (Nunes, 2010). As a document produced by the Amadora City Hall attests, between 1950 and 1970, Amadora underwent unprecedentedly sharp demographic spikes, with ten-year rates of 150 per cent and 134 per cent, due to the development of the transport infrastructure and migratory movements following the industrialisation of the metropolitan area (*Amadora XXI Census*, 2011: 13). The industrialisation of the peripheral area of Lisbon is key to understanding the intense demographic increase and upsurge of migration into this area, especially coming from southern Portugal. Together with this internal migration, many international migrants also arrived from the archipelago of Cape Verde (Pardue, 2013) during this period, especially young men looking for work (Cachado, 2013). These migrants came to make up for the scarcity of manpower caused by the high rates of Portuguese emigration towards other European countries that were undergoing reconstruction after the Second World War (Batalha and Carling, 2008). Several of the interlocutors I encountered during the research also confirmed this fact. During the period when I was conducting fieldwork, Manuela had been working as a municipal officer for the Municipality of Amadora for about ten years. When I met her, she was in charge of managing evacuation operations in the Santa Filomena neighbourhood. Manuela had extensive knowledge of the local area, especially in terms of its history. In an effort to describe the structural housing vulnerability of Amadora, she referenced the migratory phenomenon that had characterised this area for some time. In her words:

> In that period, over one and a half million people emigrated from Portugal: they were young people of working age, male. Portugal in that period was very poor and was subdued by a dictatorship. When Portugal tried to develop its own industry, there was the need for labor and this was sourced in the colonies, in the countries of P.A.L.O.P. [Portuguese-speaking African countries]:[9] Mozambique, Angola and Cape Verde, mainly. Salazar[10] used to *import* manpower. 'Import' because he obliged people to come . . . In Amadora is concentrated . . . the central nucleus of Cape Verdean migration in the country.
>
> MANUELA, Municipal Officer, interview, 27 February 2014

Amadora è terra de pretos (Amadora is a land of blacks), an activist for the rights of migrants from the former colonies told me one day with evident pride, and the Santa Filomena neighbourhood was one of the most significant places in this *terra*.[11] According to my interlocutors, these newcomers gave rise to non-compliance with existing local property laws, land-use regulations and building codes. Indeed, since the 1970s, it has been very common for people to occupy uncultivated and (apparently) abandoned land. At the same time, the existence of the informal *bairros* became socially and politically visible. While on one hand there was, indeed, an urgent demand for labour both nationally and internationally, on the other hand Portugal was not prepared to receive and adequately accommodate these migrants (ACIDI, 2011; Cachado, 2013; Cachado and Baia, 2012; Alves, 2013; Habita, 2014).

João was one of the first squatters in the neighbourhood. Born in Praia in the 1950s, he arrived in Portugal together with 800,000 other people in the year the Portuguese empire disintegrated, 1974, and then made his way to the *bairro* in 1977. From the moment he arrived, he worked as a bricklayer in the Lisbon area. When I met him, he lived in a modest two-storey house he had built by himself, using materials he was able to recover from the construction sites where he worked. The house was nestled between a tree and a larger building, and the debris of the houses that had recently been demolished made it difficult for him to reach his front door:

> At the beginning, there were few of us living here. We came from the other side of the river [Tagus]:[12] we found work here and, as these lands were abandoned, we built a house here.
>
> JOÃO, Santa Filomena inhabitant since 1977,
> interview, 17 April 2014

As João's statement suggests, succeeding in establishing a stable living space is tantamount to succeeding in one's trajectory of migration. In this sense, the illegal appropriation of lands can be understood as an act of 'systemic' repair and recuperation, characterised by intense agency on the part of migrants that compensates for a lack of public and government organisation and recuperation of an area that has been abandoned (or is at least perceived as abandoned). At the same time, forms of recuperation can also be interpreted in terms of the unexpected results these efforts produce, generating an unpredictable patchwork of services, provisions, networks or even infrastructures. In general, the first squatters of the *bairro* used to live in highly precarious conditions and in constant conflict with local institutions. According to their narratives, the migrants moved to these lands in search of an informal refuge. Research participants recounted how, in the very first moments of the foundation of the community, they were able to improvise reusing scrap and discarded materials and domesticating long-abandoned spaces. In João's words:

> At the beginning, the houses were made of cardboard, or wood, or wood and cardboard together. Then, with time, we built this one [indicating his own house]. We stayed here even if the municipality did not want [us to] . . . Here there was nobody before, then a little here, a little there, then all the spaces . . .
>
> JOÃO, Santa Filomena inhabitant since 1977, interview, 17 April 2014

João's account describes how the very first installation in the area immediately produced a renewed material world and generated positive affects: 'Here there was nobody before, then . . .' This foundation was formed of necessity and precariousness, but at the same time it can be read as a moment of makeshift through which new webs of solidarity were developed (Mayer, 2013). Emilio, another long-term inhabitant of the neighbourhood, also confirmed this perspective, when he explained that the auto-construction process was both the result of an ensemble of *bricolage* practices (Lévi-Strauss, 1962) and a method of place-making and collective organisation:

> [in the beginning] People used to build only wooden barracks. Then people got organised to build with bricks. Therefore, many times we took all the wood away from the walls [to sell it and buy more materials] and ended up with only the mattress! Then the municipality used to come to tell us that we could not build with bricks and so, to avoid this problem, people built directly inside the wooden barrack.
>
> EMILIO, Santa Filomena habitant, interview, 25 March 2014

As this description underlines, residents' continuous practices of repairing and recovering were aimed at achieving more stable living conditions, mainly in accordance with the hegemonic configuration of values and desires (Holston, 1991). As Emilio explained, in order to avoid an 'open clash' with institutions, migrants attempted to find alternative and informal solutions to continue building their own houses and to improve their living conditions. In this sense, the first period of life in the *bairro* was characterised by a general non-compliance with the existing laws regulating land use, property and residential construction. For example, the tactic of erecting a building with bricks inside an existing wooden structure,[13] possibly during the night to maintain the 'hidden transcript' (Scott, 1990) and avoid attracting unwanted attention,[14] seems to epitomise the meaning of such actions. As João reported to me:

João The municipality didn't want [us to build] or, better, wanted the houses to keep being made with wood, only wood . . . However, in wooden barracks there are no conditions [for living]! There were fields everywhere around here [*gesticulating*], there was the packed dirt floor and so we built these [houses].

Giacomo Since the municipality opposed the settlement, how did you fix it?

João Slowly. We had to do it during the night. We built only during the night and this is the result [*proudly indicating his house*]. Many houses were demolished before being finished because they were illegal . . . If they saw you while you were building, they would come to demolish . . . And so, we built some house in just one night! In one night, you could build all the walls, you could invite people to help you . . . And then, on another night, the roof . . .

JOÃO, 17 April 2014

João's words show that, at least in the beginning, the building process in Santa Filomena was regulated by three main factors. First, a lack of the economic resources needed to participate in the real estate private market; second, the possibility of obtaining preferential access to construction skills (cultural capital) and materials. In fact, the majority of the male inhabitants used to work in *construção civil* (construction industry) and this background allowed them to informally track down materials and carry out construction. And finally, mutual aid, familial and neighbourhood networks (social capital) played a fundamental role in the settlement building process: these networks were inserted in individual or familiar migratory routes (Grassi, 2006; Batalha and Carling, 2008), enormously improving the efficacy of the process of generative re-setting and re-territorialisation. In this sense, the first factor (lack of resources) demonstrates the selectivity and inequalities that determine the geography of the neoliberal city. The second provides a shining example of recuperative and transgressive responses to socioeconomic exclusion: the cultural capital of the community was activated, thus producing a makeshift urbanism that reinvented the abandoned area through acts of re-appropriation, mending and bricolage. Finally, the last factor speaks to Martin Heidegger's (1971) theory on dwelling, demonstrating the connections between building practices and the cultivation of social identity and community belonging.

Another peculiar aspect has to do with the selection of different building materials (from cardboard to wood, from wood to bricks) and illustrates the temporal dimension of dwelling, as well as existing politics of recognition, hospitality and belonging. Likewise, the quality of the building materials used in this case reflects the social and political role of the Santa Filomena community as perceived by city administrations, indicating the intrinsic social and symbolic value of such materials. For instance, while cardboard – in migrants' narrations – represents the severe vulnerability and precariousness of the initial period of occupation,[15] the transition to wood indicates an improvement in living and working conditions (in this case as well, conceded by institutions), while the final step toward the use of bricks asserts the solidity of the settlement as well as the severe opposition it encountered from local government. Paradoxically, we can read these passages through the lens of recuperation: on one side, the progression of different materials indicates the growth of local mutual aid networks, while on the other side it conveys the settlement's evolving relations with institutions. Likewise, there is an interesting relationship between repair and recuperation, two acts that the residents' oral narrations position as part of the same sphere.

This relationship emphasises the centrality of the 'house repair strategies' through which locals sought to transgress institutional bans on settling permanently in the area.

According to residents' accounts, the first phase of settlement was characterised by the need to build a primary good, a house. Settlement then entered a second phase (in the 1980s and 1990s), in which the neighbourhood was equipped with basic infrastructure: access to water and electricity, connection to the sewer system and road construction. According to the narratives I collected, when these services were finally provided in the neighbourhood, the shift produced a local conflict based on dispossessions, re-appropriations and different registers of negotiation. However, while in general the first phase of settling down was characterised by patent non-compliance with the rules in effect at the time, this second phase involved continuous negotiations with the Municipality of Amadora. The city was interested in managing the growing number of people who were settling in the area thanks to migratory chains and family networks, and one of the tools it most used was to formally legalise local housing illegality. This took place through a delicate process of bureaucratic-administrative inclusion, intended as the first step towards substantial inclusion.

In general, my research found that, from an institutional point of view, conceding Santa Filomena inhabitants access to basic resources would have been tantamount to publicly admitting that the neighbourhood existed and had a right to exist. The institutions thus feared the symbolic implications of a public recognition of their failure. That is, a public effort to 'fix' the previous mistake (the total absence of urban planning, migration and housing policies and consequent production of numerous illegal settlements such as Santa Filomena) would make this mistake widely evident to the citizenry. In the initial period, the local institutions decided to avoid becoming involved in any way in addressing this issue. As a result, the local population decided to personally provide all the infrastructural services needed to ensure better livability for the area. In so doing, the local population was reacting to a perception of political injustice. Emilio, who had lived in Santa Filomena since 1977 and participated in constructing its infrastructure, described the situation as follows:

Emilio   We are the ones who built the sanitation! . . . We built all this, we did this. The sewage system from that door, can you see it? Here and even those down there, people made them. After, what did the municipality do?! They gave the people more materials and said: 'now go on building!' . . . and this is what happened. . . . More or less in 1985. Before, there were only fountains. People used to get water there at the fountains . . . Then we made some connections with tubes at the fountain to bring water [to homes]; the municipality saw that it was losing a lot of money and started fixing it . . .

Giacomo   Did this happen in the same period as the sanitation?

Emilio   No, no, water was the first thing [fixed]. And light, too; the sewage system only came later.

Giacomo   So, it seems to me that the institutions have never done anything directly, they have only reused what people had done before. Is that right?

Emilio   Yes, it has always been like this! The municipality did none of what you see here now!

EMILIO, Santa Filomena habitant, interview, 25 March 2014

According to the information provided by Emilio, the Municipality of Amadora decided after the fact to institutionalise the residents' work in some way. In this case, the local institutions repossessed the inhabitants' appropriations, producing a *mirror trick* that reflects the complex configuration of political implications entailed by those informal practices. In reality, a municipal officer also confirmed the version of events provided by residents (interview, 27 February 2014), although without openly explaining how the infrastructure had been furnished to the community. Furthermore, the actors involved in the conflict interpreted the supply of services in different ways. From the point of view of the institutions, the necessity of equipping the *bairro* was perceived as a risky move to institutionalise the occupation and a sort of concession. On the other hand, the inhabitants, especially those who did not participate in the material construction of infrastructure, interpreted the provision of services in the *bairro* (and continuative payment of light, water, sewage and trash collection bills)[16] as a weighty symbol of a tacit and ambiguous legalisation process. Moreover, rhetorically, the Amadora Municipality interpreted the move to ensure service provision as a guarantee of democratic participation and mechanism of social inclusion, but exclusively in a formal sense. In contrast, the Santa Filomena community understood this move as an act of recognition that was more substantial than formal. In this sense, reparative self-building processes acted not only on the material level, but also – and more efficaciously – on the symbolic and mythological narrative of the local world-making praxis.

In the 1980s, the process of reparative building and dwelling proceeded, keeping pace with the residents' personal and familial investment in the territory; the social relationships they formed reinforced the foundations of a community, albeit a frail one. At this point, the neighbourhood grew into the composition of alleys, paths, cul-de-sacs and bottlenecks that continue to hold a key place in the inhabitants' memories and left traces on the ground, some still visible during my fieldwork. The *bairro* began 'filling up', in part because of constant commerce in land,[17] sometimes conducted informally and at other times in a more legalised form.[18] Excluded from the formal market and denied access to social housing for migrants (Alves, 2013), a real estate market was structured *inside* Santa Filomena. Some Cape Verdean migrants bought land and buildings from Portuguese locals and used them to build barracks in the area. Once the land had been purchased, in many cases informally and without any documentation of ownership – although many still remember the price very well! – the houses were improved and more lots of land were occupied, or purchased, thus generating a collective process of self-construction and *autogestion* (Lefebvre, 1991), as mentioned above.

Gradually, the entire area came to be 'owned'. Even though there was no documentation, the community is conscious of this territorial division of property. In the meantime, streets were given names, common spaces – not for sale or transfer – were identified and local governments began the process of partially institutionalising the neighbourhood. João (interview, 17 April 2014) underlined that many residents who sold lots or buildings were not the legitimate (legal) owners of the property in question: indeed, as trade was informal from the beginning, the person who used and occupied the land was often not the 'legal owner', the person indicated in the real estate registry as the landowner. Furthermore, for more than thirty years, the 'real legal owners' did not show up to complain and it was only in 2013 that local residents, some of them with property certificates, discovered how the territory was 'really' subdivided. At any rate, this division was revoked in 2007, when the real estate investment fund Villafundo acquired the entire area.[19]

Clearing, filling, demolishing

Reconstructing the social biography of a building reveals the valuable role practices of repair and recuperation play in the reproduction and modification of living spaces. As mentioned above, my fieldwork period coincided with the end phase of implementing a governmental rehousing programme governed by Decree-Law 63/1993, known as *Programa Especial de Realojamento* (PER). PER was formulated to regulate the massive housing emergency (Ferreira, 1994), defined by the programme as a 'huge social plague'. In the case of Santa Filomena, the programme involved demolishing the entire neighbourhood and rehousing some of its residents in public housing. The process of implementing the rehousing of local inhabitants in public housing structures produced complex dynamics of adaptation, resistance and struggle (Pozzi, 2017a–b). The Programa Especial de Realojamento offered a top-down opportunity to the municipalities situated in Porto and Lisbon metropolitan areas to proceed with the elimination of local informal settlements and, at the same time, to provide the resident population with new accommodation in public-housing buildings (Ferreira, 1994; Cachado, 2013). The rehousing process excluded many residents on the grounds that they had arrived in the *bairro* after the 1993 census. Furthermore, the land on which the neighbourhood was located was bought in 2007 by a real estate investment fund, Villafundo, that was managed by Portugal's biggest banking group, Millenium BCP (Habita, 2014), which added further impetus to the drive to 'reclaim' the area.

Although the city asserted its claim on the area with insistence and violence, the inhabitants of the *bairro* adapted their practices of local area anthropisation to the new conditions. They thus reconceptualised the destruction of their living space on the basis of the makeshift model that had characterised both the original creation of the neighbourhood and the following phase of adaptation and stabilisation. Specifically, they creatively resignified institutional policies of eviction, transforming them into new forms of dwelling. As Carsten notes: 'Houses are not of course solely the outcome of the interplay of individual lives and of familial intimacies. The forms they take and their content and resources reflect the attentions or neglect of the state and local and broader economic conditions' (2018: 105). Repair, mending and recovery played a fundamental role in this process. To illustrate and argue this point, in the following I present the sociocultural biography of a building located in the eastern part of the neighbourhood that I was able to follow throughout my fieldwork, observing how it was changed, used and resignified on a daily basis.

Maria, a Cape Verdean migrant who arrived in the neighbourhood in the first half of the 1990s thanks to familial reunification with her husband, had lived in Santa Filomena since the early 1980s. According to Maria, the building in question was constructed in the second half of the 1980s on a plot of agricultural land. A family moved in, made up of a mother, father and two adolescent boys. The father worked in construction while the mother took produce grown in the *bairro* and sold it in the area around the Amadora station area. When the eldest son had his own child, the father of the family decided to add an additional storey onto the house to accommodate the new family. With the support of other bricklayers and carpenters living in the neighbourhood, and salvaging the materials from the building sites where he worked, he quickly built the second floor. Maria described the building as occupying an area of at least 50 square meters in size and having a wall decorated with graffiti.

Jumping forward in time, the families were evicted in 2012. The family that had been living on the ground floor was rehoused in public housing on the outskirts of Amadora. The city did not offer the son's family any form of compensation for the loss of their home, since it had been built after 1993. Following the eviction, the building remained empty. Other residents of the *bairro* then proceeded to remove its doors and windows to sell them on the informal market. As I had the opportunity to observe for myself, in December 2013, the second floor was demolished because it communicated with a building located behind it that was also being demolished. The ground floor of the building remained intact. At first, it was used by some young neighbourhood residents for informal trafficking, mostly drugs, and in some cases by individuals from outside the *bairro* to consume narcotics.

Zezinha, whom I introduced at the beginning of this chapter, found herself in February 2014 with the debris of a former house and no rights to any compensation for her loss. Given her situation, she decided to use the building as a warehouse to store the goods she had collected for her trade activity, so as not to lose them. She thus asked me to help her clear out the debris and rubbish from inside the building, with the aid of some other residents. We cleared out a space she could use to store her goods. She chose a room without windows, so that her collection would not be seen and stolen and, with the help of a neighbour, filled the empty space left by the missing front door with a piece of laminated pressboard and some boards. In the end, however, Zezinha had accumulated a large store of goods and the space carved out was not big enough to hold them all: many of her items were therefore left at other homes in the neighbourhood, thus activating networks of kinship and mutual aid. Residents cleared out storage spaces, closets and other little niches so that her goods could be placed there, and Zezinha stayed for almost two months with her neighbour, Maria.

After some time, not having enough money, she decided to resell some of her goods on-site and so temporarily transformed the warehouse into a store to display the items for sale. When this failed to achieve the degree of success she had been hoping for, she moved on to selling homemade food: tuna and chicken croquettes, blood sausage and *cachupa* (Cape Verde soup). She thus decided to transform the warehouse/shop into a kitchen: using recycled materials and the help of a resident (whom she paid in kind, giving him meals), she set up a table to work on, wash basins and a hob inside the building; outside, she set up a fire to cook the *cachupa* and smoke the blood sausage. After a few weeks of earning rather well, she managed to ship her goods to Cape Verde, where they were picked up by a cousin who was in charge of selling them retail. At this point, she cleared out the warehouse/shop/kitchen. A few days later, the building was demolished, together with the neighbouring house. The day after the destruction of this house, some residents came in to begin tilling and sowing the land, taking advantage of the open space freed up by the demolition.

The biography of this building effectively illustrates the creative character of the repair, recovery and mending practices enacted in the Santa Filomena neighbourhood. It also gives us the opportunity to consider how urban living spaces – and cities as a whole – represent the effervescent fruit of these forms of makeshift urbanism. In the case of Santa Filomena, a common thread seems to weave together practices from the past, as narrated by informants, and the contemporary practices I observed first hand. Specifically, there is a certain continuity in the way inhabitants self-construct and creatively manipulate urban-planning frameworks and the local landscape. Networks of relationships, in this specific case between relatives, neighbours and acquaintances, are activated in a collective manner to resolve the critical challenges of precarious housing; at the same time, the residents' informal practices adapt to the spatiality of the area and its spatiality adapts to the residents' informal system of commerce.

Concluding considerations

In this chapter, I focused on a peculiar recovered dwelling that emerged from interactions among heterogeneous actors, representations and politics. Through the inhabitants' narratives, I explored the state of exception (Agamben, 2003) that has characterised the area since its foundation as a neighbourhood. The narratives depicted a recuperative production of space imbued with a general precariousness, the result of broader institutional neglect. As João and Emilio explained, when local inhabitants perceived a widespread lack of political will to resolve their situation, they were driven to enact various recovery tactics, with the power to transgress the permanent crisis produced by their socioeconomic exclusion. These interventions were enacted at different levels and through different registers, namely involving material, political, economic, representational and moral forms of engagement. In this sense, the recuperative makeshift urbanism that emerged in the area can be interpreted as a generative (material and discursive) world-making process. From this perspective, repair and re-appropriation interventions can be considered, not as only interpretative tropes but also as generative forms of creative cultural, political and social production.

The notion of makeshift urbanism highlights self-made 'modes of urban practice that work in the margins between formal planning, speculative investment and local possibilities' (Tonkiss, 2013: 313). The Santa Filomena case study demonstrates the epistemological centrality of marginal creative practices in anthropological analysis. Indeed, the interpretation of interstitial acts such as informal forms of dwelling allow us to shed light on a wider context by looking at its own specific borders, limits and cracks. In this sense, the social analysis of such interstitial elements forces the researcher to abandon the exclusive use of *etic* or *emic* categories and classifications and to treat the city as a method (Corsín Jiménez, 2017). This move encourages the emergence of empirical and dialectical categories that prove highly useful for the oblique and original analysis of contemporary worlds. In short, categories such as repair, recovery, transgression and re-appropriation appear to be prolific tools for a proactive anthropology devoted to ensuring that its intellectual and analytical speculations give rise to practical outcomes.

Notes

1 The term *retornados* denotes the Portuguese population of the colonies, specifically those in the colonial territories and members of the colonial administrative apparatus, who arrived in Portugal after the decolonisation process. See, for instance, Dacosta (2013) and David (2015).
2 According to the census conducted in 1993 by the Amadora Municipality, in Santa Filomena there were 442 buildings for a total of 1,945 residents, divided into 547 familiar nuclei. Estimations said that in the last twenty-five years, even if there are no coherent data in this respect, the number of buildings increased by at least one-third, with an equivalent growth of the population (Habita, 2014).
3 An archipelago located in the North Atlantic Ocean, off the shore of West Africa.

4 I tried to stick to a story or interview format. All the names in this chapter are pseudonyms in order to protect the identity of informants. The material generated through fieldwork was also cross-referenced with archival research, academic and non-academic literature, newspaper articles and reports.

5 I use 'post-crisis' to refer to the sociopolitical context created following the Troika (ECB, EC and IMF) intervention of 2011, a €78 billion economic bailout that finally ended in May 2014. In terms of housing policies, the Passos Coelho government of the time was obliged to reform its National Housing Law (Lei das Rendas), following a council held by the 'triad' conveyed by the Monitoring Committee for the Reform of Urban Housing. Generally speaking, the main changes effected worsened the situation of tenants: shorter contracts, increases in rent, a reduction of the time allotted for vacating the property if the contract lapsed, accelerated evictions and reduced compensation. This iron grip on the private market accelerated the dismantling of illegally constructed neighbourhoods, fuelling a public rhetoric celebrating more rights for those living outside the law (unauthorised immigrants who were not evicted) rather than for those who respected it.

6 This interpretative hypothesis should be considered as part of a wider conceptual framework, also characterised by ambiguities and limits. One of the main risks of this perspective is that of perceiving the interpretative categories of formal and informal as radically distinct. However, instead of regarding this as a dichotomic relation, we should consider these categories as occupying a dialectical configuration. The second risk is that of conceptualising informality as a 'social-class characteristic'. In this sense, informality functions as a metonymy of the urban poor. Nevertheless, many studies (e.g. Sassen, 2001; MacFarlane and Waibel, 2011, 2012) have demonstrated the social pervasiveness of informality in the practices of the middle and upper classes, showing the groundlessness of the equation: informality = poverty. The third risk is that of considering the social actors who engage in informal acts as exclusively 'heroic and creative entrepreneurs' (Roy, 2011): the result is a tendency to romanticise social actors and completely overlook the role of the structural causes – economic, political and social – that contribute to the production of informality.

7 Nevertheless, some references are necessary to contextualise the theoretical framework in which this ethnographic analysis has been conducted. In particular, some inspiring anthropological analyses of housing informality are Holston (1991) and Murphy (2015) for the South American context; Ong and Roy (2011), Harms (2013),

Schwenkel (2012) and Herzfeld (2016) for Southeast Asia; and Appadurai (2000) and Roy (2011) for India.

8 All the excerpts from interviews were translated by the author.

9 Países Africanos de Lingua Oficial Portuguesa. This group was established in 1996 and represents six African countries, all of them former Portuguese colonies (with the exception of Equatorial Guinea), the official language of which is Portuguese. The countries are Angola, Cape Verde, Guinea Bissau, Equatorial Guinea, Mozambique, and São Tomé and Príncipe.

10 António de Olivera Salazar, dictator of Portugal, 1932–68.

11 The Municipal Officer interviewed observes, confirming a revisionist stereotype, that the emergence of informal settlements in the area coincided with the arrival of migrants from former colonies: however, most of the informal Portuguese neighbourhoods were founded by internal migrants (Cachado, 2013) and not international ones, although from a subsequent period to the present former colonial subjects represent the main populations of these settlements (ACIDI, 2011).

12 The south side of the river is one of the oldest industrial zones in Portugal, dominated by the fishing and metallurgic industries.

13 The first time a participant described this tactic to me was when I was interviewing an activist from Habita (Roberta, 4 February 2014). The activist asserted that this tactic could be considered a primary form of informal resistance to institutional control and the ban on semi-permanent occupation in the area.

14 A social actor affirmed that, in the early 1990s, some of the residents of the *bairro* were actually spies being paid by the municipality. I am unable to confirm this statement because I was not able to locate any more accounts that mention it.

15 Remarkably, in residents' narratives of their memories, these past conditions are often compared to current ones, now that, following the implementation of the Special Plan of Rehousing and austerity regime, there is a widespread perception that the neighbourhood suffers from degradation, precariousness and discord.

16 I collected information dating back to the 1980s that show residents did, in fact, pay for lighting and water services. These documents are often treated as proof of a sort of moral contract between the supplying entity and consumer rather than an economic or legal one. This exacerbates the residents' feelings that the rehousing programme represents an example of institutional deceit.

17 This trade has always been illegal in character, in the sense that houses are built on private lots. This fact was clearly depicted by

the land registry map, which provides a graphic illustration of the 1993 census, conducted to assess the possible scope of the Rehousing Plan. Here, the land appears to be broken up into many separate lots.

18 Some residents of the *bairro*, above all those who have been living there for years, have registered their houses with the national land registry and pay the municipal property tax (IMI-Imposto Municipal sobre Imóveis).

19 The zone was valued at €25,210,590.72 and, for the investors, amounted to an additional value of €1,389,409.28 (Habita, 2014).

References

Agamben, G. (2003) *Lo Stato di Eccezione*, Torino: Bollati Boringhieri.
Alto Comisariado para a Imigração e Dialogo Intercultural (ACIDI) (2011) *Acesso à Habitação e problemas residenciais dos imigrantes em Portugal*, Lisbon: ACIDI.
Alves, R. (2013) *Para uma compreensão da segregação residencial: o Plano Especial de Realojamento e o (Anti-)Racismo*, Lisbon: Faculdade de Ciências Sociais e Humanas (FCSH), Universidade Nova de Lisboa.
Amadora XXI Census, 2011 (2011) Available at: http://www.cm-amadora.pt/territorio/informacao-geografica/estatisticas/602-pop-e-hab.html (accessed 3 August 2019).
Appadurai, A. (2000) 'Spectral housing and urban cleansing: Notes on millenial Mumbai', *Public Culture*, 12 (3): 627–51.
Batalha, L. and J. Carling (eds) (2008) *Transnational Archipelago: Perspectives on Cape Verdean Migration and Diaspora*, Amsterdam: Amsterdam University Press.
Cachado, À. R. (2013) 'O Programa especial de Realojamento: Ambiente histórico, politico e social', *Análise Social*, 206, 48 (1): 134–52.
Cachado, À. R. and J. Baía (eds) (2012) *Politicas de habitação e costrução informal*, Lisbon: Mundos Sociais.
Carsten, J. (2018) 'House-lives as ethnography/biography', *Social Anthropology*, 26 (1): 103–16.
Cellamare, C. and F. Cognetti (eds) (2014) *Practices of Reappropriation*, Rome: Planum.
Corsín Jiménez, A. (2017) 'Auto-construction redux: The city as method', *Cultural Anthropology*, 32 (3): 450–78.
Dacosta, F. (2013) *Os retornados mudaram Portugal*, Lisbon: Parsifal.
David, I. (2015) 'The *retornados*: Trauma and displacement in post-revolution Portugal', *Ethnicity Studies*, 2: 114–30.

De Boeck, F. (2015) 'Divining' the city: Rhythm, amalgamation and knotting as forms of "urbanity"', *Social Dynamics: A Journal of African Studies*, 41: 47–58.
Engels, F. (1872) *The Housing Question*, Moscow: Co-operative Publishing Society of Foreign Workers.
Ferreira, A. F. (1994) 'Habitação social: lições e prevenções para o PER', *Sociedade e Território*, 20: 8–10.
Foucault, M. (1977) 'A preface to transgression', in *Language, Counter-Memory, Practice: Selected Essays and Interviews*, Ithaca, NY: Cornell University Press, pp. 29–52.
Giuffrè, M. (2007) *Donne di Capo Verde: Esperienze di antropologia dialogica a Ponta do Sol*. Roma: Cisu.
Góis, P. (2006) *Emigração cabo-verdiana para (e na) Europa e sua inserção em mercados de trabalho locais*, Lisbon: Alto-Comissariado para a Imigração e Minorias Étnicas.
Grassi, M. (2006) *Cabo Verde pelo Mundo: o Género e a Diáspora Cabo-Verdiana*, Lisbon: Imprensa de Ciências Sociais (ICS).
Habita (2014) 'Dossier Santa Filomena'. Available at: http://www.habita.info/2014/05/dossier-bairro-de-santa-filomena.html (accessed April 2018).
Harms, E. (2013) 'Beauty as control in the new Saigon: Eviction, new urban zones, and atomized dissent in a Southeast Asian city', *American Ethnologist*, 39 (4): 735–50.
Hart, K. (1973) 'Informal income opportunities and urban unemployment in Ghana', *Journal of Modern African Studies*, 11 (1): 61–89.
Heidegger, M. (1971) 'Building dwelling thinking', in *Poetry, Language, Thought*, New York: Harper Colophon.
Herzfeld, M. (2016) *Siege of the Spirits: Community and Polity in Bangkok*, Chicago, IL: University of Chicago Press.
Holston, J. (1991) 'Autoconstruction in working-class Brazil', *Cultural Anthropology*, 6 (4): 447–65.
Iveson, K. (2013) 'Cities within the city: Do-it-yourself urbanism and the right to the city', *International Journal of Urban and Regional Research*, 37 (3): 941–56.
Lefebvre, H. (1991) *The Production of Space*, Oxford: Blackwell.
Lévi-Strauss, C. (1962) *La Pensée Sauvage*, Paris: Pion.
MacFarlane C. and M. Waibel (2011) *Learning the City: Knowledge and Translocal Assemblage*, Oxford: Blackwell.
MacFarlane C. and M. Waibel (eds) (2012) *Urban Informalities: Reflections on the Formal and Informal*, London: Routledge.
Malighetti, R. (2012) 'La centralità dei margini', in A. Koensler and A. Rossi (eds), *Comprendere il dissenso: Etnografia e antropologia dei movimenti sociali*. Perugia: Morlacchi, pp. 7–11.
Martínez, F. (2017) 'Waste is not the end: For an anthropology of care, maintenance and repair', *Social Anthropology*, 25 (3): 346–50.

Mayer, M. (2013) 'Preface', in Squatting Europe Kollektive SqEK (eds), *Squatting in Europe: Radical Spaces, Urban Struggles*, London: Minor Compositions, pp. 1–9.

Murphy, E. (2015) *For a Proper Home: Housing Rights in the Margins of Urban Chile, 1960–2010*, Pittsburgh, PA: University of Pittsburgh Press.

Nunes, J. P. S. (2010) 'Dos subúrbios citadinos aos subúrbios metropolitanos: Estrutura de povoamento e morfogénese da metrópole de Lisboa (1950–2001)', *Cidades, Comunidades e Territórios*, 20/21: 123–37.

Nunes, J. P. S. (2013) 'O programa Habitaçoes de Renda Economica e a constituiçao da metropole de Lisboa (1959–1969)', *Analise Social*, 206, 48 (1): 82–100.

Ong, A. and A. Roy (2011) *Worlding Cities: Asian Experiments and the Art of Being Global*, Malden, MA: Wiley Blackwell.

Pardue, D. (2013) 'The role of creole history and space in Cape Verdean migration to Lisbon, Portugal', *Urban Anthropology*, 42 (2): 95–134.

Pitzalis, S., G. Pozzi and L. Rimoldi (2017) 'Per un'antropologia dell'abitare contemporaneo: Pratiche e rappresentazioni', *Antropologia*, 4 (3): 7–18.

Pozzi, G. (2017a) 'Cronache dell'abitare: Pratiche di costruzione informale e rialloggiamento forzato nel quartiere Santa Filomena (Lisboa)', *Antropologia*, 4 (1): 71–91.

Pozzi, G. (2017b) '"Quebrar a luta": Etnografia di un conflitto sociale ad Amadora (Lisboa)', *Dada: Rivista di antropologia post globale*, Special Issue (1): 203–46.

Pruijt, H. (2013) 'The logic of urban squatting', *International Journal of Urban and Regional Research*, 37: 19–45.

Remotti, F. (ed.) (2002) *Forme di umanità*, Milan: Mondadori.

Roy, A. (2011) 'Slumdog cities: Rethinking subaltern urbanism', *International Journal of Urban and Regional Research*, 35: 223–38.

Sassen, S. (2001) *The Global Cities: New York, London, Tokyo*, Princeton, NJ: Princeton University Press.

Schwenkel, C. (2012) 'Civilizing the city: Socialist ruins and urban renewal in central Vietnam', *Positions*, 20 (2): 437–70.

Scott, J. (1990) *Domination and the Arts of Resistance: Hidden Transcripts*, New Haven, CT: Yale University Press.

Tonkiss, F. (2013) 'Austerity urbanism and the makeshift city', *City*, 17 (3): 312–24.

Vasuvedan, A. (2015) 'The makeshift city: Towards a global geography of squatting', *Progress in Human Geography*, 39 (3): 338–59.

Ward, C. (2002) *Cotters and Squatters: Housing's Hidden History*, Nottingham: Five Leaves.

4

Geographies of public art and urban regeneration in Lisbon

Chiara Pussetti and Vitor Barros

On a warm summer evening in July 2017, we had a fortuitous encounter with the street artist Andrea Tarli who, exactly one year before, had painted one of the flagship artworks of our event, *Paratissima Lisbon*.[1] During the span of that year, the artwork had gathered an incredible amount of attention but, when we asked if he was happy with it, he sighed heavily and said, 'Yes and no. It's a bag of mixed feelings.' We could understand his point of view. After several weeks dialoguing with the population in Mouraria – a rundown old quarter in the city centre, subject to intense regeneration in the past five years – Andrea Tarli could sense the growing disquiet of the local population with the recent touristic wave. With his activist stance, he decided to give voice to those anxieties and produced an anamorphic mural depicting a middle-aged Portuguese lady spray-painting the face of a hipster tourist holding a selfie-stick (Figure 4.1). The artwork was an instant hit among the local population, but its fame quickly spread beyond the neighbourhood. On the one hand, it became the favourite cover for articles denouncing and criticising the ongoing mass touristification and gentrification of Lisbon's historical centre. On the other hand, however, it started to be showcased in most touristic promotional materials, it was heralded as a major addition to the growing recognition of Lisbon as a capital of street art, went viral on social media and is now part of the touristic pilgrimage to the heart of Mouraria itself.

This ambiguity is certainly not strange to many cultural actors in Europe these days, especially those who work far from the institutionalised and consecrated spaces of contemporary art production and exhibition, preferring to work in the public space,

FIGURE 4.1 *Political graffiti in Mouraria. EBANO Collective.*

engaging directly with the local populations, addressing social and political issues – those involved, in short, with what has been described as 'new genre public art' (Lacy, 1994). The recognition and the demand for that kind of work has grown exponentially in recent years, coupled with the rhetorics of the democratisation of culture and empowerment of local communities (Bailey, Miles and Stark, 2004). However, in many cases, this growth is partly explained because national and local authorities have also progressively harnessed it as part and parcel of their post-austerity urban-regeneration programmes. It is, of course, of vital importance to differentiate between the implicit and explicit, private and public processes associated with it but, as cities move their cultural policy progressively from 'institutions' to 'events' (Henningsen, Håkonsen and Løyland, 2015), and its geography is shaped to accommodate a year-round calendar of cultural happenings – a 'festivalisation' of both culture and city – these encounters between art, public space, local communities, large audiences and media coverage have become 'powerful tools to attract investors, stimulate consumption-oriented industries and reshape the image and reputation of a city' (Aubry, Blein and Vivant, 2015). Some authors have expressed this ambiguity, this tension, in dialectics between the 'carnival' and the 'spectacle':

> The carnival is the vernacular, bottom-up, potentially subversive festive event, while the spectacle is the top-down strategic pageant orchestrated by the powers that be. Artists perhaps most often want to create on the side of the carnival, cracking open the everyday to turn it into a thing of wonder . . . But in the current economic and political context, artists find themselves and their works corralled into city-boosting spectacles.
> RADICE and BOUDREAULT-FOURNIER, 2017: 11

But as one unfolds the artist's ambiguity, how can one think about the role of the cultural producers, as we are? Composed by artists and social scientists, EBANOCollective has designed over the years a number of site-specific participatory projects, art interventions and cultural events that temporarily modify the urban space – inquiring into its dynamics, its geographies and its flows, mediating local relations, transforming collective imagery and narratives, revealing social inequalities, contradictions and paradoxes and opening new spaces of cultural production in an ongoing (de)constructive process. Our intention is, in short, through art and research, to render visible new paths for local populations to question the public space they live in, and collaboratively design new ones. At the same time, however, the collective did not escape the drift towards the eventification of its projects, the spectacularisation of its outcomes, the choice of given territories according to the expectations of the funding bodies and stakeholders and their belief in culture as a policy tool for urban regeneration. Place-making with the communities and *mise en place* for the municipalities; both a carnival and spectacle, subversive event and strategic pageant.

This self-analysis mirrors the diversity of visions about our projects. EBANOCollective has been the subject of several academic studies, conferences and summer schools on ethnography-based, public, site-specific and collaborative art in urban space (Coelho, 2013; Matias, 2015; Sequeira, 2015, 2016; Manfredi, 2016). EBANOCollective's urban interventions are described in these works as site-specific participatory projects, supported by ethnographic research, tackling local community issues and larger social and urban questions. Some of these studies interpret the art events, festivals and interventions we have organised as actions aimed at urban renewal and regeneration. Others maintain that our interventions were forms of collective mobilisation, activism and resistance in times of crisis and austerity, creating alternative modes of sociability. In other interpretations, considering public space as a place for spontaneous action, EBANO's initiatives stimulate new relations between the city and its inhabitants, their collective history and individual memories and narratives, involving the populations in the fate of the structures of their neighbourhood. Sequeira (2015, 2016) affirms that EBANO's art interventions constitute a clear example of how public art can effectively support reclaiming the right to the city, contributing to the development of new community dynamics and working as a critical discourse about the condition of the buildings in the city, particularly its derelict and expectant structures.

At the same time, we found pictures of public art interventions organised by our collective in several leisure magazines, cultural agendas, tourism books and apps, websites, blogs and videos for the promotion of Lisbon – sometimes, long after the event occurred. Tour guides were created exclusively to show Lisbon's phenomenon of street art, where the narrative of the beautification of the city engulfs the specificity of any given project. Time appears to lose depth, as preparation, implementation and assessment of a project are soon forgotten. The multitude of events seems to be one and the same, condensed into a small number of photos and statistics used for city-branding purposes, destined to enhance competitiveness in the global tourism market (Liu, 2014).

As agents directly involved in these processes, in this essay we will address these tensions between carnival and spectacle, critically assessing some of our own public art projects. Through the analysis of a selection of events, we will try to disclose the complex articulation between art, community and public space amidst the master economic narrative of culture-led regeneration in post-austerity Lisbon.

Ghetto Six: Artistic interactions with the social context

Curated by anthropologist and artist Lorenzo Bordonaro, one of the founding members of the Collective, Ghetto Six transformed a peripheral self-built shanty town into an unusual exhibition site, stimulating new relationships between artists, dwellers and the physical materiality of their everyday lives (Figures 4.2–4.3). Since its origins in the 1970s, the '6 de Maio' illegal neighbourhood houses a community of mostly Cape Verdean origin. Stigmatised as a public disorder and drug-trafficking area, 6 de Maio has been targeted by constant and violent police interventions and demolishing operations led by the Amadora Municipality, as part of a Resettlement Special Programme created in 1995 to eradicate shanty areas. Notwithstanding the constant unpredictability, the neighbourhood has now hosted several generations of immigrants and became a strong place of memory and identity for its residents. Not surprisingly, the presence of each bulldozer, each police car and each local official is met with fierce resistance. Based on three years of ethnographic research in the neighbourhood, the Ghetto Six ethnography-based art installation was inspired by the life stories of the residents and the contradictions and violence of postcolonial Portugal and Schengen

FIGURE 4.2 Ghetto 6. EBANO Collective.

FIGURE 4.3 Ghetto 6. EBANO Collective.

Europe. It employed the remains and debris of the houses that had already been demolished as support for the inscription of a 'portrait' of the neighbourhood itself, using mixed media. The choice of these materials, in Bordonaro's words, 'was also clearly a political statement, leading the observer of the aesthetic experience of the "work" to the dimension of structural violence that marks everyday life in Bairro 6 de Maio' (2013: 17).

After taking part in the collective exhibition *Woundscapes* at the Lisbon City Museum, the installation was moved by EBANOCollective to the 6 de Maio area in early 2013, to remain in the public space, becoming an actual part of the built environment until the final destruction of the whole area. The remains of demolition, after being exhibited as artworks in a museum, returned to its original source. The 6 de Maio territory has been almost completely demolished, while its population is being relocated, according to a scheme of urban sanitation applied to other spontaneous urbanisations in the greater Lisbon area. At the moment, however, there are still several families who live in an urban space that is half-ruined, made up of destroyed houses and dangerous debris, waiting for their time to come.

The Ghetto Six project documents this process in particular but allows us two broader reflections. The first one relies on a circular mobility that interferes with established circuits: the pieces are moved to the space of the museum; the fragments of narrative – now legitimate artworks – move back to the area and are re-inscribed on its own materiality; finally, the project will share the fate of the neighbourhood itself, disappearing in the demolition operation. The specific case of an artwork made with an asbestos corrugated roof is particularly telling. As bulldozers crack corrugated roof, asbestos fibres are released into the air, posing a major health risk for nearby inhabitants. When one infuses the history of those inhabitants into this hazardous debris and moves them to the museum, they are given value, they get an insurance, they are carefully packed, installed and unpacked by professionals, they are measured and examined, they appear in a catalogue. People in the museum are not allowed to touch – not because it poses danger, but because is an art piece – while people in 6 de Maio walk by it and on it every day, as debris are not removed and are left unattended, causing further deterioration. This relates to the second reflection: as art meets research and public intervention, the materials used in the produced works are physical evidence of both the non-legitimised creativity employed in the continuous reconstruction of the lives and homes of these migrant communities and the violence they face when their lives are forcefully conformed to the legitimate apparatuses of security, mobility and urban planning.

Mouraria light walk: New explorations, re-appropriations and 'making visible'

After this first experience of ethnography-based art intervention in the public space, the Lisbon City Hall proposed to us to create an urban installation in the district of Mouraria, using light as a vehicle for artistic intervention. Mouraria is a characteristic medieval district of the historical Lisbon centre, owing its name to the fact that, after the Christian conquest of the city, it was the space destined for Muslims, thus constituting one of the first ghettos of European history. Mouraria, originated as a thirteenth-century Moorish neighbourhood, remains the most Muslim district of Portugal, not only because of its history but also due to the current presence of different Islamic communities, particularly originating from Bangladesh, Pakistan, Mozambique, Turkey and Guinea-Bissau.

Despite the recent positive image of a neighbourhood that is popular, traditional and multicultural, Mouraria experiences an urban condition crossed by innumerable setbacks and heterogeneities. Recent ethnographic studies show that the transition from this representation of intercultural to effective practices of social mixing does not occur in a linear way, and is also the source of criticism, tensions and social conflicts, reinforcing an image of poverty and insecurity, both induced and self-reproduced (Malheiros, Carvalho and Mendes, 2013). The stigmatisation and socioeconomic precariousness of its context have contributed to the emergence of phenomena related to the sale and consumption of drugs and the sex market in the last decades – but historically, its dark and narrow alleys have long been synonymous with illegal activities and bohemian life.

Between 2011 and 2013, the territory of Mouraria and its surroundings in the centre of Lisbon were the object of a complex reform project aimed at changing the spatial, social and economic aspect of the territory. The decision to intervene in a wider area is related to the central geographic positioning of the quarter in the city of Lisbon. A neighbourhood characterised as a segregated, obscure and risky territory, a labyrinthine network of alleys without light, had to present itself to the city as a friendly, safe and attractive territory. The Lisbon Municipality's invitation to EBANO to create artistic light installations was destined also to stimulate new forms of use and exploitation of space with more positive emotional outcomes. The project took shape and, in July 2013, a three-day light and art public event called *Noor – Mouraria Light Walk* took place. 'Noor', which in Arabic means 'light', reflected our intention to give the project a historical, ethnographic and participatory character – to render visible social dynamics in the public space. Performed with light, the interventions were an invitation to new perspectives and dialogues with the invisible and forgotten dimensions of this simultaneously traditional and multicultural neighbourhood, drawing attention to its internal diversity. The route had two entry points and provided stages related to significant elements of the tangible and intangible heritage of the district, underlined by installations and interventions from different artists.

Using light as a privileged artistic language and, in its most symbolic sense, as a way to illuminate what is in the shadow, this project identified a wide urban route that crossed the whole quarter, creating an intense relationship with its residents, their stories, their memories, representing the most invisible and hidden aspects of this quarter. Each artist from the Collective worked on the basis of an ethnographic research in the territory, identifying social issues that lacked visibility. These installations shed light on aspects of Mouraria which intimately belong both to its past and to its present, recapturing memories and giving voice to those who are rarely listened to. The inhabitants of the neighbourhood accompanied their work during the preceding months, providing ideas, themes, criticism, sharing memories, showing what is hidden in the shadows of the narrow alleys and reviving the memory of the bohemian past. *Sin Street*, an installation developed by Chiara Pussetti with sex workers, in which they told their life stories through avatar-like lit mannequins is a good example – for the ability to share the experiences of a marginalised

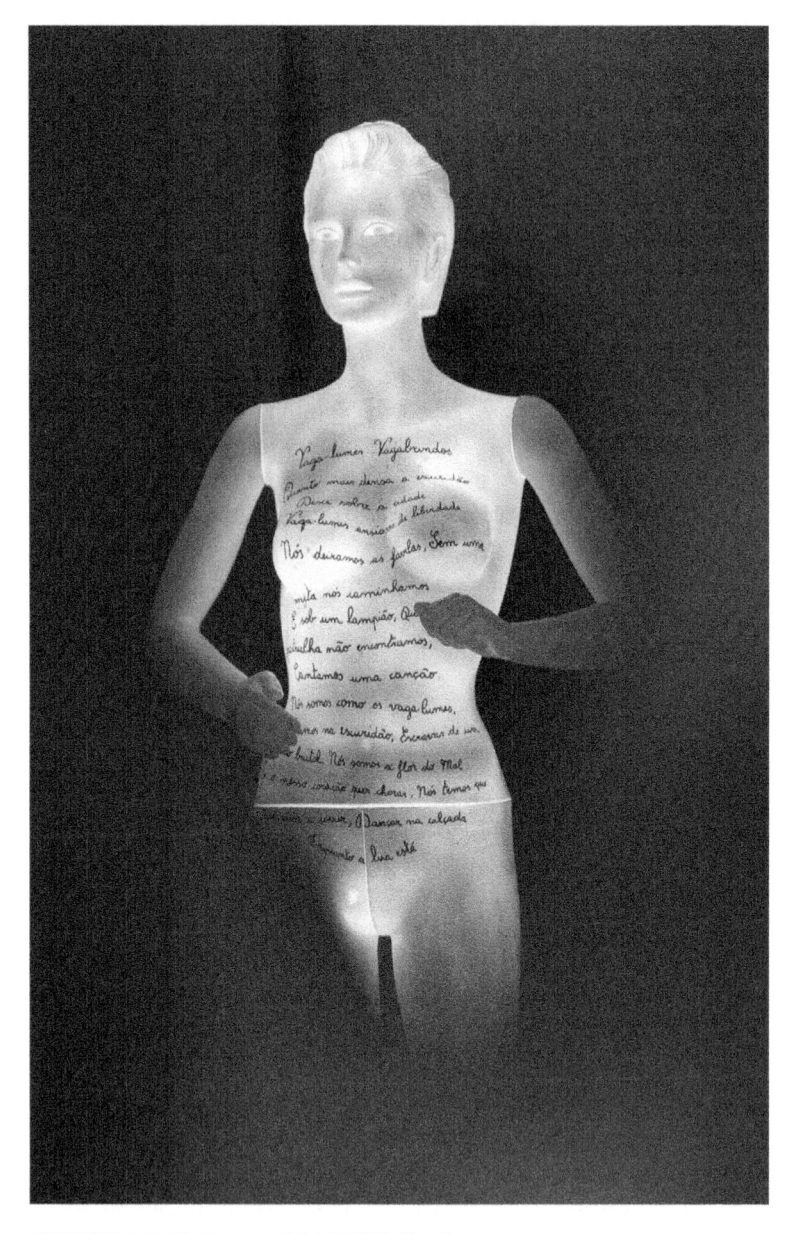

FIGURE 4.4 Sin Street. *EBANO Collective.*

social group, putting them in a noble public space like a square (instead of a corner) and driving curiosity, interaction and recognition (Figure 4.4). Another example was the participatory urbanism project done by Lorenzo Bordonaro, 'Mouraria Imagined by Children', in which the students from an elementary school were invited to redesign a neighbourhood's square as a playground since there was no equipment in the whole quarter. The drawings were, without the children's knowledge, actually produced and deployed in that square, reproducing the oneiric and playful context they had envisioned (Figure 4.5).

Mouraria Light Walk brought Lisbon inhabitants closer to the Mouraria district, which was still seen by many people as a perilous area to be avoided. During the three days of the Light Festival, over 10,000 people gathered in the streets of the neighbourhood. The *Mouraria Light Walk* introduced the public to a new way of looking at Mouraria but was also a strategy to present the neighbourhood to the wider population in a more positive light. The festival, commissioned with the aim of improving the attractiveness of the district, delivered a series of symbolic benefits that separately meet cultural policy,

FIGURE 4.5 Sin Street. *EBANO Collective.*

tourism agenda and real estate appreciation. In the following years, Mouraria has been the theatre of a real boom in the real estate market and tourism infrastructure. Our original project was based on an ideal of integration of stigmatised areas and communities, with the purpose of increasing social cohesion and rendering social problems visible. While to some extent the project has served to give a voice to specific social groups and to enhance a collective neighbourhood pride, at the same time it has contributed to a process of gentrification and touristification already underway. In the balance between carnival and spectacle, what remains? The abandoned places are still abandoned, closed heritage is still unavailable to the public, sex workers were definitely expelled from the square, where there now exists a 'fado' house as representative of a new hegemonic cultural narrative of the quarter, and the residents are still not involved in the ongoing regeneration of the public space.

Graça literary tour: Urban narratives and local identities

With the third project, also funded by the Lisbon Municipality, we want to discuss a similar paradox. In 2014, EBANOCollective organised a street art project in another central district of the city of Lisbon, the Graça neighbourhood, called 'Passeio Literário da Graça'. This project included the intervention of several street artists in a set of degraded facades of buildings in the district. The objectives of the project were, first of all, to highlight the state of degradation of the neighbourhood's heritage. Second, the project aimed to transform the bare walls into a narrative that would show its most important identity elements and the specific historical and cultural aspects that were related to this community. The route offers a series of artworks inspired by women – poets, writers, activists and feminists – who have marked the history of the neighbourhood with their presence and their work: Natália Correia, Angelina Vidal, Sophia de Mello Breyner Andresen, Florbela Espanca. The several artistic interventions on the degraded walls of the Graça, aimed to celebrate these literary figures, giving visibility to the hidden architectural heritage of the neighbourhood and distinguishing its singularity (Figures 4.6–4.7).

FIGURE 4.6 Sophia & Florbela. *EBANO Collective*.

FIGURE 4.7 Sophia & Florbela. *EBANO Collective*.

The 'graffiti' interventions became part of the collective identity of the district's inhabitants, however, at the same time, it was relaunched as a touristic route that helped to create a more contemporary and attractive image of the Graça neighbourhood. Regardless of its original aim, the Passeio Literario amplified touristic interest in Graça, increased the asset value of the district properties and worked as a strategic means of city branding. An intervention designed to strengthen the identity and social cohesion of the neighbourhood and to drive awareness to its tangible and intangible heritage is again, in spite of its intentions, an engine of touristification processes.

The case of street art – and of 'graffiti', in particular – is extremely interesting in the Lisbon context, where the practice went from a highly criminalised one to being one of the hottest skills in the artistic market in less than a decade. In 2008, the Lisbon Municipality created the Galeria de Arte Urbana or GAU (Urban Art Gallery), a specific entity to promote street art projects either in the city centre – beautifying walls, facades and urban equipment – or in social-housing neighbourhoods – making use of the numerous windowless high-rise facades in suburban so-called 'problematic' areas. Above all, the mission was to drive change in the sector, governmentalising a whole subculture: curtailing 'vandalism' by allowing the practice in particular spaces under their management, dissociating 'graffiti' from its 'illegal' nature by providing a regulated structure and framework. As street art began to be highly regarded around the world, the projects managed by GAU became more frequent, leading to a quasi-professionalisation of the sector: there are specific applications, management of authorisations, fees, grants, awards and celebrities whose work is widely used in city-branding content. The last street art event promoted by GAU in Marvila – a geographically central but socially marginalised post-industrial area at the beginning of a major regeneration process – clearly shows a process of increasing governmentalisation and commodification of culture: it was their largest festival to date, with a growing panel of internationally renowned artists, great media exposure to attract outside visitors, while creating economic agents by offering the residents the opportunity to become touristic guides in their own quarter through specialised street art training courses. The local population, however, complain about the lack of community engagement, the absence of dialogue to portray meaningful narratives of the neighbourhood itself, and the effect of a growing number of visitors coming to 'photograph the ghetto' without fostering a true revitalisation in the area.

Conclusion

In recent years, the literature on the instrumental use of the cultural dimension in urban regeneration has grown considerably, analysing the impact of mega-events (such as the European Capital of Culture), flagship facilities (the 'Bilbao effect') or the creation of artistic districts and general cultural agglomeration in the political agenda for local development and international competition (Liu, 2014; Aubry et al., 2015; Pavoni, 2015; Rahbarianyazd and Doratli, 2017; Skrede, 2015; Martínez, 2017). Lisbon's case, although surprisingly overlooked, represents a rich and complex fieldwork in the targeted way the municipality envisioned culture, in the middle of a hard-hitting economic crisis, as a major catalyst and engine of regeneration of a decadent city centre. In this context, much like in the international sphere, the cultural sector came under an increasing pressure of market-driven rationales: the master narrative of the creative industries which absorbed part of the cultural production (arts, heritage, craft) and infused it with the logics of entrepreneurship and competitiveness; the stimulus given to spectacular events with short-term gains while restraining the support for projects which do not deliver immediate, tangible benefits; and the use of the neutral, with low levels of inherent conflict, entertaining language of cultural practice in order to depoliticise major neoliberalisation and globalisation forces of urban development.

The inward reflection about the projects we brought forward in this essay intended to mirror our own ambiguities and tensions as players in both carnival and spectacle, community-based and economy-driven approaches, critical and hegemonic narratives. It is vital to be constantly aware, as we tried to be in this exercise, of the consequences of the interplay between culture and capital and the new geographies that are created in the ambitions to repair a city and a society during times of economic hardship. This is particularly relevant when those geographies curtail action instead of promoting it, disallow alternative circulation instead of nurturing it, standardise public space instead of valuing the richness of its heterogeneity and its multiple uses, and impose alternative identities without securing the local ones – in short, when those culture-led new geographies are less democratic, less participatory and narrow down conditions of possibility instead of fostering the creative development of new ones.

Notes

1 This article is part of a research project on culture, heritage and urban regeneration named ROCK (Regeneration and Optimisation of Cultural Heritage in Creative and Knowledge Cities), funded by European Union's Horizon 2020 Research and Innovation Programme (Grant Agreement N. 730280). Authors' address: Instituto de Ciências Sociais, Universidade de Lisboa, Av. Professor Aníbal de Bettencourt 9, 1600-189, Lisboa, Portugal.

References

Aubry, A., A. Blein and E. Vivant (2015) 'The promotion of creative industries as a tool for urban planning: The case of the *Territoire de la culture et de la création* in Paris Region', *International Journal of Cultural Policy*, 21 (2): 121–38.

Bailey, C., S. Miles and P. Stark (2004) 'Culture-led urban regeneration and the revitalization of identities in Newcastle, Gateshead and the North East of England', *International Journal of Cultural Policy*, 10 (1): 47–65.

Bordonaro, L. (2013) 'Ghetto Six: A antropologia ocupa espaço', *Próximo Futuro*, 12: 16–19.

Coelho, A. M. (2013) 'Sharawadji. Casos de Ruído de Vizinhança na Cidade de Lisboa', MA thesis, Faculdade de Ciências Sociasis e Humanas (FCSH), Universidade Nova de Lisboa.

Hall, T. and I. Robertson (2001) 'Public art and urban regeneration: Advocacy, claims and critical debates', *Landscape Research*, 26 (1): 5–26.

Henningsen, E., L. Håkonsen and K. Løyland (2015) 'From institutions to events: Structural change in Norwegian local cultural policy', *International Journal of Cultural Policy*, 23: 352–71.

Lee, H.-K. (2014) 'Politics of the "creative industries" discourse and its variants', *International Journal of Cultural Policy*, 22 (3): 438–55.

Lidegaard, C., M. Nuccio and T. Bille (2017) 'Fostering and planning urban regeneration: The governance of cultural districts in Copenhagen', *European Planning Studies*, 26 (1): 1–19.

Liu, Y.-D. (2014) 'Cultural events and cultural tourism development: Lessons from the European Capitals of Culture', *European Planning Studies*, 22 (3): 498–514.

Lucy, S. (ed.) (1994) *Mapping The Terrain: New Genre Public Art*, Seattle, WA: Bay Press.

Malheiros, J., R. Carvalho and L. Mendes (2013) 'Gentrification, residential ethnicization and the social production of fragmented space in two multi-ethnic neighbourhoods of Lisbon and Bilbao', *Finisterra*, 96: 109–35.

Manfredi, F. (2016) 'The participatory video: An identity definition workshop', *Humanistyczne Ksztalcenie, w teoriee i w praktyce*, Wybrane Zagadnienia, Pultusk, 294–309.

Martínez, F. (2017) '"This place has potential": Trash, culture and urban regeneration in Tallinn', *Suomen Antropologi: Journal of the Finnish Anthropological Society*, 42 (4): 1–20.

Matias, A. R. (2015) 'Um outro bairro na cidade: práticas de intervenção sócio urbanística no bairro da Mouraria', MA thesis, FCSºH, Universidade Nova de Lisboa.

Menezes, M. (2004) *Mouraria. Retalhos de um imaginário: significados urbanos de um bairro de Lisboa*, Oeiras: Celta Editora.

Pavoni, A. (2015) 'Resistant legacies', *Annals of Leisure Research*, 18 (4): 470–90.

Radice, M. and A. Boudreault-Fournier (eds) (2017) *Urban Encounters: Art and the Public*, Montreal: McGill-Queen's University Press.

Rahbarianyazd, R. and N. Doratli (2017) 'Assessing the contribution of cultural agglomeration in urban regeneration through developing cultural strategies', *European Planning Studies*, 25 (10): 1–20.

Sequeira, Á. (2015) 'Letting the walls of the city speak: The route of a sociological research project on Lisbon's street art', *Street Art and Urban Creativity Journal*, 1 (2): 82–8.

Sequeira, A. (2016) 'Ephemeral art in impermanent spaces: The effects of street art in the social construction of public space', in P. Guerra, P. Costa and P. Neves (eds), *Urban Intervention, Street Art and Public Space*, Lisbon: Urban Creativity, pp. 65–74.

Skrede, J. (2015) 'What may culture contribute to urban sustainability? Critical reflections on the uses of culture in urban development in Oslo and beyond', *Journal of Urbanism: International Research on Placemaking and Urban Sustainability*, 9 (4): 408–25.

5

The compost of recuperation

Fabricating social ties in the interstices

Marcos Farias Ferreira and Francisco Martínez

As the financial crisis came to hit Europe in the first semester of 2010, after a series of rebounds moving from one side of the Atlantic to the other, the multiple effects followed by contagion were met with austerity policies that redistributed financial risks and exacerbated social divisions by neoliberal design. These austerity measures not only involved the application of scarcity, but also entailed specific notions regarding what the relations between the state and society should be (Bear, 2015; Tellmann, 2015).[1] As a process of political engineering, the policy assembling of austerity measures went hand in hand with social de-assembling, producing both new orders and disorders. Yet, as with what occurs in ecology, decomposing is simultaneously a process of composing, creating something new out of the worn-out and leftover. The immediate weakening and regression of the welfare state and its public policies (health, education and pensions) mobilised the citizenry to occasionally take part in demonstrations, but it also triggered a series of rather tactical responses aimed at resisting the dissolution of the social at the local level. They appeared in the form of spatial coagulations, collective authorship and social *bricolage*, lacking a clear design and working with the material and social wreckage wrought by financial crisis and austerity policies. Grassroots organisations started establishing interstitial spaces around Lisbon, with pragmatic strategies for the sharing of resources and skills, recycled and put together for collective benefit. These recuperative practices emerged against what was perceived as the assault of new strategies of sociopolitical engineering, insolidarity and resource depletion. They have been conquering spaces of autonomy, which partly replace traditional hierarchical planning and paper over the cracks in the system.

Specifically, this chapter focuses on the People's Assembly of Algés (PAA), established in May of 2013 in the Oeiras district, at Lisbon's gates. A group of neighbours started to act at a grassroots level with a programme of solidarity and community-rebuilding, aimed at advancing alternative social configurations. The Spanish movement 15-M (Los Indignados) emerging from the *acampada* at Puerta del Sol in Madrid in May 2011, inspired similar movements around Lisbon of disparate groups of people assuming the need to act locally on the basis of a more deliberative democracy and other ideals proclaimed against the erosion of political institutions. The PAA emerged in the aftermath of that mobilisation effort, embodying contestation at a grassroots local level of politics, composing, in turn, new urban constellations of critique.

Social *bricolage*

This chapter develops a framework for understanding the experience of recuperation through political composting – meant to represent a society's capacity for self-building through practices of public repairing and social *bricolage*, thus paying attention to the relationship between the medium and the form of recuperation. We argue that recuperation is characterised by a practice of recombination that goes hand in hand with the reconstitution of the public space. Also, we foreground the fact that recuperation might not be accomplished with a single, specific type of intent, but rather it is practiced as a plural way of reinhabiting and reclaiming the public space through situated practices of meaning, place and value-making.

The research draws on the concept of 'intravening', proposed by architects Alberto Altés and Oren Lieberman (2013). It refers to attempts at transforming the world through the intermediate, through fragile acts of care and making-do, focused on the within of already existing spaces, and by so doing, redefining the edges of cities and reconfiguring what is possible to think and do socially. Making-do is most often understood as a way of getting by that encompasses an array of material practices that are ready at hand. Yet, this form of *bricolage* also has an infrastructural capacity, based on occurrence, assembling, experimentation and reflexivity.[2] Hence, what we are going to describe here is a fragile infrastructure of encounters for material and social intervention from within (Estalella and Sánchez Criado 2019) (Figures 5.1–5.3).

The research was conducted between September 2013 and May 2014, and assumed the form of an explorative, theory-building ethnography. We took part in the weekly open gatherings of the People's Assembly at a public garden in downtown Algés as well as in the activities of the Fabrica de Alternativas (Factory of Alternatives) of Algés, a semi-public space, organised as a common-interest civic association under Portuguese law and functioning at an old, dismantled textile factory in uptown Algés. Our research started with an invitation extended to Marcos by one of the individuals involved in the PAA, initially just to document through film the assembly discussions and the expanding activities at the factory. As the documentary project developed, the camera participated in foregrounding reflections, working as a trigger for discussing the assumptions, achievements and drawbacks, as they unfolded, of both the People's Assembly and the factory-mobilisation effort. One of our roles was to document how different perspectives were entangled, yet filming turned into a key technique of our research repertoire and not simply a form of documentation. The camera itself became a device of fieldwork engagement, generating meaningful tensions and questions about the publics and ethical implications of our research (Waltorp, 2018).

FIGURES 5.1–5.3 Fabrica de Alternativas of Algés. *Marcos Farias Ferreira.*

If reconsidering the space of betweenness from which we were producing our own accounts, we can also draw parallels between our research practice and the work of composting. In our case, the methodology did not follow a clear design and rather imitated the composting character of the object of study, connecting knowledge-production and intervention from within. Our claims are thus constructed by making use of a diverse range of epistemic materials combined in a non-linear manner. The ten print screens of *verité* scenes included in the chapter work as glimpses into what could be known, but also as forensic evidence of something simultaneously strong and vulnerable – the atmosphere of sharing. These images are constitutive of knowledge at the margins of political theory and anthropology, calling for a response and helping us to understand our disappearing field of study. The visual material of the essay is meant to preserve some of the excess, ambiguity and complexity of the interactions taking place in the field, which often went beyond our own methodological tools and even cognitive frames (Figures 5.4–5.7).

Our fieldwork took place through processes of material and social intervention, in which we ourselves participated. Often, we felt that the field site was throwing out questions to which we did not have the answers, challenging our concepts and changing our notions of evidence (Sánchez Criado and Estalella, 2018). The field itself was a social *bricolage*, with actions and meanings negotiated by the participants through their own mixtures of rituals, makeshifts and manipulations of the space and any available resources. During the research, we had the opportunity to ask people about the origins and motivations for intervention, yet we ourselves engaged differently in the field. Marcos played more the role of an activist researcher, being personally engaged in the political struggle in question and professing solidarity with the cause under study, while Francisco acted more as a cultural critic, not directly involved in the assembly but observing their discussions and activities as well as studying the relationship between participative practices and their different publics.[3] The terms of our distance or implication in the site were not established beforehand, but, rather, learned through repeat encounters. Our knowledge was constructed in these social interactions and through the very forming of supposedly non-research relationships (Martínez, 2018). Already from the first day of our research, we found ourselves

FIGURES 5.4–5.7 Fabrica de Alternativas of Algés. *Marcos Farias Ferreira.*

'in a haptic space in the middle of things' (Stewart, 2008: 71) and with 'all sorts of cross-cutting and contradictory personal commitments' (Marcus, 1995: 113) that resemble more a form of complicity than of rapport (Holmes and Marcus, 2012).

Engaging with social damage

As in the case of compost, social fertility requires the combination of multiple factors and agents (such as moisture, carbon, oxygen, the right temperature, time and several microorganisms), mixed together and decomposed. Among those involved in the factory of Algés, the idea of social repair was ubiquitous and could be found mainly in the desire to forge alternative means and links outside market relations. As João, an activist at the factory, explained: 'If society, as it is, does not provide the solution to people, then people have to look for it themselves.' The challenge of articulating alternatives took form as a means of building demonetised transactions, reducing environmental impacts and preventing resource depletion. Social transactions and money were central subjects of discussion, defining the kind of space the factory would strive to be henceforth. For instance, a bank of time was created as the mode of functioning for the factory activities, but it proved difficult to implement. The basic idea was that each factory associate would dedicate a certain amount of time to providing specific activities and would, therefore, be entitled to attend activities provided by other associates. The maintenance of the space would be guaranteed by a schedule involving all the associates. In this way, no money would be involved and all transactions would obey the principles of reciprocity and communality. Two main challenges emerged. First, the factory had to find a solution for individuals who wished to take part in activities but did not want to become associates. For this, a symbolic amount was established for the participation of non-associates in activities, allowing them to help pay for the rent as well as water and electricity bills of the factory. But money was also involved in small transactions at the bar that started operating inside the factory as the movement of people steadily increased.

Spatial coagulations such as the one at the Factory of Algés drew on a variety of formats that facilitated encounters between different traditions and sensibilities, yet what they enabled could not be fully controlled and anticipated by any design (Lezaun, Marres and Tironi, 2016). The PAA originally emerged to articulate public concerns in new ways, as a form of decentred politics, intrinsically perspectival and polyphonic. Social composting is an oblique way of making claims on the state, which might well contribute to challenging the established parameters of what constitutes political participation, influencing other people and events tangentially, without people being fully conscious of the consequences of their agency and the processes at play (Ortner, 2006). Such a process of composting in the interstices is never alien to resistances, incapacities, unexpected bifurcations and the systemic forces trying to limit it. Yet, even so, they can make alternative forms of organisation to flourish in relation to a different notion of the politics of participation (Corsín Jiménez and Estalella, 2013; Tonkiss, 2013; Färber, 2014; Hilbrandt and Richter, 2015).

Induced by the crisis and austerity measures, many people started to relate to each other differently, looking to transform the existing orderings while at the same time project alternative visions. The cracks in the city infrastructure generated a rich array of physical transformations as well as further cracks in the social and epistemic fabric of Lisbon. With respect to the financial crisis in Spain, Adolfo Estalella and Tomás Sánchez Criado (2019) note how, similar to Portugal, traditional forms of knowledge and epistemic authority are being questioned and challenged, emerging, in turn, with new forms of urban collaborations. We can see this also in the case of the factory and how people engaged in experimental makeshiftness, tinkering also with ways of making knowledge, with formats, styles and the arrangements of different types (Figures 5.8–5.9). Moreover, our case shows that recuperation can be experienced as a form of place-making and as small-scale resistance (Scott, 1990), producing a hybrid form of space, offstage, in which people meet, often with very mixed intentions, and converse horizontally about what needs to be done. When combined, these spaces of hope start further to shape urban qualities and relations, bringing into practice formerly unthinkable possibilities and multiplying the forms that politics might take (De Boeck and Plissart, 2004; Simone, 2010).

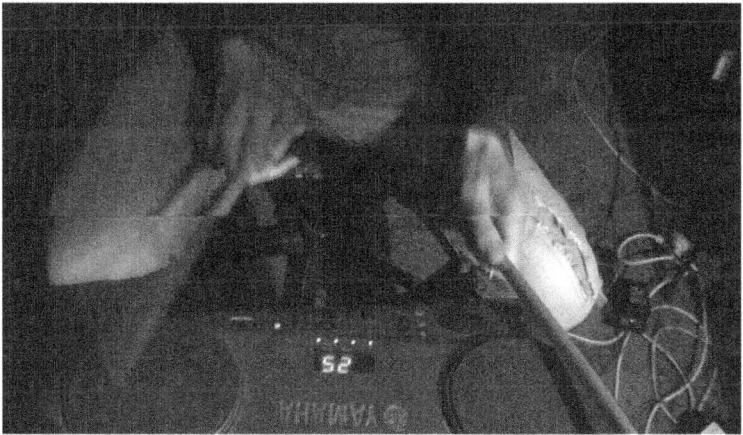

FIGURES 5.8–5.9 Fabrica de Alternativas of Algés. *Marcos Farias Ferreira.*

A factory of resilience and resourcefulness

Marcos notes that he cannot forget the first time he set foot in the factory. It was a sunny afternoon in late September, and the autumn light invaded the two-storey building through its overwhelming panels of glass. On the inside, all kinds of objects interacted in their immobility with tired machines, textile leftovers and mannequins.

The factory had been turned into a warehouse in those days, one full of old furniture and toys, waiting for the mortgage to be paid. From September onwards, Marcos' camera would witness the transformation of the factory, from a mass of leftovers into a bubble of alternative activities meant to recuperate and provide shelter from the growing commodification of society. At a general PAA meeting in late October, it was decided to accept the symbolic rent asked by the proprietor and start the makeover of the space. Henceforth, it would be known as the 'Factory of Alternatives'. The first collective endeavour spanned several weeks and involved dealing with the leftovers from previous textile activity and making the space of the former Materna textile factory free and clean. People from different backgrounds started gathering at weekends, after PAA meetings, moving stuff, sorting out and registering textile leftovers, cleaning and getting rid of rubbish, mending the floor and engaging in different kinds of restorative acts and, bit by bit, the space opened up to collective action. It was not uncommon, though, that the leftover items had been returned to the same place over the weekend, perhaps due to some whim of the proprietor, and so the cleaning and the moving would start again, but not where they had left off the week before.

Material relations are central to the process of recuperation, and for the PAA the reuse of remains played an important role in keeping the factory open to multiple spatial imaginaries and practices. If the first step was to clear the ground floor of the weaving machines and materials, often reusing them as well as any existing material, then the next step was to correlate the space design with the social initiatives that the factory was starting to host. Also, as a result of different voluntary initiatives, the walls became decorated with artistic works and collected stuff that had been thrown away and donations, such as books from a public library. As the members of the PAA explained, learning and doing politics were intertwined. The learning opportunities were not limited to books and seminars, but also extended to such initiatives as yoga, sewing, drawing, recycling workshops, theatre, dance classes, cinema and so forth, filling in the gap left by the retreat of public services and infrastructures. Until the middle of December, the factory functioned with a list of weekly alternative activities supervised by social organs through regular meetings. This narrative must not forget, however, that since the very beginning, there was an underlying tension in people's actions and decisions, with some favouring the idea of the PAA and the factory as alternative, counter-hegemonic structures and others willing to act within the context of the law, regulating common-interest civic associations in order to acquire public capacities. After a series of tense meetings and debates, it was decided that the PAA would retain a distinctive informal profile and that the factory would become a formal civic and law-abiding association.

Opening up the ideological debate had been at the crux of the creation of the PAA and its Saturday assemblies, but the penchant to act as a civic association would grow as more people began to join. Indeed, many people started to approach the factory with the will to find a space of solidarity, in which they could develop their creativity, share resources and competencies, learn new skills or simply spend time together doing meaningful things. Most often, the activities engaged with local realities rather than with specific cultural trends or artistic platforms. Unlike media debates, the factory offered a space to recuperate what was lacking outside due to the increasing privatisation of services, carving out spaces of mutuality, where a process of learning together could be organised. A sense of social dissolution was felt as demanding alternative ways of doing things and interacting with others. In this regard, the social *bricolage* of the factory was as much a perception of crisis as an answer to them, willing to transform politics by actively engaging with the surrounding materiality.

By facilitating the gathering of different social *bricoleurs*, the factory aimed at the possibility of weaving together alternative relationships as free as possible from marketisation and, therefore, at odds with resource depletion and environmental impacts. As the factory started operating, reflection and practice were clearly articulated in ways that underlined the centrality of these two concerns. Apart from a number of debates that promoted the presence of specialists and focused on such issues as degrowth, the factory dynamics came to reflect, to a certain extent, the ideal of a local, self-sustaining community united in solidarity. Self-sustainability and solidarity were closely linked in, for instance, workshops dedicated to crafts and the manufacturing of homemade products like toothpaste, soap and cleansers. But they were also visible in multiple activities promoted on behalf of the fragile uptown Algés population, like providing assistance to elderly people and schoolchildren or promoting intergenerational relationships. Taking advantage of textile leftovers and the knowledge of older women, a sewing workshop was set up with the goal of recycling resources, passing skills on to the younger generations and promoting creativity as well as the productive use of free time by unemployed people or pensioners. In our view, this generational interweaving of efforts came to represent the true potential of the factory as an alternative community capable of addressing social de-assembling.

The relational emergence of political action

In close connection to what was mentioned above, and in a way bringing together the increasing number of activities and workshops at the factory, one should give attention to shared meals as the corollary of this community. It all started during the early days of space conversion. People involved in the cleaning and other tasks were asked to take food and drinks with them to be shared at community meals. Later on, these meals became more participatory, as different people – and not only associates – came to attend weekly workshops and other activities. Food ceased to be shared in the same sense as before. What became established then was a form of 'reaping' (*respiga*) as a sustainable practice of providing food for which attendants had to pay a symbolic amount of money. On a weekly basis, factory associates would travel to the large supply market on the outskirts of Lisbon in order to obtain the leftovers that sellers refused to sell at the end of the day. People participated in the cooking process according to the schedule and mealtime became a true moment of communion. Occasionally, these meals were thematic in nature, as when Davud, a factory associate of Iranian origin, organised an evening of Persian poetry readings.

This last detail brings us to yet another central feature of the factory. The factory itself, though registered as a civic association, was seen by its associates as a means for cultural transgression in a broken city in the sense that it allowed for new forms of expression and self-fulfilment that underscored the limits of normalised daily life. Among these practices, Marcos' camera had the opportunity to document

FIGURE 5.10 Fabrica de Alternativas of Algés. *Marcos Farias Ferreira.*

open-air book exchanges and poetry readings, theatrical performances, musical jam sessions or evenings dedicated to practising traditional dances. All of them, in one way or another, highlighted unconventional ways of being together and doing politics, producing a new order of spatiotemporal continuity, characterised by a multiplication of relations and capacities (Figure 5.10).

In the factory, recuperation became topological. This interstitial, hybrid space was able to convey different capacities, evolving as both an instrument and dimension of people's sociality (Corsín Jiménez, 2003), one where people could try an alternative type of urbanism (Tonkiss, 2013). As a site of textile production, it had been inactive for some years and was the last in a series of textile factories to close in uptown Algés. The story of the factory is thus closely connected to the social history of Portugal, namely to the rise and fall of the textile sector throughout the twentieth century. Until the 1980s, the success and modernisation of the sector pushed the old factories out of the urban centre to the outskirts of town, to places like Algés. After the 1980s, a rapid decline coincided with the country's integration in free-trade associations and the reorganisation of domestic retail, new fashion demands and the textile market at large, well into the first decade of the twenty-first century.

In this sense, the PAA, together with its interstitial spaces, does not merely illustrate a collective response to the economic difficulties afflicting large sectors of Portuguese society at that particular juncture. Rather, it can be seen as a deeper movement in search of radical recuperation and community rebuilding (see, Farias Ferreira and Terrenas, 2017), and as a site whereby social *bricolage* and political engineering could encounter one another. By working through society's interstices, the factory brought about grassroots forms of resistance and transformation, creating a platform for different forms of being together and alternative arrangements of urban life at large (Corsín Jiménez and Estalella, 2013). Different people, from different backgrounds and from different generations, mobilised to foster new spaces of hope, solidarity and meaning-making in collaborative ways, showing how recuperation is an experience that reconstructs the identity of people, too. Paradoxically, the openly politicised activities were given less attention, in favour of the communitarian activities organised at the factory.

Concluding remarks

Compost is simultaneously a space and a technique for recuperation. Accordingly, the term 'composting' is proposed in relation to social sustainability and with the aim of conceptualising a process of recuperation that includes many heterogeneous elements, factors and actors and which differs from recovery – understood as a restitution of whole systems (Guyer, 2017). The factory itself was an intrinsic part of this compost – as a form of intervention from within (Altés and Lieberman, 2013), and as 'living proof that other ways of thinking and acting are possible' (Rosol and Schweizer, 2012: 713).

In Lisbon, the financial crisis deepened the tension between those who conceive of the city as a space of capital accumulation and those who live in it as a place of daily practice (Brenner, Marcuse and Mayer, 2011). Since May 2013, the PAA and the factory had been established as spaces for contesting the actual ordering of things and as spaces to sustain acts of recuperation. Hence, these spaces were created, not beyond or at the margins of the political system, but in tension with the official spheres of legality, economy and order. In fact, that very ordering was perceived as the source of crisis itself and justified the setting-up of spaces, where alternative social interactions could be discussed and put into practice. Arguably, and as part of the politicisation at both the park and factory in Algés, individuals reclaimed the right to gain access to these areas and as a means of creating a civic bond with the city, turned them into spaces of society-making. This act of insubordination was potentially transgressive, in that it instantiated an alternative spatial community that did not renounce the desire for open and fluid interactions (no formal membership in the factory was instituted).

Since we started taking part in and documenting PAA activities, we felt that a greater reflexivity and vocabulary were needed that would help us reconsider how knowledge is created and incorporated through makeshift practices. The factory became the centre of collective mobilisation itself – an interstitial space with a particular potency and capacity as the somewhere of social relationships and as a distributed agency (Corsín Jiménez, 2003).[4] The continual porosity of the PAA was visible in the way eclectic cultural expressions found their space in the factory, but also in the assumption that transgression could become the accepted normality of a space freed from conventional morality and fixed practices and hierarchies. The dynamics at the factory illustrate how grassroots recuperation worked in a patchwork manner – as always evolving readaptations and infrastructures and overlapping relations, services and provisions. However, much recuperation proved to be an active choice made by a group of Algés dwellers. What we could attest is that it developed as a complex process, taking place mostly without a detailed design or conscious planning. Rather, it was a reconstitutive process of composting, turning the old and deteriorated into something new and fertile (Saltzman, 2005).

The refurbishing of the former factory generated affects beyond the physical dimension of the intervention, enabling, in turn, a living laboratory where social relationships could be recreated. Indeed, the second life of the factory meant a new beginning for many people. In this sense, recuperation was the product of a process of negotiation among subjectivities and interests that interpreted in disparate ways the interstitial character of the process and strived to organise it according to particular views on, for instance, how the relationship between state and society has to be structured, how to take profit from and enlarge the spaces of freedom that liberal democracies enshrine in their constitutions, or how to balance individual and group interests within this kind of grassroots movement.

Our research also exemplified the plurality of ways in which visual rendering can expose people's political stakes. Further, it could be seen as a *bricolage* method itself, patchwork-like, i.e. one made up of multiple decisions about what storyline to build on, what to document and where to film, and which characters to follow given the fluidity of relationships between individuals and space. It underlines the importance of methodologically eclectic approaches, implying the recognition that, at certain junctures, one has to adopt a loose attitude toward disciplinary interactions and be able to apply more adaptive methods (Barker, 2014), allowing circumstance to shape the methods employed (Kincheloe, McLaren and Steinberg, 2011), tinkering in and with fieldwork and documentation (Sánchez Criado and Estalella, 2018).

In our case, the most troublesome aspect of the process was certainly the decision of when to stop filming. The answer came with the decision by PAA associates to organise at the garden, in downtown Algés, an open day with all the factory activities on display to mark its first year of existence. This turned out to be a festive occasion that, to my documentary gaze, came to stand for the perfect closure of a cycle. One year before, a number of Algés neighbours had started gathering at that very garden, on a weekly basis, to discuss possible lines of action in the face of a mounting crisis. In the first months, the garden had become the centre of a deliberative process and grassroots mobilisation, addressing a strategic plan for turning resistance and solidarity into day-to-day practice. Local and global issues were at stake, and often the articulation of both came into play, such as when free trade agreements became the focus of all attention. But when the decision was made to operationalise tinkering in the form of a factory of alternative actions, the dynamics started changing. Garden meetings were scheduled on Saturday mornings as before, but the factory steadily took over as a space of hope for the many who came looking for shelter and recuperation (occasionally, shelter in a very literal sense for some who had lost the roof over their heads and a job). One year on, the factory took to the garden, to its roots, for associates wanted to show, with pride, the achievements of grassroots mobilisation, resistance and solidarity in times of crisis. Moreover, they showed how this mobilisation effort can move beyond the strictly utopian dimension and become effective in the reconstitution of the public sphere.

That was the last day of Marcos filming at the factory. He would go back there months later, with a group of students from an international master's degree programme, and was told about the mounting problems with the proprietor. Eventually, they were evicted because the latter was offered better proposals on how to make more profitable use of the space it would seem. Without the space, a downturn in the PAA quickly followed, even if for some time the municipality provided a small apartment in downtown Algés for activities to be continued. As with similar movements emerging in the Lisbon area in those years, sustaining activities and keeping them in line with the original goals proved extremely difficult. Among the reasons for the difficulty, one can count the change in the political landscape from 2015 onwards, the public perception that crisis was waning when a left-wing government took over that very year and, last but not least, the harsh touristification that has hit Lisbon since then. But this would already be another story and another research project.

Notes

1 Afflicted by mounting fiscal imbalances that were the product both of the expansive policies of previous decades and European-backed policies for the immediate post-crisis period, the Portuguese government ended up asking for a bailout from the European institutions and the IMF – the so-called Troika – which, in turn, exposed society to deep fiscal cuts in all sectors of an already fragile welfare state. The need for an external bailout and the subsequent austerity policies were a way of tinkering with the cycles of instability intrinsic to capitalism and which in society were perceived as a case of systemic brokenness, as a public disjunction that needs to be repaired (Pina Cabral, 2018; Martínez, Introduction in this volume).

2 The French word *bricoleur* describes a handyman who makes use of the tools available to complete a task. Some connotations of a *bricoleur* attitude involve trickery, but also new ways of seeing and

joining, retrieving and recombining previously unrelated knowledge (Lévi-Strauss, 1962).
3 See Hale (2006) to learn more about the distinction between activist research and cultural critique.
4 By underlining reflexivity, we stress the turn to thinking about human practices as social ontologies in the sense of historically constituted interactions and transactions, therefore making them contingent and embodied in specific language games, power plays and discourses.

References

Altés, A. and O. Lieberman (2013) *Intravention, Durations, Effects: Notes of Expansive Sites*, Baunach: Spurbuchverlag.
Barker, S. (2014) 'Playing by whose rules? Social life as an interdisciplinary playground', *Journal of Political Power*, 7 (2): 318–25.
Bear, L. (2015) *Navigating Austerity*, Stanford, CA: Stanford University Press.
Brenner, N., P. Marcuse and M. Mayer (eds) (2011) *Cities for People, Not for Profit: Critical Urban Theory and the Right to the City*, London: Routledge.
Corsín Jiménez, A. (2003) 'On space as capacity', *Journal of the Royal Anthropological Institute*, 9 (1): 137–53.
Corsín Jiménez, A. and A. Estalella (2013) 'The atmospheric person: Value, experiment, and "making neighbors" in Madrid's Popular Assemblies', *HAU: Journal of Ethnographic Theory*, 3 (2): 119–39.
De Boeck, F. and M.-F. Plissart (2004) *Kinshasa: Tales of the Invisible City*, Ghent: Ludion.
Estalella, A. and T. Sánchez Criado (in press, 2019) 'DIY anthropology: Disciplinary knowledge in crisis', in F. Martínez (ed.), 'Changing Margins and Relations within European Anthropology', *ANUAC: Journal of the Italian Association of Cultural Anthropology*, Special Issue.
Färber, A. (2014) 'Low-budget Berlin: Towards an understanding of low-budget urbanity as assemblage', *Cambridge Journal of Regions, Economy and Society*, 7 (1): 119–36.
Farias Ferreira, M. and J. Terrenas (2017) 'The People's Assembly of Algés: Heterotopia and radical democracy in crisis-stricken Portugal', in I. David (ed.), *Crisis, Austerity and Transformation*, Lanham: Lexington, pp. 91–108.
Guyer, J. I. (2017) 'Aftermaths and recuperation in anthropology', *Hau: Journal of Ethnographic Theory*, 7 (1): 81–103.

Hale, C. R. (2006) 'Activist research v. cultural critique: Indigenous land rights and the contradictions of politically engaged anthropology', *Cultural Anthropology*, 21 (1): 96–120.

Hilbrandt, H. and A. Richter (2015) 'Reassembling austerity research', *Ephemera*, 15 (1): 163–80.

Holmes, D. R. and G. E. Marcus (2012) 'Collaborative imperatives: A manifesto, of sorts, for the reimagination of the classic scene of fieldwork encounter', in M. Konrad (ed.), *Collaborators Collaborating*, Oxford: Berghahn, pp. 127–43.

Kincheloe, J., P. McLaren and S. R. Steinberg (2011) 'Critical pedagogy and qualitative research: Moving to the bricolage', in N. K. Denzin and Y. S. Lincoln (eds), *The Sage Handbook of Qualitative Research*, London: Sage, pp. 163–77.

Lévi-Strauss, C. (1962) *La Pensée Sauvage*, Paris: Pion.

Lezaun, J., N. Marres and M. Tironi (2016) 'Experiments in participation', in U. Felt, R. Fouché, C. A. Miller and L. Smith-Doerr (eds), *Handbook of Science and Technology Studies*, Cambridge: MIT Press, pp. 195–222.

Marcus, G. (1995) 'Ethnography in/of the world system: The emergence of multi-sited ethnography', *Annual Review of Anthropology*, 24: 95–117.

Martínez, F. (2018) 'The serendipity of anthropological practice', *Anthropological Journal of European Cultures*, 27 (2): 1–6.

Okely, J. (1992) 'Anthropology and autobiography: Participatory experience and embodied knowledge', in J. Okely and H. Callaway (eds), *Anthropology and Autobiography: Gender Implications in Fieldwork and Texts*, London: Routledge, pp. 1–28.

Ortner, S. (2006) *Anthropology and Social Theory: Culture, Power, and the Acting Subject*, Durham, NC: Duke University Press.

Pina Cabral, J. (2018) 'Familiar persons in dark times', *Social Anthropology*, 26 (3): 376–90.

Rancière, J. (2006) *Politics and Aesthetics*, London: Continuum.

Rosol, M. and P. Schweizer (2012) 'Ortoloco Zurich: Urban agriculture as an economy of solidarity', *City*, 16 (6): 713–24.

Saltzman, K. (2005) 'Composting', in O. Löfgren and R. Wilk (eds), *Off the Edge: Experiments in Cultural Analysis*, Copenhagen: Museum Tusculanum Press, pp. 63–9.

Sánchez Criado, T. and A. Estalella (2018) 'Introduction: Experimental collaborations', in A. Estalella and T. S. Criado (eds), *Experimental Collaborations: Ethnography through Fieldwork Devices*, Oxford: Berghahn, pp. 1–30.

Scott, J. (1990) *Domination and the Arts of Resistance: Hidden Transcripts*, New Haven, CT: Yale University Press.

Simone, A. (2010) 'Urban geography plenary – On intersections, anticipations, and provisional publics: Remaking district life in Jakarta', *Urban Geography*, 31 (3): 285–308.

Stewart, K. (2008) 'Weak theory in an unfinished world', *Journal of Folklore Research*, 45 (1): 71–82.
Tellmann, U. (2015) 'Austerity and scarcity: About the limits and meanings of liberal economy', *Ephemera*, 15 (1): 21–40.
Tonkiss, F. (2013) 'Austerity urbanism and the makeshift city', *City*, 17 (3): 312–24.
Waltorp, K. (2018) 'Intimacy, concealment and unconscious optics: Filmmaking with young Muslim women in Copenhagen', *Visual Anthropology*, 31 (4–5): 394–407.

6

The place of recuperation

Limits and challenges of urban recovery in post-austerity Portugal

Luís Mendes and André Carmo

Introduction

This chapter focuses on the analysis of the new urban lease regime as a practice of neoliberal urbanism in Portugal, which promotes eviction, displacement and residential segregation. Against this background, it is argued that post-crisis recuperation efforts carried out by urban social movements should be acknowledged as modest attempts to deal with broader political, economic and anthropological transformations brought on by austerity policies, which profoundly reshaped urban environments and severely compromised the right to housing and to the city. In recent years, state-led gentrification has been used with the goal of creating a more dynamic housing market and fostering competitive urban renewal processes; however, we contrapose the regeneration planned by official economic policy with recuperative initiatives promoted by the civil society, showing how the two have radically different objectives and understandings of what recuperation means.

During the last couple of years, the urban landscape of the largest metropolitan areas of Portugal have changed rapidly. Among the most relevant instruments for this process to take place, one finds the new urban lease regime, in Portuguese, the *novo regime do arrendamento urbano* (NRAU). Arguably, by looking at the NRAU and how a political economy of housing operates at multiple scales, it is possible to provide a better understanding of the ways in which Portuguese cities have changed in recent years. This essay intends to shed light on recent processes in the reconfiguration of the Portuguese urban landscape after the financial crisis. In order to do so, we look at one of the most relevant instruments used with the goal of creating a more dynamic housing market, and thus fostering urban renewal and regeneration processes. Likewise, we also study how urban social movements have addressed the social consequences of the new urban lease regime and the way in which several recuperative efforts have been made in order to mitigate the harsh effects of the NRAU, especially in Lisbon and Porto.

The chapter begins with a description of how neoliberal urbanism has been inscribing itself into the Portuguese urban landscape, and discusses the role played by the state in this process. A detailed description of the implementation of the NRAU, here considered to be a pivotal instrument of state-led gentrification, is provided, focusing on how it has been implemented. Its immediate and potential consequences are also taken into account, against the backdrop of the most recent political changes that have occurred in Portugal. Finally, and based on the empirical evidence provided by a direct first-hand involvement with Habita – the Association for the Right to Housing and to the City – a reflection about the potential of urban social movements as agents of recuperation is put forward, acknowledging this concept mainly as a wide repertoire of urban solidarity practices and everyday expressions of care (Hall and Smith, 2015). We conclude that the emergence of these social movements is a manifestation of post-austerity fixing-up, intending to function as recuperation agents that redefine the realm of possibilities, generate specific meanings for social alternatives, and make certain experiences and narratives more viable in the post-crisis scenario (Amin, 2013). Moreover, we argue that, in the sense of urban politics, recuperation can be understood as an attempt to address and deal with the transformations brought by austerity policies during the financial crisis that began in 2008, developing resilient responses and mobilising people and resources.

Neoliberal urbanism, Portuguese style

In a context of increasing worldwide economic globalisation and interurban competition, urban policies should be analysed within the framework of an overarching tendency towards the neoliberal financialisation of the economy and society, particularly if considering Southern European cities (Mendes, 2013; Tulumello, 2015; Seixas et al., 2015; Zwiers et al., 2016; Rodrigues, Santos and Teles, 2016). Urban authorities and governments have been following managerial models, in which public resources are provided so as to attract investment. The provision of multiple social services has now been taken over by market forces and the private sector, and public–private partnerships have been upgraded (Brenner, Peck and Theodore, 2013). Indeed, the centrepiece of urban entrepreneurialism is the notion of public–private partnership (Harvey, 1978). In many regards, this has meant that the public sector assumes risk and the private sector gets all the benefits. Concomitantly, urban neoliberalism has spread across the globalising world through the entrepreneurialisation of local governments, the privatisation of public services and the commodification of urban spaces (Künkel and Mayer, 2012).

Despite failures such as the austerity policies that were carried out in Southern European countries to deal with the financial crisis, neoliberalism continues to reign. This ideology is often seen as the only possible solution, while failing to fulfil most of its main objectives (Millot and Toussaint, 2013; Rodrigues and Silva, 2015). In the 'entrepreneurial city', local authorities act as cost reduction business actors, running their cities as if they were enterprises. This has resulted in fewer services for citizens and less investment, especially in the affordable housing sector. Far from inciting institutional change oriented towards the repair of the system, the outcome in terms of policy is a redoubled effort to extend the neoliberal agenda further. Indeed, social recovery has never been the point, the drive for austerity was about using the crisis, not solving it (Harvey, 2014; Sevilla-Buitrago, 2015).

In Southern Europe, especially in Portugal, the effects of the urban crisis were more intensely felt due to the collapse of an already fragile housing market based on encouraging the purchase of houses in recent decades, supported by easy access to cheap credit in parallel with the development of a model of urban expansion based on the mass production of new construction, especially on the outskirts of metropolitan areas, leading to a gradual indebtedness of individuals. These facts, in conjunction with the outbreak of a very strong economic downturn since 2008, accompanied by rising unemployment, higher taxes for the working class and cuts in social support to the most socially and economically vulnerable groups, resulted in a significant increase in credit default by Portuguese families.

The Portuguese housing problem is not new, however. João Rodrigues, Ana Santos and Nuno Teles (2016) argue in their study on financialisation of the Portuguese capitalism, that the impact of this process in the housing sector is not exclusively derived from the liberalisation and deregulation of financial markets. That is, in fact, a process of financialisation of the whole of the Portuguese economy and society as a social and historical product. The authors stress the central role that the state plays in its driving or standing and international integration of the Portuguese economy. The semi-peripheral condition of Portugal, in combining the features of the developed and less developed countries, makes our country particularly vulnerable to external pressures (including those arising from the European integration process), thereby conditioning its trajectory of evolution in the financialisation of capitalism. Indeed, the historical weaknesses of the Portuguese economy and society, as well as a context of an insufficient welfare state, favoured the option of creating a private market of housing dominated by finance, in which the state never ceased to play a decisive role.

Since the 1970s, Portugal featured an intense constructive dynamic, reflecting the strong expansion of the real estate market. The Portuguese housing stock has always maintained a fast-paced growth, and, specifically, the rate of change of the number of households, until recent years, has always been above 20 per cent (although the rhythm has gradually slowed), but also much higher than the variation in the number of families, denouncing the presence of a speculative logic in this sector. During 1981–2011, housing dynamics largely outpaced the evolution of the number of households. Starting from a relatively balanced situation in 1981, the situation inflated rapidly, i.e., whereas in 1981 the number of houses was only 16 per cent higher than the number of families, in 2011 the figures reached 45 per cent. In addition to the high rate of construction evidenced by the dynamics of the Portuguese housing stock, it is also necessary to consider changes concerning home ownership, alongside a 'static' rental market and a high proportion of empty houses, several of them in an advanced state of degradation.

The socioeconomic transformations of contemporary Portuguese society and the political system have had a huge impact on the way public intervention in the housing sector was conceived and implemented. To a large extent, the debate on housing dynamics neglected the social meaning and function of housing and merely focused on market issues, such as the balance between supply and demand. In fact, whereas 'for most European countries, the quantitative need for housing is seen as a problem of the past and housing policies are now seen as responses to specific social groups more than global strategies of access to housing' (Guerra, Mateus and Portas, 2008: 10), in Southern European countries, the 'housing problem' still means the existence of serious shortages, informal construction and the lack of a consistent and systemic public intervention in the sector.

Otherwise, several contradictions can be found in the implementation of urban regeneration policies devised by the previous Portuguese government (see, Salgueiro, André and Henriques, 2015). For instance, urban regeneration actions make use of beautification strategies of public space, giving priority to areas that can offer unique amenities to attract private investment and revitalise the urban economy. Also, the results have been disappointing regarding the rehabilitation of poor and marginalised urban areas, meaning less attention to matters of social integration and sustainability. Likewise, difficult access to credit has resulted in the worsening of living conditions not only in the poorest neighbourhoods, but also in those inhabited by segments of the middle class (severely hit by austerity policies and the rise of unemployment in recent years).

Then, in the case of urban renewal and housing policies, it can be said that instead of the systematic destruction of public provision of goods and services, neoliberal policies have pushed urban governance towards a sophisticated restoration of state power at the local scale, thus making fiscal incentives and public–private partnerships instruments of urban life commodification. The Portuguese framework of housing policies and urban regeneration that has emerged in the twenty-first century should, therefore, be understood against the backdrop of this mode of urban governance to promote social recuperation through the maximisation of real estate profits and market initiatives (Martínez, 2017).

The new urban lease regime, or how to promote state-led gentrification

Historically, the traditional centre of Lisbon has been home to diverse groups of people. Over the past ten years, in particular, however, property values have increased. This, coupled with the economic crisis, the financial austerity, the NRAU (bulwark of a neoliberal turn in legal and urban policy frame) and escalating rents, destabilising the local housing market and the supply of houses for rent, have pushed out the poor people, elderly and immigrants. The financial crisis provided an adequate environment to impose the adoption of new models for the management and development of the Portuguese real estate and housing markets, as those models were seen as important to safeguard the 'success' of the International Financial Assistance Programme, which obviously conditioned the performance of the state and other public and private sectors. The Memorandum of Economic and Financial Policies, also known as Memorandum of Understanding or Plan Troika, was signed in May 2011 by the Portuguese state, the ECB, EC and IMF, and was intended to balance public accounts and promote the development of the Portuguese economy.[1]

The structural reform of the rental market was assumed as a priority in the domain of housing (Mendes, 2014; Alves, Pereira and Rafeiro, 2015). Therefore, the memorandum includes a specific chapter on the housing market, aimed at improving access of families to housing, promoting workforce mobility, improving the quality of existing houses and their better use, and reducing incentives to family indebtedness. Three themes are addressed – the rental market, administrative procedures in terms of rehabilitation and taxation of real estate – each one of them with specific measures being put forward. Regarding the first theme, the document suggested that the Portuguese government should present measures to change the new urban lease law (Law No. 6/2006) in order to assure a more balanced relationship between the rights and obligations of landlords and tenants. Under the second theme, the Portuguese government was recommended to adopt legislation to simplify administrative procedures regarding rehabilitation. Finally, on the third theme, the government was advised to review the legal framework of evaluation for tax purposes of existing real estate and land, to modify taxation of real estate with the goal of levelling incentives to lease with the own-house purchase, and to carry out a broad analysis of the functioning of the housing market with the support of international renowned experts.

The most significant of these recommendations was the first, as it paved the way for the promulgation, in 2012, of the new urban lease regime (NRAU; Law No. 31/2012, 14 August), an initiative that was subject to vigorous social protests as it could mean rising costs in rents. The new law facilitates contract termination and eviction processes on a varied basis. For instance, if a tenant does not pay the rent for a two-month period, or if the rent is paid with more than eight days of delay – four times during one year – contracts can be terminated and evictions can take place immediately without recourse to a court of law. Likewise, if the landlord claims the house for his/her own personal usage or the use of his/her descendants, or to conduct structural works or profound repairs, it is enough to inform tenants within two years of antecedence to terminate the contract.

In fact, the NRAU promoted negotiations between both parties. Obviously, landlords and tenants do not have the same negotiation power and this lease regime, contrary to the previous one, does not protect tenants as the negotiation process is organised in a way that allows landlords to put forward a new lease value that can be subject to a tenant submitting a counterproposal. If both reach an agreement, rent values increase the month after. If not, landlords can offer a compensation of 60 times the average of both proposals, and unilaterally terminate the contract. Moreover, if landlords have no capacity to compensate the tenant, the contract duration automatically turns to five years, with a maximum rent corresponding to 1/15 of the real estate taxation value.

This way, the government sought to terminate older contracts and facilitate the displacement of tenants. An additional service was also created: the national lease counter, responsible for a new special procedure aimed at accelerating and dejudicialising eviction processes and widening the possibilities for landlords to terminate contracts. During a ten-year period, ending in 2022, for tenants of 65 years of age and above and for those handicapped with more than 60 per cent incapacity, although they can have their rents increased, their contracts cannot be terminated nor can evictions be carried out. However, after that 'protection' period, free market lease values enter into force. In 2022,[2] the transitional period ends for the NRAU and for those tenants who have not yet signed a new contract. They will then be faced with the choice of either having their rent substantially increased or being evicted from their current home. Or, as many feared, they will not even get an offer to renew their contract, as the profitability of rental to tourists is more attractive for landlords nowadays. In this sense, the NRAU can be acknowledged as a state-led gentrification instrument as it accelerates the replacement of older residents and economic activities with new ones, more in line with the neoliberal urbanism ethos described above. Arguably, this mechanism has become very important for Portuguese cities, in particular Lisbon and Porto, where nearly 200,000 contracts were signed before the 1990s.[3]

It is important to point out that in spite of its recent trajectory in the gentrification processes in Portugal, the largest metropolitan areas are still at a primary stage, with relatively low levels of displacement, when compared to other European metropolises. This is characteristic of Southern European cities, where there was a kind of 'pocket gentrification' (Mendes, 2014). However, new trends in urban policies, from the beginning of the twenty-first century, mainly oriented to a touristification in the historic districts of Lisbon and Porto, have fostered the emergence of more aggressive forms of tourist and commercial gentrification creating sacrificed zones. This process of the destructive production of the space leads also to displacement, residential segregation and sociospatial fragmentation.

Physical structure and dwelling conditions have changed and the poor, immigrant and aged populations have been displaced from inner-city areas, with higher income groups then moving into these areas. In this sense, the NRAU can be taken as a pivotal instrument to accelerating the destructive production of the space and extending sacrificed areas, in order to make cities more 'friendly' environments towards neoliberal capitalist interests, while promoting an ever-growing pressure in the displacement of thousands of inhabitants, especially those living in the historical neighbourhoods. This shift was implemented in a context of generalised austerity, in which Portugal had a pro-Troika government. Nowadays, the country has an entirely different political situation, with the potential to stop (or at least minimise) the destructive power of the NRAU. In fact, the prorogation of the transition period of the law during 2017–22, can already be seen through this lens.

The place of recuperation

Urban movements constitute specific configurations of social struggle with the potential ability to transform structurally dominant dynamics and processes (Pickvance, 2003). This is conducted in a highly diversified manner, and there are numerous strategies, tactics, organisational arrangements, ideological stances, sociotechnical apparatus, media connections and state-movement nexus. Arguably, each urban movement is site-specific and structurally contingent. This means that they are deeply embedded in the particular historical-geographical contexts from which they emerge and unfold. As such, they often seek to achieve a delicate and challenging balance between supporting the long-term sociopolitical struggles taking place in urban environments while, at the same time, paying attention to the materiality and infrastructures that makes everyday micro-powers possible. This corresponds to the time-space of recuperation, that is, the framework within which small-scale gestures, continuous repair practices and involvements aimed at improving living conditions and the quality of sociospatial environments are carried out.

The experience of Habita is used here to illustrate this argument and provide some evidence as to how recuperation practices materialise in relation to urban change, namely those regarding the NRAU effects. The authors of this chapter were directly involved in the activities of Habita, which is considered to be one of the most consistent and dynamic collective action groups built around housing issues and the city as a whole in contemporary Portuguese society. Although the association was formally constituted in 2014, the more recent creation of a collective of engaged and compromised people around housing and the right to the city took place in 2012. Its embryonic existence as an urban social movement with a more organic and less institutionalised configuration can be traced back nearly a decade, when a specific group dealing with housing was created within an association called Immigrant Solidarity. Then, just like now, housing problems severely affected migrant populations.

Hence, Habita also considers that everybody is entitled to the right of the city, meaning equal access and fruition of its various social spaces, and active participation in its production and appropriation processes. Despite both being intertwined, it is also underlined that the right to the city challenges the multiple processes of segregation, insecurity, discrimination, vulnerability and expulsion that limit the right to housing, as well as services, equipment and public spaces. Housing and urban development should be constitutive of a truly participatory public policy and instrumental in the struggle against all forms of speculation. Likewise, Habita also addresses the commodification of housing, a process that excludes the most vulnerable and precarious people, who are evicted from their homes and living places when they are unable to afford the inflated and speculative prices that have favoured real estate and banking sectors for decades.

As part of its political and strategic orientation, the association also seeks to foster self-organisation and raise awareness about such enduring problems. In so doing, Habita promotes a critical reflection about the existing barriers and obstacles that limit the right to housing and to the city, while at the same time stimulating direct action, political pressure and organisational networking in order to achieve changes in legislation, policy-making, people's consciousness and sociospatial justice. In Habita, there has been a continuous effort to keep in touch with people's problems and needs, being present in their neighbourhoods, providing immediate support and solidarity whenever their rights are under attack, establishing fruitful and honest dialogues, building bridges and giving voice to those who often remain silent and impotent while tragic events such as evictions or demolitions take place.

Similar to what Iker Barbero (2015) described as the anti-eviction activism for Spain, entire families unable to continue paying their mortgages because of unemployment or insecure employment, are being involved in urban struggles by refusing to leave their houses. In effect, they are responding to the crisis by claiming and affirming their right to decent housing. In response to the neoliberal rationale that sees the evicted families and individuals who have defaulted on the payment of their mortgages as incapable, irresponsible and lazy, Habita respects their dignity and seeks to help them move away from the hegemonic rationality of vulnerability towards a new political subjectivity made of active and engaged people, reclaiming their rights to decent housing.

In this regard, benefit concerts and weekly accompaniment sessions also played an important role, although in the latter case most situations were not directly related to the NRAU. Instead, most of the people who attended were affected either by evictions and the concomitant demolition of informal settlements (mainly on the peripheral outskirts of Lisbon), or by the high increase of rents in public social housing (mostly in Lisbon) due to changes in specific legislation. A series of factors may explain this absence, such as an already accumulated experience dealing with the most deprived urban areas in the Lisbon region, a significant incapacity to make Habita visible to a wider audience, and even the fact that most probably the NRAU affected many people who perceived their situation as an individual failure, instead of a wider problem with deep socioeconomic roots, hence their feeling ashamed and unable to adopt a more proactive stance towards the process.

Furthermore, Habita also organised an educational activity oriented towards children living in the city, in which mothers, families and educators united by the importance they ascribe to care, and the creation of cities that are more children-friendly, facilitating mutual aid, exchange networks and solidarity, came together to share ideas and practices aimed at building new ways to educate, take care of one another, play and live non-commodified lives in urban spaces. The association has carried out a series of initiatives that seemingly revolve around the idea of alleviating the effects of neoliberal urbanism, in the sense that they intend to minimise social suffering and pain, through the valorisation of togetherness and creating safe places for communication, sharing and pleasure, that intended to strengthen the human capacity of preparedness and resilience to anticipate, resist and recover from adversity. These small-scale time-spaces fill up the interstitial gaps between activists and people directly affected, fostering cohesion, self- and mutual confidence, and also strengthen the political position of Habita and its potential social impact. Moreover, and up to a certain extent, these are also privileged places to promote, from a non-paternalistic stance, self-education and raise political awareness, as people who seek out Habita often show low levels of civil and political engagement and self-confidence.

Conclusion

The overview of Habita's initiatives illustrates the relevance of urban movements as agents of alleviation of the effects of austerity measures. Social participation is pivotal for the development of any collective action of repair, and these processes are often consolidated from the small gestures that humanise political struggle, giving a face and a voice to social needs and desires. This does not mean, however, that the struggle for the right to housing and to the city, in this specific case very much oriented towards an anti-gentrification agenda, should only be about compassion and merely resisting shocks coming from austerity (the idea of resilience), without stimulating the capacity to devise alternative political imaginaries widening the horizon of possibilities.

The challenge is thus to generate and maintain critical movements capable of enhancing new subjectivities and transformative social practices as well as spaces of alternative ordering that not only mitigate damage being made by neoliberal urbanism, but also put forward consistent and long-term recuperative agendas. Yet, while recuperation is acknowledged as a priority for a post-crisis situation, it is important not to internalise the idea that communities and neighbourhoods at the local level are responsible for the capitalist crisis, thus becoming trapped in a neoliberal discourse which does not recognise the production of sociospatial inequalities as an intrinsic feature of neoliberal urbanism and silently resigns to find mitigating interventions, devoid of motivation for a transformation of the system itself.[4]

Notes

1 The document, which came in force in May 2011, was characterised by pro-market fundamentalism, putting forth financial policies of deep austerity (e.g. cuts in social spending, contraction of public investment, tax raises) and a series of structural reforms that have resulted in a real assault on labour and social rights (i.e. facilitation of lay-offs, reduction of the duration and cost of unemployment benefits, etc.). Every three months, a team of unelected foreign bureaucrats came to Portugal to evaluate the implementation of the memorandum, and decide on the release of a new tranche.

2 In its original formulation, the NRAU defined a five-year transition period, scheduled to end in 2017, to protect those living below the poverty line. In October 2016, it was extended up to 2022, and low-income people were no longer protected.

3 However, it is important to point out that despite its recent trajectory, gentrification processes in Portugal's largest metropolitan areas are still at a primary stage of gentrification, with relatively low levels of displacement, when compared to other European metropolises.

4 We acknowledge the financial support from the FCT (Fundação para a Ciência e a Tecnologia), I.P., under the project HOPES: HOusing PErspectives and Struggles. Futures of housing movements, policies and dynamics in Lisbon and beyond (PTDC/GES-URB/28826/2017).

References

Alves, R., M. Pereira and M. Rafeiro (2015) 'O memorando de entendimento e as reformas no mercado de arrendamento e na reabilitação urbana', in M. L. Rodrigues and P. A. Silva (eds), *Governar com a Troika: Políticas Públicas em Tempo de Austeridade*, Coimbra: Almedina, pp. 237–59.

Amin, A. (2013) 'Surviving the turbulent future', *Environment and Planning D: Society and Space*, 31 (1): 140–56.

Barbero, I. (2015) 'When rights need to be (re)claimed: Austerity measures, neoliberal housing policies and anti-eviction activism in Spain', *Critical Social Policy*, 35 (2): 270–80.
Brenner, N., J. Peck and N. Theodore (2013) 'Neoliberal urbanism: Cities and the rule of markets', in G. Bridge and S. Watson (eds), *The New Blackwell Companion to the City*, Oxford: Wiley Blackwell, pp. 15–25.
Eckardt, F and J. Sánchez (2015) *City of Crisis: The Multiple Contestation of Southern European Cities*, Bielefeld: Transcript.
Guerra, I., A. Mateus and N. Portas (eds) (2008) *Contributos para o Plano Estratégico da Habitação 2008–2013. Relatório 3 – Estratégia e Modelo de Intervenção*, Lisbon: Instituto de Habitação e Reabilitação Urbana (IHRU).
Hall, T. and R. Smith (2015) 'Care and repair and the politics of urban kindness', *Sociology*, 49 (1): 3–18.
Harvey, D. (1978) 'The urban process under capitalism', *International Journal of Urban and Regional Research*, 2 (1–4): 101–31.
Harvey, D. (2014) *Seventeen Contradictions and the End of Capitalism*, Oxford: Oxford University Press.
Künkel, J. and M. Mayer (eds) (2012) *Neoliberal Urbanism and Its Contestations*, New York: Palgrave Macmillan.
Martínez, F. (2017) '"This place has potential": Trash, culture and urban regeneration in Tallinn', *Suomen Antropologi: Journal of the Finnish Anthropology Society*, 42 (3): 4–22.
Mendes, L. (2013) 'Public policies on urban rehabilitation and their effects on gentrification in Lisbon', *AGIR: Revista Interdisciplinar de Ciências Sociais e Humanas*, 1 (5): 200–18.
Mendes, L. (2014) 'Gentrificação e políticas de reabilitação urbana em Portugal: uma análise crítica à luz da tese rent gap de Neil Smith', *Cadernos Metrópole*, 16 (32): 487–511.
Millet, D. and E. Touissant (2013) *A Crise da Dívida. Auditar, Anular, Alternativa Política*, Lisbon: Círculo de Leitores.
Pickvance, C. (2003) 'From urban social movements to urban movements', *International Journal of Urban and Regional Research*, 27 (1): 102–9.
Rodrigues, J., A. Santos and N. Teles (2016) *A Financeirização do Capitalismo em Portugal*, Lisbon: Actual.
Rodrigues, M. L. and P. A. Silva (eds) (2015) *Governar com a Troika: Políticas Públicas em Tempo de Austeridade*, Coimbra: Almedina.
Salgueiro, T. B., I. André and E. B. Henriques (2015) 'A política de cidades em Portugal: instrumentos, realizações e perspectivas', in P. Neto and M. M. Serrano (eds), *Políticas Públicas, Economia e Sociedade: Contributos para a Definição de Políticas no Período 2014–2020*, Alcochete: Nexo Literário, pp. 49–82.

Seixas, J., S. Tulumello, S. Corvelo and A. Drago (2015) 'Dinâmicas sociogeográficas e políticas na Área Metropolitana de Lisboa em tempos de crise e de austeridade', *Cadernos Metrópole*, 17 (34): 371–99.

Sevilla-Buitrago, A. (2015) 'Crisis and the city: Neoliberalism, austerity planning and the production of space', in F. Eckardt and J. Sánchez (eds), *City of Crisis. The Multiple Contestation of Southern European Cities*, Bielefeld: Transcript, pp. 32–49.

Tulumello, S. (2015) 'Reconsidering neoliberal urban planning in times of crisis: Urban regeneration policy in a "dense" space in Lisbon', *Urban Geography*, 37 (1): 117–40.

Zwiers, M., G. Bolt, M. Van Ham and R. Van Kempen (2016) 'The global financial crisis and neighborhood decline', *Urban Geography*, 37 (5): 664–84.

7

Secondary agents of recuperation within the Hindu community in Lisbon

Inês Lourenço

This chapter discusses the retrieval of legacies within a Hindu community of the Great Lisbon area connected to the construction of a Shiva temple in Santo António dos Cavaleiros (Loures). Based on ethnographic data on the community of Indian origin in Portugal, the research explores how different projects of retrieve in a congregational building had undesigned effects of recuperation beyond the initial purpose of the maintenance of domestic and ritualistic traditions. Two different ethnographic cases illustrate the processes of recuperation of and within a Hindu community, where material culture – exemplified by the refurbishing of the Shiva Temple and through the transmission of books of *vrat katha*, ritual stories accompanied by fasting – have a central role in consolidating community ties. An active engagement with the material culture of the community contributed to the consolidation of the community ties through material things, correlating refurbishing and reconnection unexpectedly, turning the building into a device for participation and recuperation. Accordingly, one of the key arguments of this essay is that retrieve initiatives can also contribute to the strengthening of community ties, generational dialogue and the materialisation of recuperative dynamics.

The research draws on the work of Alfred Gell (1998), who argued that things (especially artworks) function as agents in social relations, in the sense that they cause events to happen in their milieu and simultaneously allow a past and a future in a present. Also, Jane Guyer (2017) has exposed how memory and materiality are two central elements in the recuperation of the ties of a group, functioning as a means of activating identity and assembling what appears fragmented. An important issue in this matter is the question of intentionality, in other words, to what extent things are designed for the social outcome they might produce. For Gell, individuals can distribute their agency through things, which function as secondary agents and surrogates of intentionality. Through their design, manufacture and function, things are formulated as active players, 'calling out various responses' (Dant, 1999: 222), triggering and mediating feelings through systems of values and intentionality.

Hindu communities of the metropolitan area of Lisbon

According to the *High Level Committee Report on the Indian Diaspora* (Singhvi, 2001), approximately 33,000 Hindus live in Portugal, distributed between Porto, Coimbra and Greater Lisbon.[1] Most Portuguese Hindus are from Gujarat and participated in the Hindu-Gujarati migration from India to East Africa during the colonial period. Therefore, they mirror other European Hindu-Gujarati settlers, especially in the UK, where the Gujarati community is bigger and is studied from different points of view. Some of these Gujarati families came from Diu, which, as well as Goa and Daman, were under Portuguese colonial rule until 1961. Most of the families from Diu who migrated to East Africa chose to settle in Mozambique, another Portuguese colony, which gained independence in 1975. The majority of Hindu-Gujarati families residing in Portugal migrated from Mozambique to the Lisbon Metropolitan Area in the early 1980s, following the civil war taking place in Mozambique.

Since the early 1980s, Hindus in Portugal, particularly in Lisbon, have settled in residential areas with specific patterns of access to housing.

Those who went to live in informal settlements, such as the Quinta da Holandesa and Quinta da Vitória, in very central areas of Lisbon, were afterwards resettled from these shanty towns to resettlement neighbourhoods between the 1990s and 2000s. Hundreds of Hindu-Gujarati families also settled in Santo António dos Cavaleiros. In the early 1980s, this was a new suburban area in northeast Lisbon, inhabited by a diverse immigrant population originating from former Portuguese colonies with several cultural backgrounds.

The district of Santo António dos Cavaleiros belongs to the Municipality of Loures, located in the Lisbon Metropolitan Area. This place was the centre of a housing expansion that began in the 1960s and 1970s, which called for the establishment of many families from the former colonies from the late 1970s. With 21,947 inhabitants, Santo António dos Cavaleiros has a very diverse population group originating from different countries, with different religious and cultural references. The Hindus living there constitute a community that is highly heterogeneous from a socioeconomic point of view. It is made up of people from various points across Gujarat, some of whom were originally from the island of Diu and others from the province of Saurashtra in South Gujarat (e.g. Rajkot, Porbandar or Junagadh) and, therefore, comprise diverse social groups and cultural references.

In addition to temples belonging to specific religious movements, such as the Hare Krishna (ISKON) and Swaminarayan, there are three Hindu temples in the Greater Lisbon Area. In 1983, in addition to their small domestic shrines, the Hindus began the construction of the Jay Ambé Temple in Quinta da Vitória at the same time as they were building their own homes in this neighbourhood. The temple has recently been relocated to the building where many Hindu families have been rehoused. Although only recently officially recognised as a place of Hindu worship, this was the first Hindu place of worship in Portugal and a statue of the goddess Ambé, which was transferred from a previous temple in Mozambique, can be found there.

In 1985, the Hindu Community of Portugal was formally set up and immediately embarked on building the Radha-Krishna Temple in Lumiar, which was completed around a decade later. This is the most high-profile Hindu place of worship in Portugal, located in central Lisbon. Completing this overview of Hindu religious diversity, the

FIGURE 7.1 *Current Shiva Temple building, Santo António dos Cavaleiros. Inês Lourenço.*

Shiva Temple was opened in Santo António dos Cavaleiros in 2001 (Figure 7.1). This process began in 1991, when the Shiva Temple Social Solidarity Association was officially recognised as representing the Hindu residents of the neighbourhood. The Hindu congregation living there grew substantially in the 1990s, making it urgent to obtain their own space to allow for its congregation and socialisation.

The construction of a Hindu temple in the district began in 2001, preceded by the blessing of the land (*bhumipujan*) by Swami Satyamitranand, as well as in a plot of land given by the Municipality of Loures, in Torres da Bela Vista. In the meantime, the community used to meet in rented spaces, such as the Neighbourhood Association of Santo António dos Cavaleiros or the local abandoned high school. As there has not been a permanent priest and laity until recently, women have been responsible for the religious activities of this community. Its activities include *puja* (worship) on Mondays. In the days of great festivities, such as the Navratri,[2] local Hindus and others coming from other communities in the metropolitan area of Lisbon, attend the religious performances at the Shiva Temple. In addition, weddings, religious ceremonies and cultural programmes are sponsored by the management of the temple. This was also the meeting space for groups that developed religious and cultural activities, such as youth groups, Gujarati school, dance rehearsals, women groups and the management of the temple itself. Many of these activities have disappeared in the last few years, as I will analyse further.

The constitution of a temple appeared as a new beginning for the community, containing both a retrieve and a promise of change, thereby introducing new activities and forms of community organisation and contributing to the consolidation of a diaspora consciousness. Yet when Portugal was plunged into a financial crisis, this community started to face difficulties in attracting youth; consequently, the temple was forced to close the Gujarati school for lack of students, dance and children's programmes were declining and the group's cultural activities became gradually focused on the older members. Also, due to their exposure to global cultural products, younger generations of Hindus were progressively detaching themselves from the cultural traditions of their parents and grandparents, originating a generational gap that threatened the continuity of the group.

The loss of the Gujarati language and the closing of the Gujarati school symbolised the growing detachment of the younger members from the traditions of their families, and the older members of the community began to state pessimistic concerns about the future of the congregation. This revealed a huge generational gap in opposition to their children and grandchildren, who became progressively more integrated into Portuguese society and detached from the Hindu and Gujarati traditional references, such as language and religious beliefs and rites:

> Our youngsters don't want to know about our traditions. They don't eat our food. They like to eat roast chicken, fries . . . They no longer know how to speak Gujarati. Some still understand but don't want to learn it. They just want to speak Portuguese . . . Now there are fewer [young] women working in the temple, helping. It's just us, the older ladies, and we're becoming less and less: M. and S. often go to the UK, to visit their daughters, they stay there for a while. L. She's getting sicker, she doesn't leave home any more. We are getting less and less . . . in a while it's all over . . .
>
> Field notes, 26 March 2015[3]

Further on, the precariousness generated by the financial crisis had profound consequences on the lives of the Hindu community, especially among the youth, leading to situations of vulnerability and exclusion, difficulties in emancipation and housing autonomy, and emigration – mainly to the UK, Angola and Brazil (Bastos and Bastos, 2006; Padilla and Ortiz, 2012; Soeiro, 2014). Thus, the financial crisis was correlated with family and an identity crisis within the Hindu community, which became a frequently discussed topic by Hindu merchant families and also by the temple head:

> With the crisis people began to move away from the temple, to move away from the community. You know? We are almost all business people. Most are small businesses, some are marketers . . . with the crisis many businesses were going through difficulties. Hindu families had to invest more in business and no longer had time for their families or to come to the temple. Thus, the youngsters disconnected from the religion and the traditions of their parents. They have disconnected from their roots . . . Of course, they were born in Portugal and their identity is Portuguese, they have to integrate, but it is important to know about the religion and culture of their ancestors. With the new priest, many youngsters returned to the temple. He had answers to their doubts, he clarified them about things that were not clear to them.
>
> Field notes, 2 February 2017

Many families have encountered serious difficulties in continuing their businesses, investing all their spare time in duplicating efforts to maintain business. This additional effort obviously had family repercussions and the previously non-existent 'resource' – the priest – has proved to be an important contributor to attenuate the effects of these multidimensional crises. After the investment in the fixed priest in the temple, whose personal expenses are guaranteed by the association that manages the temple, the panorama of this generational gap has diminished. In a post-crisis moment, this community had already been drawing concrete strategies, such as the return of the Gujarati school, the creation of a restaurant with reduced prices and the implementation of yoga classes, open to all the population surrounding the temple area. All these activities are associated with a greater objective: the symbolic materialisation of this group through the construction of a new temple.

Constructing a new temple or refurbishing the old one?

The actual Shiva Temple has existed in the form of a temporary construction since 2001. For several years, the definitive construction of the temple was a distant reality, and the need to recuperate the community ties and maintain cultural legacies was not originally identified with the materialisation of a permanent temple for the congregation. The long-term contact with the congregation under study allowed me to observe different processes over the years. For instance, in my previous fieldwork (2009), I analysed the key role of women in the maintenance of the religious, and cultural, activities of the community, initially because the congregation lacked a fixed *pujari* (priest), and once he arrived, by pushing a decentralisation of rituals and festivities (Lourenço, 2011).

In 2016, during a visit to the Shiva Temple to attend the festival of Navratri, I came upon a huge image of the future temple, printed on a decorative canvas. The head showed it to me with pride, to my amazement as I had not heard of the future temple before. As they said, he was about to build the temple soon. It was all planned, but they were lacking the financial capacity to do so. After the visit of architects from India to study the project, two funding scenarios were outlined for the construction process. The first would be a root construction on the same ground, as it was projected since the beginning. The other, a *low-cost* alternative, that the community representatives call 'Plan B', was to adapt the existing hall to the architectural features of a traditional Hindu temple, changing its exterior characteristics without demanding unbearable financial costs for the community. Specifically, Plan B involved enlarging the roof of the existing building, supporting it with columns all around and placing a dome on top in a fibreglass material. The choice of material makes it much more economical and much lighter, a material that has recently been adopted by Hindu communities in the United States, which facilitates transportation, hence its lower cost. In fact, my surprise was due to the enterprise by the temple in investing in a project that had been successively postponed. The multiple crises that this community experienced demonstrated the need to invest in something whose visibility was strongly symbolic, both for the community and for the surrounding society.

As explained above, the construction of the building appeared as an answer to the multidimensional crises faced by the congregation, rather than a strategic and well-planned move for the reinvigoration of community ties and the group's identity. When the community was about to start refurbishing Plan B, they finally managed to secure enough funding for the most expensive plan with the support of international diaspora institutions and some private donations. The new Shiva Temple is meant to display, in a more prominent visual sense, the Hindu presence in the area, thus evidencing an effort at identity retrieval within the community. Also, the symbolic refurbishing is having significance for the visibility of the Indian community in the public space, which is thus understood as a step towards agency and participation in Portuguese society. For instance, one of my female interlocutors mentioned the reactions of non-Hindu neighbours to their ritual practices, which always begin in the temple but might move between different floors and go to the entrance of the building:

> Our neighbours are curious. Usually they ask us the meaning of our ceremonies. We explain that we do certain rituals to protect the family, to bring luck to the bride and to the groom. They like to know more about us. They often say that our clothes are very beautiful.
>
> Field notes, 15 January 2009

Once a year, the temple is visited by guests from outside the community: representatives of local associations and local authorities, but also friends and visitors, attracted by the loud sound of the music that is heard over nine nights. Navratri, or Nortah, as it is commonly referred to, is a festival of nine (*nav*) nights (*rat*), deeply prominent in Gujarat, the state of origin of this community, and is dedicated to the Mother Goddess, the Mataji, also called the Great Goddess, the Mahadevi. The worship of the Goddess during Navratri takes place through dances – traditionally associated with agricultural rites of cereal crops – around the *garbo*, an octagonal wooden structure, illuminated with a central lamp and decorated with images of the various manifestations of the Goddess, placed in the middle of the circle of devotees. This is the most expressive festivity in the community, and as such, it is also the one that invites more visitors from outside, attracted by the performance. Despite occurring inside the temple, this festivity transcends the physical building by the sounds heard from outside and by the frenetic movement between the Santo António dos Caveleiros residential area and the temple, by the constant movement of Hindus during this period.

In addition to the construction of the temple, strategies, such as the construction of a restaurant and the promotion of yoga classes open to the local population, contribute to the investment in the public visibility and interaction of the group. At the community level, the impact of this refurbishing strategy has also had surprising results. This process of cultural recovery and revitalisation of the group also acquired a strong religious component and began with the *Sabha* – conversations about Hinduism – sessions, in which the priest, using English to reach the youth, clarified central themes of the Hindu scriptures and rituals, for which young people had long waited for answers, as my research showed (Lourenço, 2011). These sessions have gradually attracted the youth, and now counts hundreds of participants. On this issue, the head of the Shiva Temple states that:

> youngsters are not like us. Our parents told us to go do this *hawan* [fire ritual], and we would go, we could not even ask. Young people do not, they want to know what they are doing and what the meaning of that ritual is. And I think they are quite right!
>
> Field notes, 2 February 2017

Over the past few years, diverse retrieving and refurbishing strategies to face multidimensional crises and restore identity were employed through the materialisation of the temple. The project evolved from an initial temporary construction to a low-cost renovation plan and then, finally, to a root construction of a big temple, with areas dedicated to worship, festivals and cultural events that can host large audiences. These changes resulted from different upheavals related to the funding capabilities of a community that rises in a post-crisis moment, demonstrating how the process of retrieval takes place in relation to specific emotions, normativities and social conditions.

Safeguarding cultural heritage in a diaspora setting

Material culture is, as we know, a central axis through which communities construct, reconstruct and reproduce their identity references, and is often associated with symbolic objects of extreme relevance. The relationship between migratory processes and material culture have already been examined (Svašek, 2012); also, how the movement of populations according to the most diverse circumstances is associated with issues of materiality (Basu and Coleman, 2008). Also, there is literature about the complex ways in which religious devotion is practised, not just as adherence to an abstract set of norms but as a dynamic process that uses materials and aesthetics (Mohan, 2017). Yet, an emphasis on the relationship between social engagement with things and how it enhances shared identities and connections with the homeland allows us to focus on the centrality of affective transmissions of fixing, mending and refurbishing (Martínez, Introduction in this volume). Further, this perspective reveals a material dimension behind the practices that involves human recuperation, evidencing the centrality of objects in these processes and their role in grounding cultural identities (Meyer and van de Port, 2018; Martínez, 2018). In the case of Hindus, we can also see that a myriad of objects is indispensable to ritual performance. The *vrat katha*, ritual religious storytelling followed by fasting, is an example of a domestic feminine rite that requires a series of specific objects: *murti* (picture or statue) of divinity, *divo* (lamp), incense and *kumkum* (ritual red powder). In addition, since it is a practice followed by specific kinds of fasts, certain foods are associated with it.[4]

Bina, who is 42 years old, is frequently engaged in activities to promote Indian and Gujarati culture. In 2016, she published, along with the anthropologist Rita Cachado, who developed long-term fieldwork in the Quinta da Vitória neighbourhood of Portela de Sacavém, in which she lived until 2016, a cookbook entitled, *Coentros e Garam Masala. Uma Cozinha Indiana-Gujarati em Portugal* (*Cilantro and Garam Masala: An Indian-Gujarati Cuisine in Portugal*). Since then, she has been invited even more frequently to events promoting Indian culture in Portugal. For Bina, the publication of this book was a way of spreading a very important trait of her cultural heritage: food. The Gujarati gastronomic culture is a very marked trait in the Gujarati origin community in Portugal. In the case of Bina, this book served to keep this reference of identity for future generations who, like their children, prefer *fast food* to homemade recipes. And obviously, a way of sharing a heritage highly valued by the community of Indian origin in Portugal through its food. However, Bina is not only involved in this project. Her concern to bring to the younger generation, the traditional Hindu values which, in her opinion, are being lost, was reflected in the need she shared with me for some time, of transcribing *vrat katha* to Portuguese. *Vrat kathas* are religious histories originating in the Puranic texts, read or recited in domestic rituals, and separately particularly by women, together with fasts (*vrat*; see, Narayan, 1992), in order to obtain family and domestic balance.

According to traditional Hindu values, in addition to their reproductive role, women should also call for divine protection of their home and family, by vowing to realise family stability. In exchange for their requests, women make vows, offerings and fasts. Placing the responsibility of family survival on women drives them to control their destiny and that of their family through negotiation with the gods (Knott, 1996). Old books are the central object of this process as, over time, they have achieved a symbolic role that reveals the centrality of material culture in this diasporic context. Throughout my fieldwork, I realised how *vrat kathas* were so important for social and cultural transmissions through women. Thus, I recently started collecting short stories from a book which was about 30 years old and which Bina considers to be the most indicated source. Although choosing this older version does not imply, for Bina, that there is a need for authenticity. Paradoxically, *vrat kathas* are often altered and updated, and this fact does not detract from their importance as a central portable cultural heritage among the Hindu diaspora.

Bina travelled from Mozambique to Portugal after her marriage in 1993. The daughter of a priest from Rama Temple in Salamanga, Mozambique, she inherited several religious objects, among them

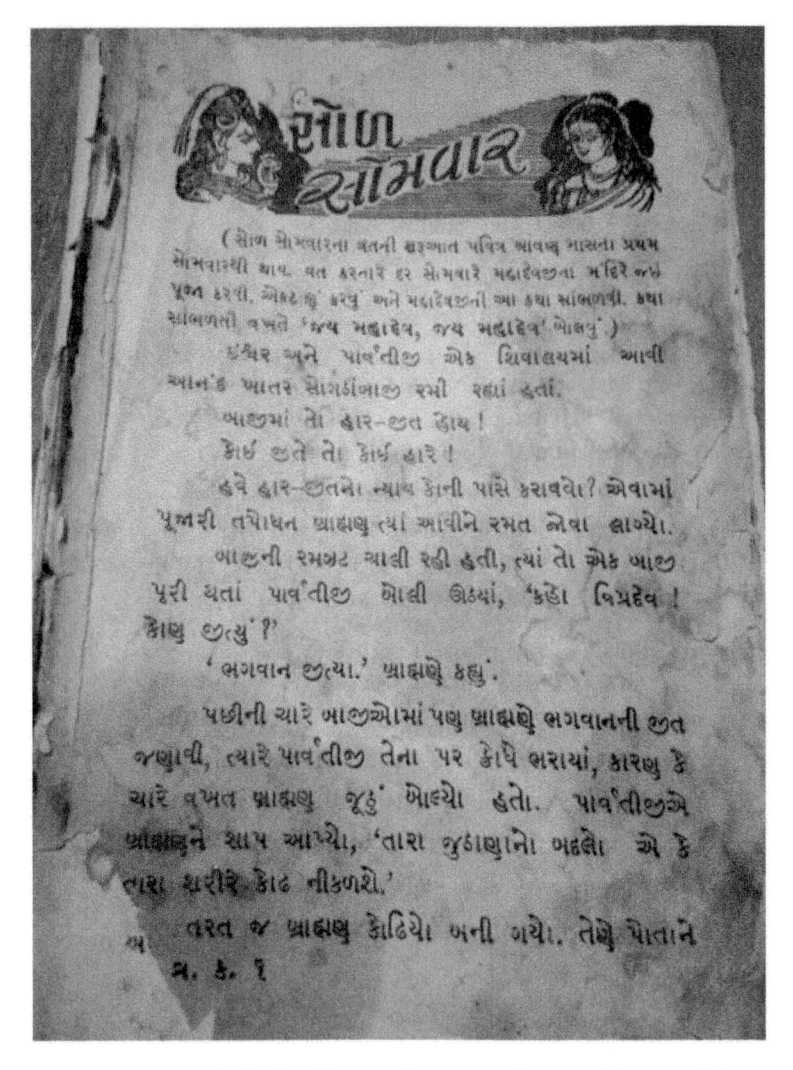

FIGURE 7.2 Vrat katha *book carried to Portugal in 1993 by Bina Achoca from Salamanga, Mozambique. Inês Lourenço.*

this book, which she carefully stored throughout her journey from Mozambique to Portugal, and then in Portugal, after successive house changes (Figure 7.2). She has always used it to do the *vrat kathas* readings and she asked me to keep it during the process of translation. Hence, the safeguarding and retrieval of the book plays a central role for the identity construction and preservation within the Hindu community.

Otherwise, in the case of the Shiva Temple refurbishment, investment in the translation and dissemination of these texts among the younger generations comes precisely at a time when the economic and social crisis was felt in Portugal. Thinking about her adolescent children and reconsidering the identity crisis within the community, Bina decided to activate the religious heritage using an object that she brought with her from an earlier migratory context and carefully preserved during all these years. Bina's effort to reactivate community bonds by recovering old objects that also function as a mode of recuperation, and despite having access to newly published books, attributes a special character to the old one because of its antiquity, acquiring a symbolic role in the process of reactivation.

The connection between authenticity and tradition also extends to ideas of diaspora and identity (Kasfir and Yay, 2004). A glance at the cultural survival of the African diasporas resulting from slavery processes might help us to understand the relevance of the relationship between migration and the maintenance of a heritage from generation to generation, thus transforming the process of transmission (most often passing from orally based to materially based) as a required adaptation to the new environment (Nettleford, 2004). *Vrat kathas* have been transmitted in the same way (before being popularised in the written version, also orally) from generation to generation. These are intended to supply cultural foundations for certain behaviours or ways of thinking that integrate a specific religious and cultural heritage and that help to preserve diasporic identity references in Portugal. Thus, the study of this immigrant and portable heritage will allow the inclusion of minorities in the heritage studies, exploring 'practices and forms of knowledge that are strongly tied to a sense of identity, to place and to memory' (Naguib, 2013: 2181).

Concluding considerations

Over the years, my long-term contact with the Hindu communities in the Lisbon area has enabled me to perceive different crises and different reaction waves to these crises. Currently, the Hindu congregation is in a period of transition, in which the former priest was replaced by another priest and a new temple is being built. As such, it is a period of implementation of further measures of recuperation, which are intended to have even more impact in attracting young Hindus. For most of my informants, enhancing intergenerational dialogue was a key concern and a form of community sustainability, which, paradoxically, is achieved through the retrieval of past things.

Relying on Gell's idea that material things might function as secondary 'social agents' (1998: 7), endowed with the formation and manifestation of intentional actions, this essay makes evident how the retrieve of material legacies activated feelings of commonality within the Indian diaspora in Lisbon, allowing the congregation to recuperate itself and leading, in turn, to a stronger visibility of the community in question. Likewise, the Hindu community in Santo António dos Caveleiros gained confidence from the refurbishment of the temple, repairing the community itself through it, transforming the building into a device of participation and recuperation. Eventually, this case reveals how recuperative projections towards the future can be materialised, consolidating ties, in turn, not only within the community but also with the surrounding society.

Notes

1 These figures cover both People of Indian Origin (PIOs) and Non-resident Indians (NRIs).
2 Nine night festival dedicated to the Goddess Mahadevi, celebrated on the equinoxes of spring and autumn, are very popular in Gujarat.
3 Words quoted in this chapter are from the author's ethnographic research, which was done with the consent of the subject and an awareness that these words could end up in print.
4 For example, *samo* (millet) is a cereal indispensable to the accomplishment of the *Sama Pancham* – also called *Rishi Pancham* – *vrat katha*.

References

Bastos, S. P. (1991) *A Comunidade Hindu da Quinta da Holandesa: Um Estudo Antropológico sobre a Organização Sócio-espacial da Casa*, Lisbon: Laboratório Nacional de Engenharia Civil (LNEC).

Bastos, S. P. and J. G. P. Bastos (eds) (2006) *Filhos Diferentes de Deuses Diferentes. Manejos da Religião em Processos de Inserção Social Diferenciada*, Lisbon: Observatório da Imigração (ACIME).
Basu, P. and S. Coleman (2008) 'Introduction: Migrant worlds, material cultures', *Mobilities*, 3 (3): 313–30.
Dant, T. (1999) *Material Culture in the Social World: Values, Activities, Lifestyles*, London: Open University Press.
Gell, A. (1998) *Art and Agency: An Anthropological Theory*, Oxford: Clarendon Press.
Guyer, J. (2017) 'Aftermaths and recuperations in anthropology', *Hau: Journal of Ethnographic Theory*, 7 (1): 81–103.
Kasfir, S. and J. Yay (2004) 'Current debate: Authenticity and diaspora', *Museum International*, 56 (1–2): 190–7.
Knott, K. (1996) 'Hindu women, destiny and Stridharma', *Religion*, 26 (1): 15–35.
Lourenço, I. (2011) 'Religion and gender: The Hindu diaspora in Portugal', *South Asian Diaspora*, 3 (1): 37–51.
Martínez, F. (2018) *Remains of the Soviet Past in Estonia*, London: UCL Press.
Meyer, B. and M. van de Port (eds) (2018) *Sense and Essence: Heritage and the Cultural Production of the Real*, Oxford: Berghahn.
Mohan, U. (2017) 'When Krishna wore a kimono: Deity clothing as rupture and inefficacy', in D. Jeevendrampillai, A. Parkhurst, T. Carroll and J. Shackelford (eds), *The Material Culture of Failure*, London: Bloomsbury, pp. 39–55.
Naguib, S.-A. (2013) 'Museums, diasporas and the sustainability of intangible cultural heritage', *Sustainability*, 5: 2178–90.
Narayan, K. (1992) *Storytelers, Saints and Scoundrels: Folk Narrative in Hindu Religious Teaching*, Delhi: University of Pennsylvania Press.
Nettleford, R. (2004) 'Migration, transmission and maintenance of the intangible heritage', *Museum International*, 56 (1–2): 78–83.
Padilla, B. and A. Ortiz (2012) 'Fluxos migratórios em Portugal: do *boom* migratório à desaceleração no contexto de crise. Balanços e desafios', *Revista Intedisciplinar da Mobilidade Humana*, 39: 159–84.
Reis, J. (2012) 'Austeridade', in *Dicionário da Crise e das Alternativas*, Coimbra: Almedina, pp. 33–4.
Singhvi, L. M. (2001) *High Level Committee Report on the Indian Diaspora, Ministry of External Affairs of India*. Available at: https://www.mea.gov.in/images/pdf/1-executive-summary.pdf (accessed 3 August 2019).
Soeiro, J. (2014) 'Da *Geração à Rasca* ao *Que se Lixe a Troika*. Portugal no novo ciclo internacional de protesto', *Sociologia*,

Revista da Faculdade de Letras da Universidade do Porto, 28: 55–79.

Svašek, M. (2012) 'Introduction: Affective moves – Transit, transition and transformation', in M. Svašek (ed.), *Moving Subjects, Moving Objects. Transnationalism, Cultural Production and Emotions*, Oxford: Berghahn, pp. 1–40.

8

Recuperation and vice versa in Portuguese folk art

Maria Manuela Restivo and Luciano Moreira with photos by Nuno Marques

In this visual essay based on interviews, archival material and fieldwork, we engage with the notion of recuperation – which inherently assumes the existence of a previous crisis – in the arena of Portuguese folk art. Contrary to what happens in other regions of the world, where we are witnessing processes of emancipation through folk arts and crafts, in Portugal, actual practices of recuperation are not led by the artists themselves but rather by external (and emergent) agents. These are, namely, the municipal and touristic operators, who, in their quest to develop the country's economy and market relations, try to reinvigorate a sense of locality through encounters with 'authentic' local people and materiality.

When we look at the Portuguese context, there is a general belief that folk art has not been given its deserved attention (Leal, 2004), and that it still occupies a problematic status in Portuguese museology (Dias, 2015). However, this has not always been the case. During the Estado Novo regime (1926–74), folk art was given a crucial place in the cultural politics and national identity-at-large, allegedly embodying ideas of simplicity, modesty and humility (Alves, 2007). The close association of folk art with the Estado Novo resulted, as we believe, in a generalised absence of folk art in some circles and its appearance in other spheres. During the years that followed the Portuguese revolution in 1974 (and until very recently), folk art was seen primarily as craft and not as art. For instance, it was promoted by the Instituto de Emprego e Formação Profissional (Institute for Employment and Vocational Training) as a simultaneous mode of self-employment and of preserving local craft techniques, and several crafts markets were created. However, at the same time, folk art lost its presence in museums and universities, resulting in a surprising absence of folk art from the academic fields (particularly acute in the domain of art history), remaining as a field that is being given residual attention.

As a way of reversing this situation, we started a project in 2015 called *Arte Popular Portuguesa de Ana a Zé*,[1] which was designed to document, promote and research the field of Portuguese popular, traditional and outsider arts. One of the key aims of the project was to create a visual, digital archive for Portuguese folk art, documenting key artists,[2] materials and techniques and contextualising them. By making such data publicly available through the website, we aimed to increase their visibility and to invite people to reflect on their situated knowledge in terms of constructed yet embodied skills, contribution to place-making and the potential representation of local values. Additionally, we intend to produce an anthropological analysis based on the perceptions and beliefs that the artists have about their own work and the ways they position themselves towards the actual 'folk art world'.[3]

With the preservation urges that are underlying the creation of 'local crafts' – ranging from the increasing denomination of protected origin (DOP) and denomination of controlled origin (DOC) products through heritage labels – folk artists are being involved in top-down processes of classification that are usually alien to their own working and selling practices.[4] Consequently, disagreements between governments and artisans take place.[5] In fact, the fieldwork that we have made so far leads us to argue that folk art in Portugal is characterised by a certain degree of autonomy and marginality. In general, folk artists are elder and have lower levels of formal instruction. Most have lived and worked outside the city centres, usually in smaller villages, and almost all of them are self-taught or, as is most common in some contexts, have learned with someone close to them, usually family or neighbours. Generally, they work with local materials (like clay and wood), or materials that once existed in the region (as is the case of clay in Bisalhães). Most of the creators have their workshops at home, sometimes occupying part of a division of their house. Indeed, it is not uncommon that the boundary between work and personal affairs is thin and the time dedicated to these different dimensions is not as strict as it is in other fields. Júlia Côta, for example, works in her dining room, and she might even invite you to eat with her and her family (see Figure 8.8, further down). Folk artists sell their objects in local or national crafts markets, but also in some stores that buy their works to resell. However, in most cases, they sell their work directly to those who visit their workshops, which is sometimes the artists' main source of income.

The characteristics of production and the selling circuits of the objects in a way make them operate in a kind of parallel economy. As they are self-employed, often working and selling from home, they find themselves beyond the reach of regulatory and supervising powers. Some artists do not make objects as their main work activity and are not registered in the financial system. And even when they are, a considerable percentage of the sales generally goes unreported. When it comes to selling the objects, most of the objects go directly to the hands of clients and collectors. In sum, the universe of Portuguese folk art remains, thus far, in a marginal domain, in terms of location, production and circulation of the objects. This marginality, though, is being reshaped by recent circumstances, thus forcing artisans to take part in new and redefined settings, as in the following examples.

Lazarim

In the small northern village of Lazarim, famous for its traditional carnival where the wooden masks are the protagonists, a small interpretative centre dedicated to the Iberian mask (CIMI) opened in 2017. Recently, the municipal government decided to apply the Lazarim mask to the UNESCO Intangible Heritage List, and they are now in the research phase of the project. Although there is a general satisfaction with the dynamics that the promotion of the mask is causing in the village, Adão de Castro Almeida, one of the maskmakers, told us that the centre, as a way of growing its collection, tries to accord a value with the artisans for the masks that is below the market value, which dissatisfies them (Figures 8.1–8.4). Despite the folk artists recognising the importance of the centre, it is interesting to see that they do not feel they need to adapt to the needs of the centre, but precisely the opposite.

FIGURE 8.1 *Adão de Castro Almeida's workshop and his masks in Lazarim. Nuno Marques.*

FIGURE 8.2 *Daniel Silva, a young apprentice, making a mask in Lazarim. Nuno Marques.*

FIGURE 8.3 *Lazarim masks at the Iberian Mask Interpretative Centre (CIMI). Nuno Marques.*

FIGURE 8.4 *Carnival of Lazarim, where the masks are publicly used. Nuno Marques.*

Bisalhães

The black pottery of Bisalhães in the north, was inscribed in 2016 in UNESCO's List of Intangible Cultural Heritage in Need of Urgent Safeguarding. Extensive research was conducted with the active involvement of the potters, some books were published and an exhibition was organised. However, two years later, the landscape is somewhat disappointing: street signs to the village of Bisalhães remain few and old, resulting in a difficulty to find the village and the creator's workshops, and there were no successful safeguarding measures. Two years later, the techniques are still in the hands of the same five potters, four of whom are aged over 70 years (Figure 8.5–8.6).

FIGURE 8.5 *Querubim Rocha's workshop in Bisalhães. Nuno Marques.*

FIGURE 8.6 *Querubim Rocha's workshop in Bisalhães. Nuno Marques.*

Among the potters, there is a generalised feeling of unfulfilled promises, and they are still waiting for the improvement of their work and life conditions, as well as the continuation of the craft traditions, of which only they are the guardians. Although the classification enabled the local government to have access to some European funds, the artisans, as they told us, 'didn't see any money', and nothing has changed for them.

Barcelos

Barcelos, in the north-west, is, when it comes to folk art, probably the most successful example in terms of the preservation and vitalisation of some traditional artistic practices. When it comes to the clay figures of Barcelos, the *figurado de Barcelos*, which date back at least to the end of the nineteenth century, a growing group of people, some of them young, are producing clay figures and giving them their own interpretations and styles. Contrary to the previous examples, the clay figures of Barcelos were not, at least until now, involved in UNESCO classification processes. Instead, in 2005, the Barcelos Municipality developed a certification that identified the materials, motifs and techniques of what could be considered the 'traditional' *figurado*. As inevitably occurs with these processes, there is an inherent inclusion and exclusion of some producers that is not consensual between the crafters themselves. Júlia and António Ramalho are suspicious of this certification, either for the artists whom the certification leaves out or because they feel it is not useful for them (Figure 8.7). As Júlia told us, they would sell their objects anyway. Moreover, Júlia does not want to donate her pieces to the museum after her death, insisting that she does not recognise the local museum, the Museu de Olaria, as the appropriate actor in the safeguarding of her family legacy, although they dedicated a solo exhibition to her in 2016. For Júlia Côta's space in the village, see Figure 8.8.

Through processes of classification as heritage – either locally or UNESCO-related – folk artists are being called upon to abandon their marginality, engage in defining and categorising what they create and take part in a complex net of negotiations between them and

FIGURE 8.7 *Júlia and António Ramalho's workspace in Barcelos. Nuno Marques.*

FIGURE 8.8 *Júlia Côta's work space in Barcelos. Nuno Marques.*

multi-scalar institutional powers. The strategy is to strengthen local identities while developing the potential of cultural consumption, thus creating an ambiguous relation between the spheres of cultural heritage and tourism. Furthermore, and contrary to what we witness in conventional artistic institutions, folk artists do not seem to recognise the new institutional actors as validators of their work, showing a kind of resistance towards them. As Adão de Castro Almeida from Lazarim suggested, 'when they arrived, we were already here'. Folk artists seem to claim a certain ontological precedence over the newcomers.

This visual essay is an invitation to reconsider what is being recuperated, and for which purposes. It is also an invitation to think about what will happen to folk artists and to their work, in the face of this new, changing landscape. How will they cope with growing pressures to submit their work to alien regulations and standards? And how will they come to participate as equally as possible in an uneven, multi-scalar arena of economic and political interests?

Actual policies of cultural reconnection and revaluation through the retrieval of folk art are meant as constitutive of recuperation, yet one that is imposed and based on alien terms. Its failures or limited achievements then come as surprises.

Notes

1 Available at: www.artepopularportuguesa.org (accessed 9 March 2018).
2 In this text, we will use the terms 'artist', 'artisans', 'creator' and 'producer' as an equivalent, leaving the classifications for others to decide. This project shows us that the dichotomies between artist/artisan and art/artefact are not absolute.
3 Following the term 'art worlds', coined by Howard Becker to refer to everyone involved in producing, commissioning, presenting, preserving, promoting and selling art (Becker, 1982).
4 Although our project is dedicated to folk arts in general, by which we roughly mean an opposition to erudite forms (in terms of apprenticeship, techniques and circuits of circulation of the artists and works), it is useful to make a distinction between the creators who operate within a local tradition (with its particular materials, techniques and motifs) from the ones who create any outside

conventions, which are also called 'outsider artists' in English. In Portugal, these terms have no consensual correspondence, so we take the term 'folk' (in English) as a translation of 'popular' (in Portuguese) to include both categories. Although we are aware of the risks of essentialising the concept of folk art, we believe in its usefulness in the Portuguese context, specifically in trying to remark and overcome its artistic and academic marginalisation. In this essay, due to its characteristics, we are only approaching the folk arts rooted in shared artistic local traditions. The 'outsiders' remain detached from a specific location, and for that, are not being 'appropriated' by cultural and touristic operators.

5 The conflicts between governmental policies and craft communities are very common when it comes to the safeguarding of Intangible Cultural Heritage. One of the principles of the UNESCO Convention states that: 'those who practice the traditions should have the major responsibility for their safeguarding' (Kurin, 2004: 71). For an overview of the problems of the Intangible Cultural Heritage convention, see ibid.

References

Alves, V. M. (2007) 'A poesia dos simples: Arte popular e nação no Estado Novo', *Etnográfica*, 2 (1): 63–89.

Arte Popular Portuguesa de Ana a Zé. Available at: www.artepopularportuguesa.org (accessed 9 March 2018).

Becker, H. (1982) *Art Words*, Los Angeles, CA: University of California Press.

Dias, N. (2015) 'Preface', in A. Shelton (ed), *Heaven, Hell and Somewhere in Between: Portuguese Popular Art*, Vancouver: MOA/University of British Columbia, p. viii.

Kurin, R. (2004) 'Safeguarding intangible cultural heritage in the 2003 UNESCO convention: A critical appraisal', *Museum International*, 56 (1–2): 221–2.

Leal, J. (2004) 'Metamorfoses da arte popular: Joaquim de Vasconcelos, Vergílio Correia e Ernesto de Sousa', *Etnográfica*, 6 (2): 251–80.

9

Recuperative dances
Reconnecting through *kizomba* in a crisis context

Livia Jiménez Sedano

Introduction

This chapter puts the focus on the couple dance called *kizomba*, its iterations and reformulations, and the kind of effects these have generated among practitioners in Lisbon.[1] Associated with a modern and cosmopolitan African-ness, and since the 1990s commodified, *kizomba* did not, however, fade away during the times of austerity but transformed itself qualitatively. The research looks at the commodified *kizomba* dance culture that developed in Lisbon as a contemporary ritualised practice of recuperation that makes sense precisely in the actual context of crisis. Participants in these dancing venues have been escaping from the stress and suffering of everyday life in conditions of austerity through embodying an imagined African-ness in their nightlife. The ethnographic material shows how the rule of verbal silence that governs the dance floor invited people to focus on their bodily experiences. Likewise, the slow *kizomba* tempo inverts the progressive acceleration of social life, and close proxemics symbolise the opposite of fraying social ties. Moreover, many participants reported how dancing activated their kinetic memory of *bailarico* – the village celebrations around communal dance they experienced in their childhood. To some extent, there is an implicit feeling of reviving a sense of belonging to a warm community through kinetic symbols without renouncing to the cosmopolitan ethos that this way of imagining Africa projects on the dance floor.

The couple dance popularly known as *kizomba* became fashionable in the 1980s in Portuguese-speaking *African* communities who lived in Africa and Europe, connected through transnational ties (Jiménez, 2018b). In the 1990s, it was commodified in Portugal and had a great success in dance schools and clubs. One of its most appealing features consists of a proxemics unusual in the world of commodified genres: the two partners dance in a close embrace, allowing for tight body contact, a characteristic often interpreted as 'too sexual' by many other dance aficionados that prevents them from practising it. The romantic beat of the music is accompanied by coordinated slow and sinuous rhythmic movements that sometimes end up with navel shocks,[2] and sometimes turn into almost imperceptible slow-motion moves. These traits, combined with the aficionados' habit of closing their eyes on the dance floor, turn the dance into quite an intimate experience, frequently shared with unknown partners. Throughout the commodification process, teachers gradually introduced new acrobatic and complex steps, stemming from other ballroom styles such as salsa, tango and bachata.[3] As a result, the kinetic languages of commodified *kizomba* dance floors evolved in diverging paths.

In the first section, I will describe how, during the financial crisis, while many discos of Lisbon went into bankruptcy, the *kizomba* craze bloomed instead of fading away. The next section argues that we can only understand this phenomenon through analysing the social meanings of the encounter at the commodified *kizomba* dance floor: the need to find conventional ways of recuperation from the social suffering produced by the financial crisis. We will explore how the participants produced a specific context, where the social order was inverted by reproducing the rules of an imagined and idealised '*African* culture'. The main contrasting characteristics of the dance prove slow dancing rhythm instead of everyday life acceleration, placing the focus on the silenced body as a means of communication, and performing with physical proximity to feel reconnected and symbolically reverse the frailty of social relations under the conditions of neoliberal austerity. Moreover, we will see how the dancing experience made the dancers' bodies activate kinetic memories of village parties they had experienced in their childhood (*bailarico*) and correspondingly helped to symbolically regain a former sense of belonging to a solid community. At this level, African-ness helped to remove an embarrassing vulgarity linked to rural dance, which allowed the participants to experience this revival without renouncing to a cosmopolitan ethos. The last section describes how the explicit discourse of 'love for African culture' that makes up part of the commodified *kizomba* public message did not lead aficionados to immerse themselves in the so-called *African discos* of the city – here understood as an example of how many postcolonial tensions are still alive.

Dancing *kizomba* in times of crisis

People speak more about communication, contact, heat, well-being, love and solidarity as long as those values leave the social field. In these meaningless times, specialists in communication, contact, heat, well-being, love and solidarity proliferate. Specific places, times, products and services planned for those ends display those social obligations in little bits, leading the subject to search in the private sphere what he cannot expect to find in ordinary life . . . Intimacy becomes a key value of modernity, including the search for new experiences, body well-being and self-exploration; it requires contact with others but always in a measured and controlled way

LE BRETON (1995: 154).

In late modernity, the advancing neoliberal system has made life and working conditions extremely hard at the global level: unstable jobs, greater exigence of mobility, rapid adaptation to changing conditions, increasing dismantling of social welfare and the progressive acceleration of social rhythms of life (Comaroff and Comaroff, 2001; Harvey 2005; Jameson, 1984; Le Breton, 1995; Martínez, 2015). In such a complex global scenario, the financial crisis has aggravated the hardness of living conditions in Southern Europe.[4]

According to different scholars, as a result of the austerity measures imposed by the so-called 'Troika',[5] South European populations have acquired a new sense of common belonging, based on shared suffering instead of on cultural commonalities (Knight and Stewart, 2016; Baumgarten, 2013). The drastic austerity politics have undermined basic public health, education and labour rights acquired through historic political struggles in both Spain (Narotzky, 2016) and Portugal (Accornero and Pinto, 2015). In Portugal, the middle classes have reached levels of precariousness they had never experienced before. The combination of rising unemployment rates and severe cuts in basic public services has had a negative impact in several areas, such as the population's health (Sakellarides et al., 2014), domestic finance, the quality of family relationships (Ribeiro et al. 2015) and economic investment in leisure activities (Mauritti and da Cruz Martins, 2014). Also, protest movements such as *'Que se Lixe a Troika'* (Accornero and Pinto, 2015) and *'Geração à Rasca'* (Gray, 2016), with a strong influence of the Spanish *'Indignados'*, had their greatest impact during the period spanning 2010–13.

However, the *kizomba* phenomenon under analysis does not represent an example of protest, and neither is it an explicit attempt to actually repair the social fabric. Instead, the dance floor turns into a context to escape from the harnesses of everyday life, without an open aim of transforming the situation. In any case, by stating its apolitical nature, I do not wish to reinforce the stereotype of an essentially 'passive Portuguese civil society' (cf. Accornero and Pinto, 2015). In fact, the *kizomba* boom took place during the hardest times of the financial crisis during 2010–13, when the streets of Lisbon became the scene of demonstrations of sizes that had not been seen since the military coup revolution of 1974 (Gray, 2016; Accornero and Pinto, 2015; Baumgarten, 2013), and, indeed, the same analysis applies to the case of Madrid. Summing up, these dancing encounters belong to a complex set of different reactions to the financial crisis. Some of them involved protesting against its consequences on everyday life, while others focused on producing collective ways for escaping from reality and dreaming of an alternative/lost social order.

During the first year of fieldwork in 2013, I followed the weekly encounters of *kizomberos*[6] in Madrid: each night, this dancing community gathered at different discotheques. Since the commodified version of the dance was introduced successfully in the city in 2007, it soon spread all over the country. Simultaneously, I witnessed how many of my friends-informants lost their jobs during that period: Maria[7] (35, biologist) and Juan (34, industrial engineer) spent a long time looking for something else; Pedro (40, telecommunications director) had a stable and promising position; Pablo (42, international expert in internet security) started searching abroad; Sara (32, secretary) had worked for the same company for years; Altagracia (32, marketing manager from the Dominican Republic) lost her job and only found a new one when her visa was about to expire; Elena (55, beautician) lost most of her clientele and had to close her beauty shop and start receiving clients at her home to reduce costs and Fernando (42, account manager at an important bank) told us that the company had fussed with another and the new boss was cutting down on staff to save costs. Each morning, someone was fired.

With such a situation, I wondered if the *kizomba* nightlife business would survive for long. Surprisingly, instead of disappearing, new *kizomba* events bloomed during 2013. One night, at the *But* disco, I had an informal conversation with Alfredo, a salsa promotor who had recently decided to enter the *kizomba* market as well. He explained why he wanted to start up this risky business in the middle of the financial crisis. According to him, the number of dance aficionados had not decreased:

> I ask Alfredo how many *kizomba* students he has . . . and he answers that there are around 80 people as a whole . . . I ask him if the number of clients attending dance discos has fallen down considerably. As he has worked in the salsa business for the last 30 years, he has a historical perspective. He says that the number of clients has not declined, or maybe just a little bit, but nothing significant. The real difference is the amount of money clients spend. The same people come to the disco, but instead of buying one or two alcoholic drinks – what they used to consume before, now they take just the free refreshment included in the ticket. They pay the entrance ticket and that's all. Having the disco as crowded as always, you can earn per night half the money you used to get before.
>
> Excerpt from fieldwork diary, 10 June 2013

In September 2014, I started doing fieldwork in *kizomba* contexts in Lisbon, where the financial crisis had had an even greater impact than in Madrid. According to all the disco owners and managers interviewed, the situation had severely affected the nightlife business industry. Many clubs had gone bankrupt and, in this period of accelerated changes, new ones opened, closed and changed owners faster than ever before. In the world of dance aficionados, ephemeral parties attended by a changing audience substituted the old club culture based on a clientele loyal to their local sense of belonging. In the middle of the chaos, the disco considered the temple of salsa in Lisbon was still alive: Barrio Latino. It was born in 2004 and was devoted to the salsa community, but things changed when *kizomba* stole the crown from salsa and became the queen of the night around 2006. Interestingly, this shift took place during the period of the financial crisis. Zé Ferreira, Barrio Latino's owner during the research, reflected on this phenomenon in an interview:

ZF [The period of great success of *kizomba*] started in 2006. The house was incredibly crowded, in this room[8] you could not even breath . . . They [the former owners] had to make the room bigger, because there were too many people here. Now, something different is happening: there were so many people here that we started playing *kizomba* in the big room and salsa in the small one . . . It has to do with what people search, and it also derived from the crisis. Salsa aficionados started staying at home . . . [They became] unemployed, dance schools lost salsa students, and that's why they decided to compensate for the economic loss by organising parties. In the field of parties, the concurrence is bigger. We used to be the only ones working on dance nights and every salsa aficionado came to Barrio Latino. Now you have many parties, Jazzy [a dance school], many options. In the area of African music, even though there is concurrence as well, people never forgot Barrio. I think it was in the time of the crisis, during the peak, but anyway, we always had people . . .

L Do you mean that the crisis affected salsa more than *kizomba*?

ZF Yes, that's it . . . Maybe because salsa aficionados are older. Anyway, Barrio's clients are a bit older,[9] they got frightened because, from my point of view, ten years ago nobody knew how their situation would be three months later. That's true, many people decided to stay at home and not go out at night any more. Some people went out once in a month, or twice in a month, because they didn't know how long it [the crisis] would take. We were falling down, we reached a situation in which the crisis got worse, we could see it month by month, hardly anybody came to salsa parties. It was frustrating, with good DJs, good music for salsa parties and nobody came. *Kizomba* also decreased but not to that point. For example, this club didn't work during the summer and it started working successfully during the summer . . . I think that it was because of the crisis too, people didn't have money for travelling in the weekend, in the summer, for spending the holidays outside, they stayed here and spent the money they had in the city nightlife . . . The summer used to be rather weak and now the summer is really strong, here in Barrio Latino . . . Algarve[10] was not full of Portuguese people any more, there were more foreigners than Portuguese people. They stayed here and spent the money they had by going out at night.

Interview with ZÉ FERREIRA, 24 April 2014

During my fieldwork, something I was struck by was what I perceived to be an obsessive-compulsive attitude towards the dance floor. It was not only about having fun in a relaxed way: people were eager to release their pain on the dance floor. *Kizomba* dancing encounters became an alleviating context for the increasing levels of uncertainty and stress:

When Maria arrives to Ramdall [Madrid], she tells me that she is passing through a rather difficult moment in her life, she feels lost, she doesn't know what to do, it's a long time she can't find a job and that is stressing her too much. She says that she cannot go on like this, and she has sent CVs abroad, to Brazil . . . Then she says: 'I don't want to think. I am going to dance.' She smiles and goes to invite someone to dance.

Excerpt from fieldwork diary, 2 April 2013

In Lisbon, I witnessed the same kind of situations with unemployed or unstable working *kizomba* aficionados going out every night. Most of them were single people in their thirties and forties, as well as separated fathers and mothers who spent their nights free of children at the *kizomba* venues. Some of them had lost their previous networks of support and usual friendships after a divorce or, for example, after being left the only unmarried members of their group. As I could observe from many informal conversations, these situations were lived with an ambiguous combination of feelings: joyful freedom and painful isolation. The relative solidity of social networks and stable jobs they had seen in their parents' generation seemed to have vanished. Uncertainty about the future produced a high level of stress and silent suffering that only gave a short break during the dance.

Distress and anxiety became more obvious when, for some reason, there was a delay in reaching the dance floor. In December 2013, I accompanied a group of five self-labelled *Portuguese* aficionados during their trip from Lisbon to a *kizomba* festival in Madrid. Marcos (36, accountant), Sandra (35, administrative) and Amalia (36, researcher) were single and had no children. Jesus (42, sales manager), Gonçalo (40, sales manager) and Pedro (43, marketing manager) were separated; the two latter each had a child in shared custody with their former partners. They all had a job at that moment. They met at a dance school and used to go out dancing together. We rented a car and left Lisbon on Thursday night. The objective was to arrive on time to enjoy the opening party that finished at 5 a.m. There were three days ahead of non-stop dancing, but they did not want to miss a minute. The need to rest after a hard week of work could not compete with the strong need to dance. After a six-hour night trip, nobody wanted to go to bed: everyone was anxious to get on the dance floor. The unity of the group was not the main objective but it was instrumental to allow the individual pleasures of the dance floor:

> Pedro arrives late, under stress and still working, making phone calls during the first part of the journey. Until he finishes, we cannot talk or put on music . . . He also calls his son to check out if everything is alright with him . . . As we arrive, there are moments of stress, acceleration and separation of the group, nobody wants

to miss a single moment of the dance night . . . Pedro and Gonçalo don't even wait for us, we stay at the hotel reception but they get ready quicker than the rest and leave before. As we arrive, they are negotiating about how to access the ballroom. There is only one hour of party left and the stand where tickets are sold is already closed'.

Excerpt from fieldwork diary, 5 December 2013

In fact, one of the most widely used metaphors in the field was that of *kizomba* as a drug and dancing as an addiction. People did not hide their anxious attitude towards dancing: on the flip side, it was considered fun. Aficionados laughed in complicity with the feeling of sharing a forbidden secret pleasure (Figure 9.1). In the next section, I will propose an anthropological interpretation to understand the deeper sense of this 'addiction': the meeting at the disco as a means to compensate for social suffering in precarious conditions. Suffering is understood here not just as a psychological phenomenon but 'as a broader aspect of ill-being that combines personal life events and wider historical, economic and political processes' (Pussetti, 2013: 570).

FIGURE 9.1 Kizomba *dancing at* Ondeando disco, *Almada, 2014. Livia Jiménez Sedano.*

Kizomba addicts: Meeting at the disco as a ritualised practice of recuperation

The relevance of the *kizomba* gatherings in this austerity context can only be understood if we go beyond the ethnocentric perception of social dancing as some frivolous activity, beyond the scope of the 'hard' political issues that social sciences are interested in (cf. Farnell, 1999). To give a few examples, dance has been analysed as a means of communication (Hanna, 1979; Giurchescu, 2001), a public declaration of one's relational composition (Wolffram, 2006), a system of knowledge (Kaeppler, 1999; Daniel, 2005; Grau, 1998; Buckland, 1999; Farnell, 1999) and a powerful political tool (Giurchescu, 2001; Quintero, 2009; Browning, 1995), among others. In this specific case, I propose to look at *kizomba* events in Lisbon as a type of conventional practice of recuperation with a high level of ritualisation. That is, the set of the social rules of the dance floor is rather fixed and the sequence of action is quite predictable, making participants construct a sense of belonging around these shared codes. This kind of ritualised gathering provides social groups with a situation to intensify their links or reconstruct them (García and Velasco, 1991) so that they become especially important in times of crisis. This characteristic was already highlighted in the classical theories of ritual, with Malinowski (1948) arguing that rituals also have an effect at the psychological level, in providing a sense of control over menacing events. More recently, Buckser (2001: 547) also noticed that 'rituals provide a context to liberate repressed emotions collectively'.

For all of these reasons, these kinds of highly ritualised gatherings become especially important in times of transition, when social structure becomes weaker (ibid.). This is exactly the kind of historical context in which the *kizomba* boom has taken place in Lisbon. The regular meeting at the disco is a good example of the kind of secular gatherings that have spread in contemporary societies. According to Martine Segalen, many of these social practices, which she calls 'contemporary rituals', take place around leisure activities:

> Contemporary rituals, some of which are expanding notably, such as those derived from sports, politics and companies, or even private life, have some features that make of them phenomena of

their time. They are vectors of new forms of local, rural or urban identity, or even protest. Their festive dimension is often expanding in relation to the nucleus they are based on, so that their validity is under suspicion. Anthropologists who study non-European societies are also surprised that some of the 'big rituals' were celebrated in a low solemn atmosphere, full of familiarity and relaxation.

2005: 169

In the same line of thought, Marvin Harris (2011) considers leisure activities and spaces as serving the same ends as religious gatherings: they alleviate anxiety in difficult moments, reinforce the feeling of togetherness and community and produce a sense of belonging to a social group. Rock concerts, attraction parks and sporting events are some of the examples the author gives.

In the case of *kizomba* encounters, social and psychological recuperation takes place through a symbolic inversion of daily life. Agreeing with Honorio Velasco (2007), the system of parties and celebration organises the community's time and, correspondingly, we can consider nightlife in general as the realm opposed symbolically to daily routines to some extent. However, the crisis has transformed the pre-existing night social rules. In this concrete historical situation of intense social anxiety and suffering, the dance floor started to play a more specific repairing role. In these night contexts, certain features of sociability are opposed to those of everyday life. This inversion takes place through a process of masking – just like in Carnival, people mask themselves to behave differently (cf. Caro Baroja, 2006). At *kizomba* events, participants implicitly accept playing the role of 'Africans' as part of the game of 'reproducing African culture' in such a way that they allow themselves to interact with social rules rather different from the usual ones. The structure of time, the hierarchy of verbal and bodily communication and the proxemics etiquette are inverted for the occasion. The neoliberal social order is suspended temporarily and the dance choreography symbolises its contrary: small community, close relations, slow rhythms and the silenced body as the main agent of the social encounter. The body, acting as an *alter ego* (Le Breton, 1995), performs a play of recuperation, without actually reconnecting individuals with society.

Recuperative silence: Shut up and dance

The social encounter works to some extent as an antithesis of the world outside. One of the *kizomba* dance-floor implicit rules is keeping conversations to a minimum. While in daily life most communication acts are based on verbal and written exchanges, in this context all (or as far as possible) communication takes place through coordinating body movements to the sound of music. Dance anthropologist Judith Hanna (1979) developed a well-known theory of dance as a means of non-verbal communication, with Brenda Farnell (1999) making a broader statement through the expression 'action-sign' to avoid the Cartesian dichotomy of mind vs body, implicit in the contrast between verbal vs non-verbal action. However, from the *emic* point of view, participants experience talking as opposed to moving. During the event, time is considered a scarce resource that should be invested in dancing as much as possible. Correspondingly, chatting before, during or after dancing is regarded as a loss of time and energy, and someone who tries to keep a conversation for more than five minutes is spoiling the others' night. In other words, talking is a kind of antisocial behaviour in this context. The proper place for long exchanges of ideas and impressions for this community is Facebook. During fieldwork, many attempts at informal conversation were aborted through an invitation to dance. Indeed, they were interpreted as a prolegomenon to an invitation. By contrast, in the so-called 'African discos' of Lisbon under research, people would talk a lot, sitting down and chatting for a long time. The amount of time spent in dancing was much less and, even during the dance moment, advantage was usually taken of body closeness so as to have a conversation. In this excerpt from the fieldwork diary, we can observe the astonishment of a disco owner of Cape Verdean origin when looking at the attitude of *kizomba* aficionados on his dance floor:

> In general terms, he established a clear distinction between people who learn to dance since childhood and people who learn to dance at schools. He laughs at the latter, he says that, 'they dance with such a serious attitude, in a mechanical way, they don't

enjoy it, they don't laugh, they don't speak, they don't joke, they are always so serious'.

Excerpt from fieldwork diary, 29 January 2014

This rule of verbal silence places the body as the main media of communication. It is not a coincidence that the play of recuperation takes place through the dancing body. As Quintero (2009) explained, dance became essential in conditions of slavery for people forced to move from Africa to America during the colonial period. When the body became the property of another agent, dance movements helped recover their agency during the night. In a similar line of thought, several authors have stressed that spirit-possession female ritualised practices in several African contexts release through the body the tensions created in a situation of crisis and dramatic social change (Rausch, 2000). In colonial Africa, many of those new ritualised practices expelled symbolically the coloniser from the social body. Similarly, when the financial crisis pushed the bodies to hard conditions, the need to dance grew. Even when conditions were getting harder, people did not stop going out, dancing *kizomba*.

Recuperative rhythm: Flowing in slow motion

The structure of time is in reverse, too: instead of reproducing the acceleration and fast changes of everyday life, the night flows in slow motion through a simple basic rhythm of around 90 beats per minute (BPM). Participants in the event do not get tired of moving to the same pace for hours. Interestingly, in the so-called *African discos*, the situation is rather different: as I could observe during fieldwork, slow *kizomba* music is played just as a brief romantic section in the night, in a course of more dynamic rhythms and music styles. This is the way DJ Sabura put it in an interview:

> In an Angolan place . . . you listen to 60 per cent semba, 20 per cent zouk retro[11] . . . And then 20 per cent Afro House, Brazilian music, soukous, music to dance on your own, music for fun . . . there are more women than men . . . for those women, that music is really good to release energy and dance freely . . . Thus, the

ambience is more friendly for everyone. It is not so focused on kizomba, tarraxinha, in . . . couple dance.

Interview with DJ Sabura, 19 March 2014

For this audience of *African discos*, keeping the *kizomba* section on for hours would be extremely boring and annoying. By contrast, participants in *kizomba* venues symbolise their alternative experience of time as something authentically *African*: in informal conversations, they talked about an imagined idealised Africa out of stress, flowing slowly, connected to the rhythms of nature, a paradise lost before modernity introduced craziness.

Recuperative proxemics: Embodying African heat

When asking informants what they felt when dancing *kizomba*, the most repeated answer was 'connection'. Indeed, that seemed to be the reason for their addiction: through dancing, they got to feel connected, tuned in to the others. The concept of 'attunement', widely used in ethnomusicology to discuss an intensified awareness of and sympathy with the surrounding sonic environment (Schafer, 1993), has been developed in the discipline of dance movement therapy as 'kinesthesic empathy' (Berger, 1972) and 'affective attunement' (Stern, 1996). At these *kizomba* venues, music and dance played their role as one of the most powerful symbolic means to make people enter the same emotional state together (cf. Feld, 2012) and build what Miller calls 'a community of sentiment' (2008). A strong collective feeling of alienation in everyday life is repaired on the dance floor at the symbolic level. The experience of proximity is obtained by dancing slowly in coordination at a close body distance, much closer than any other dance and much closer than the usual proxemics for aficionados in Portugal and many other parts of Europe. Proxemics are, in fact, one of the most difficult cultural traits of the dance that make many students feel embarrassed in the beginning. It is also one of the main reasons why many others decide not to give it a try. The general idea is that 'this is an African dance' and, as such, 'it is hot'. In symbolic terms, the fray of social ties is inverted through sewing the dancers' bodies. Growing distances outside are compensated through getting close tight in the dancing context. Embodying the ethnic other becomes the medium to operate this alchemy and make it acceptable. The tacit agreement that they need to perform African-ness in order to dance proper *kizomba* makes people do things they would not do outside the disco.

Moreover, belonging to a dance school or a club helps to overcome the feeling of isolation in practical terms. Some of my informants in Lisbon (but not all of them) used to go out in relatively stable groups that formed in schools and danced regularly with the same people they met at the disco. Nevertheless, it does not mean that in *kizomba* contexts people create a new strong community that challenges the structure of power relations behind the conditions of their suffering. The kind of social relations built in *kizomba* contexts is ephemeral and instrumental for the event. Bonds last as long as the individual continues going to the disco. Most participants had scarce information about the other's lives and very often they did not even know the names of their usual dance partners. This type of sociability is very similar to what Luis-Manuel García (2011) defined as 'liquidarity' for social life in electronic dance music contexts, based on Bauman's notion of 'liquid bonds' (cf. Bauman, 2000):

> Despite all the uncertainty and fluidity, a partygoer can swim his or her way through this pool of swirling relations and still feel connected to something solid. Further parallels with Berlant's notion of intimate publics begin to appear: while the concept of an intimate public describes how we can sense a belonging to something without explicitly articulating the terms of belonging, liquidarity describes how we can feel connected without explicitly articulating the terms of those relations. Like intimate publics, liquidarity thrives in this vagueness, which allows a diverse group of strangers, acquaintances and friends to act as if they were a solid group with already-established norms of relation and engagement. Both of these concepts describe a collectivity that coheres (loosely but powerfully) at the level of affective attachment while being incoherent at the level of explicit discourse and membership structure.
>
> GARCÍA, 2011: 158

In the *kizomba* context, participants create a sense of community that does not transcend the dance floor. Society is not restructured, ties are not recuperated in a strong sense. These fluid bonds created in dance events make sense only to socialise in these liquid gatherings. Many of my informants used to go to the disco on their own and come back home alone, and had not created any sufficient ties for any purpose other than that of participating together in *kizomba* events. This type of socialisation, instead of being revolutionary against neoliberal conditions, produced a choreography that expressed the features of late modern society outside the disco.

In this sense, it is especially interesting that informants connected the dance floor experience, not only with an imagined *African* society, but also with their own childhood experiences of belonging to a community. Many aficionados reported explicitly that dancing *kizomba* had brought them memories of summer village parties, a dance event called *bailarico*.[12] In other words, these dancing practices helped participants regain symbolically a former state or condition through recuperating elements from the past (see Martínez in this volume), that in this case consist on embodied kinetic symbols of community bonds. For example, Pedro, a Portuguese aficionado, explained during an interview how his first *kizomba* workshops activated his kinetic memory back to the first celebrations he had experienced as a child at his village, Trás-Os-Montes:

> It's very similar to our *bailarico* danced on *pimba* music,[13] isn't it? Imagine, if you go to your homeland and there is a party, a village party, what they dance is not so different from the kizomba basic steps. If you meet people who have danced it, imagine, in their villages, they learn easily . . . That was my perception in those times, that it was very similar to *bailarico*, because I came from Trás-Os-Montes, from a village, and I used to dance it . . . People dance to Portuguese popular music at village parties . . . It is usual to see parents dancing with children in those parties, isn't it? People dance with those they know, imagine, a woman will not dance with any man, she dances with her father, with her mother, with her brother, with her nephew . . . that's it!
>
> Interview with PEDRO, 29 January 2013

On the one hand, we can see how the dance floor activates memories of holiday travelling with their parents to their original villages, a trope rather frequent in informal conversations with informants. Therefore, there is an implicit sense of reviving to some extent the sense of belonging to a warm and welcoming community that they keep in their childhood memories. This nostalgic attitude towards the past relates to the current frailty of intergenerational links, a problem that interestingly also underpins Inês Lourenço's ethnographic case (in this volume). In rural contexts, solid village social networks were celebrated through musical and embodied dancing symbols at certain moments of the year. On the other hand, the cosmopolitanism and modernity associated with exotic new *African* dances such as *kizomba* helps free the gathering from the connotations of unsophistication and vulgarity involved in the emic conception of *bailarico*, a complex that seems to affect the perception of popular national music in general in Portugal (Nunes, 2003).

We may argue that the *kizomba* scene in Lisbon eventually helps to maintain the status quo, as people get the energy and alleviation necessary to carry on with their precarious daily lives, without trying to change the situation. It even encourages suffering individuals to stop thinking about the problem or exchange ideas about it. Unlike the assemblies in Algés described by Marcos Ferreira and Francisco Martínez in this volume, the *kizomba* culture is useful to keep society unchanged. It helps participants to get a feeling of what it is like to recuperate social ties for a moment, during the event, just in an ephemeral way, through effective shared symbols of African-ness. However, as they leave the disco, a suffering, fraying and accelerated society is awaiting them outside. And inside.

Africa inside and Africa outside: Unsolved postcolonial conflicts

Most of my informants in Lisbon referred to a feeling of pride in watching how a cultural form from an Africa closely related to Portugal had such a great international success. The Portuguese-speaking Africa, immigrants coming from those countries and everyone deemed in connection with them, had acquired value in these contexts. Both in Spain and Portugal, I found the widespread idea among *kizomba* aficionados that *Portuguese* people could dance much better than other *Europeans* because, as they were culturally closer to Africa (that is, the part of Africa where *kizomba* came from, according to the dominant discourses), they 'got the feeling of the music' (Jiménez, 2019). In other words, there was a transnational consensus of the idea of a common structure of feeling that connected *Portuguese* people with the Portuguese-speaking Africa: they carried something of Africa inside. It had empirical consequences on the dance floor: during fieldwork in Madrid, I witnessed how, whenever a man labelled *Portuguese* visited a *kizomba* party, women would wait in line to dance with him. It was considered a great chance to learn and to enjoy a 'dance with real feeling'. At the end of one of those nights, Rebeca (31) came complaining because she had not succeeded in reaching a *Portuguese* man after waiting for a long time: 'Sara and Ana have kidnapped the *Portuguese* guy the whole night! They think that they are the only ones who have the right to dance with him because they have a high level, that´s enough! We all have the right to dance with *Portuguese* guys!' This assumption also had symbolic efficacy at international *kizomba* festivals, where people from many countries gathered. As I could observe, aficionados produced an *emic* hierarchy of value of the dancers based on national categories, in which those labelled *Portuguese* were one of the best positioned, after the so-called *French* of African descent. In the context of the commodified *kizomba* social world, Portuguese-ness had become a sign of prestige. In this way, the feeling of national pride – weakened in times of crisis – was enhanced on the dance floor through a symbolic special connection with an imagined Africa.

In the dance floor context of meaning, most *kizomba* aficionados reported during interviews and informal conversations that one of the reasons why they chose this dance was their love for '*African* culture'. Nevertheless, as argued before, what they called '*African* culture' was a symbolic construction efficient for their play of recuperation but independent from what the so-called *African* people actually did in their night life.[14] A long history of colonisation, followed by traumatic wars of independence and labour migrations, have resulted in a society crossed by deep structural inequalities that place people labelled *African* in the worst positions. As a whole, these citizens suffer a combination of residential segregation (Cardoso and Perista, 1994; Pussetti and Barros in this volume), the most precarious labour conditions (Machado and Abranches, 2005; Almeida, 2000) and a subtle and not-so-subtle everyday racism (Machado, 2001; Almeida, 2000) that has resulted in an ethnically structured night life (Jiménez, 2019). In such a context, the *kizomba* boom unsurprisingly did not awake in *Portuguese* students the desire to visit those *African* discos spread throughout the city (the 'Africa outside'), in which flesh-and-blood *Africans* performed the dance every night. Actually, unsolved historical conflicts, mutual fears and suspicion, would make the task of going to *African discos* a highly stressful experience more than an enjoyable and pleasant moment. In other words, these *kizomba* aficionados did not want to explore another culture: they actually needed to create their own culture based on the imagined African-ness that made sense for them. A domesticated, colourful and 'exotic' African-ness, offered and purchased by *kizomba* teachers and party organisers, became highly attractive for this audience. The few who decided to go to *African discos* reported hard experiences, such as the following:

> (Leonor) tells me that, in those African discos nobody invites you to dance, and you spend the night alone. She says that she has gone out many times and that's what she has seen: what happens, she says, is that those are closed ambiences . . . People go there with their mates or their group of friends, and they spend a good part of the night sitting down. They dance just a little bit and, in case they dance, they do it with their mate or with people of their group of friends. 'I have been invited,' she tells me, 'it's uncommon but in some occasions I have been invited, and what I have felt is that their friends don't like it. They don't think it's ok because you are supposed to invite the women of your group first, not outsiders. And African women don't like it at all seeing their men dancing with us, White women.'
>
> Excerpt from fieldwork diary, 6 March 2014

Last night, I had an interesting conversation with Gonçalo at *B.leza*. When I tell him that I am exploring African discos, he says that he went once to an African club in Oporto that maybe I should visit. He says that he went with a friend and he didn't like it. As he tells me, from the moment they went downstairs they could see many Black men and they were the only two Whites in the place. They stared at them with hostility, he continues, and he even felt afraid for his physical integrity. He doesn't like to drink alcohol, he just wants to dance, but that night what his friend and he did was going to the bottom of the bar and just drink and watch. They didn't dare to invite to dance anyone. He says that African men are rather territorial and they consider women as their property.[15] Thus, in order to invite a woman to dance, she has to ask permission to the man sitting next to her, and if he doesn't accept that she cannot dance. He says that, as soon as they closed the disco's door and got in, he felt as if he was not in Oporto any more and he had travelled to Angola. 'In that place,' he adds, 'I felt totally lost and I didn't know the rules. I was afraid of doing something wrong.' He felt rather uncomfortable, he didn't dance with anybody, and so he decided he would never get back there.

Excerpt from fieldwork diary, 2 February 2014

As a consequence, in general terms, the *kizomba* commodification during the 1990s did not lead to an actual mixing up of social dancers, but, rather, it generated a new context – specific for students. The dance marketers produced a new version of depoliticised Africanness that fulfils the expectations of potential middle-class European consumers, without needing to visit the so-called *African discos*. As the main reasons for consuming *kizomba* lie somewhere else than the desire to actually socialise with people labelled *Africans*, this fact has not become an obstacle for the development of this dance market.

Conclusion

In this chapter, I explored two dimensions of the *kizomba* gatherings in Portugal and Spain in times of crisis: first, as a way of recuperating the community experience through kinetic symbols, which feels like an urban sophisticated version of *bailarico* childhood memories. This involves a combination of recuperating the past without renouncing to a cosmopolitan modern ethos. Nowadays, far away in time and space, they perform current liquid social links in commodified dance contexts. Even if this could apply to other modern couple dances such as salsa or tango, *kizomba* appears as more efficient in symbolic terms because of its specific features. The rule of silence, slow rhythm and close proxemics prove the symbolic means through which the recuperative alchemy operates. Moreover, *kizomba* contributes to fixing national pride in the context of international festivals due to the connection with the Portuguese-speaking Africa. Second, aficionados build the dance event metaphorically as 'a drug' to escape from the harnesses of everyday life under austerity conditions. In this sense, dancing gatherings help people to escape symbolically from their accelerated, isolated and uncertain daily lives under austerity conditions. This involves dreaming of an alternative society in motion, imagined as an *African* moral community. However, due to unsolved postcolonial tensions, flesh-and-blood labelled *Africans* are avoided and their living cultures remain mostly separated in parallel nightclubs and events.

In a context of social crisis, this dance helps people to temporarily feel reconnected with a community, synchronising personal and societal temporality by letting their silenced bodies speak collectively. However, it is remarkable that many of the recuperation practices described in this volume (see, for example, Ferreira and Martínez, and Pussetti and Barros), although trying to reverse the current liquid logics of social networks and its effects, paradoxically rely on the creation of communities that prove ephemeral. It looks as if the attempts at weaving a new social fabric or reinforcing a previous one, search for their roots in the quicksand of the neoliberal order and hence end up vanishing. In other words, it seems that recuperation also constitutes a phenomenon that leans on the kind of 'liquidarity' we find on the dance floor. In line with the critical insights given by Mendes and Carmo (in this volume), when looking at the effects of these practices, we may wonder how far recuperation can be deemed a goal, a dream, a desire or a real ongoing process nowadays in Portugal.

Notes

1 Words quoted in this chapter are from the author's ethnographic research, which was done with the consent of the subject and an awareness that these words could end up in print. I want to express my gratitude to all the participants in this research, who generously shared their thoughts and experiences. I also wish to thank Francisco Martínez, Tomás S. Criado and Valerio Simoni for their insightful comments on previous versions of this chapter.
2 See, Travassos (2004) for an overview of the 'navel shock' (*umbigada* in Portuguese) family of *African dances*.
3 For a commodified version of the dance, I suggest watching the video performed by the teachers, A. Rojas and S. López, which became rather popular among aficionados during fieldwork, available at: https://www.youtube.com/watch?v=29DT-71bk-M (accessed 3 August 2019).
4 I carried out fieldwork in *kizomba* dancing contexts in Spain and Portugal between 2013 and 2015, with participant observation in the so-called *African discos*, *kizomba* dance schools and *kizomba* international festivals. This was complemented by interviews with DJs, dance teachers, dance students, disco owners and organisers of *kizomba* events, as well as public relations. In order to enrich the analysis, I also collected material such as debates on Facebook, radio (mainly RTP África) and television (mainly TPA, Angolan public television). The chapter stems from my postdoctoral project, 'Dancing Ethnicities in a Transnational World', which aims at exploring the diverse ways in which ethnicity is constructed out of social dance contexts. *Emic* categories appear in italics in this text. As ethnic and ethnonational categories are considered objects of analysis and not scientific categories (cf. Brubaker, 2002; Díaz de Rada, 2008; Jiménez, 2018a), they appear in italics, too.
5 The name given to the European Central Bank (ECB), the European Commission (EC) and the International Monetary Fund (IMF), together.
6 The name that *kizomba* aficionados give themselves in Spain.
7 All the names of participants are pseudonyms to protect the anonymity of informants, except for those who have a public professional profile in the world of *kizomba* (teachers, promotors, disco owners and DJs).
8 There are two dance rooms in the club. Here, Zé Ferreira refers to the small room, where the interview was taking place.
9 Most clients are in their thirties and forties.

10 A region of south Portugal, famous for its beaches and typical holiday destinations in the country.

11 Music styles usually performed as couple dances.

12 This rope of village homesickness is explored in the Portuguese film, *Aquele querido mês de Agosto* (Our Beloved Month of August), based on a popular song. See the trailer, available at: https://www.youtube.com/watch?v=wmF0pAuylhU (accessed 3 August 2019).

13 The label widely used to refer to popular party music that conforms to the preferred soundtrack of public celebrations in Portugal, involving connotations of rural life, sexual double-meaning and a lack of sophistication. See, Nunes (2005) for a brief history and description of this music label.

14 See Delgado and Muñoz (1997) for a development of the concept, 'every night life'.

15 In these stories and perceptions, there is a rather interesting gender issue that deserves attention. For reasons of space, I cannot develop this matter here, but I wanted to stress its importance.

References

Accornero, G. and P. R. Pinto (2015) '"Mild mannered"? Protest and mobilisation in Portugal under austerity, 2010–2013', *West European Politics*, 38 (3): 491–515.

Almeida, M. V. (2000) *Um Mar da Cor da Terra. Raça, Política e Cultura de Identidade*, Oeiras: Celta.

Bauman, Z. (2000) *Liquid Modernity*, Cambridge: Polity.

Baumgarten, B. (2013) 'Geração à rascal and beyond: Mobilizations in Portugal after 12 March 2011', *Current Sociology*, 61 (4): 457–73.

Berger, M. R. (1972) 'Bodily experience and the expression of emotions', in *American Dance Therapy Association*, Monograph 2, Columbia, MD: American Dance Therapy Association (ADTA), pp. 191–230.

Browning, B. (1995) *Samba: Resistance in Motion*, Oxford: Westview.

Brubaker, R. (2002) 'Ethnicity without groups', *European Journal of Sociology*, 2: 163–89.

Buckland, T. J. (1999) 'Introduction: Reflecting on dance ethnography', in T. J. Buckland (ed.), *Dance in the Field: Theory, Methods and Issues in Dance Ethnography*, New York: Palgrave Macmillan, pp. 1–10.

Buckser, A. S. (2001) 'Ritual', in T. Barfield (ed.), *Diccionario de Antropología*, Barcelona: Bellaterra, pp. 545–7.

Cardoso, A. and H. Perista (1994) 'A cidade esquecida: pobreza em bairros degradados de Lisboa', *Sociologia: Problemas e Práticas*, 15: 99–111.
Caro Baroja, J. (2006) *El Carnaval*, Madrid: Alianza.
Comaroff, J. and J. Comaroff (2001) *Millenial Capitalism and the Culture of Neoliberalism*, Durham, NC: Duke University Press.
Daniel, Y. (2005) *Dancing Wisdom*, Champaign, IL: University of Illinois Press.
Delgado, C. F. and J. E. Muñoz (1997) *Culture and Dance in Latin/o America*, Durham, NC: Duke University Press.
Díaz de Rada, Á. (2008) '¿Dónde está la frontera? Prejuicios de campo y problemas de escala en la estructuración étnica en Sápmi', *Revista de Dialectología y Tradiciones Populares*, 63 (1): 187–235.
Farnell, B. (1999) 'It goes without saying – but not always', in T. J. Buckland (ed.), *Dance in the Field: Theory, Methods and Issues in Dance Ethnography*, New York: Palgrave Macmillan, pp. 145–60.
Feld, S. (2012) *Sound and Sentiment: Birds, Weeping, Poetics, and Song in Kaluli Expression*, 3rd edn, Durham, NC: Duke University Press.
García, J. L. and H. Velasco (eds) (1991) *Rituales y Proceso Social*, Madrid: Minesterio de Cultura.
García, L.-M. (2011) '"Can you feel it too?" Intimacy and affect at electronic dance music events in Paris, Chicago, and Berlin', PhD thesis, University of Chicago. Available at: https://lmgmblog.wordpress.com/2011/06/09/can-you-feel-it-too/ (accessed 3 August 2019).
Giurchescu, A. (2001) 'The power of dance and its social and political uses', *Yearbook for Traditional Music*, 33: 109–22.
Grau, A. (1998) 'On the acquisition of knowledge: Teaching kinship through the body among the Tiwi of Northern Australia', in V. Keck (ed.), *Common Worlds and Single Lives*, Oxford: Berg, pp. 71–94.
Gray, L. E. (2016) 'Registering protest: Voice, precarity and return in crisis Portugal', *History and Anthropology*, 27 (1): 60–73.
Hanna, J. L. (1979) *To Dance is Human: A Theory of Nonverbal Communication*, Austin, TX: University of Texas Press.
Harris, M. (2011) *Antropología cultural*, México D.F.: McGraw Hill.
Harvey, D. (2005) 'The neoliberal state', in *A Brief History of Neoliberalism*, Oxford: Oxford University Press, pp. 64–86.
Jameson, F. (1984) *Postmodernism, or the Cultural Logic of Late Capitalism*, Durham, NC: Duke University Press.
Jiménez, L. (2012) 'On the irrelevance of ethnicity in children's organization of their social world', *Childhood*, 19 (3): 375–88.
Jiménez, L. (2018a) *Etnicidad: un juego de niños*, Barcelona: Bellaterra.
Jiménez, L. (2018b) 'Ritual roles of "African nights" DJs in Lisbon', *Cadernos de Arte e Antropologia*, 7 (1): 15–26.

Jiménez, L. (2019) 'Bodies that cannot listen', *Anthropological Journal of European Cultures* 28 (1): 73–7.
Kaeppler, A. L. (1999) 'The mystique of fieldwork', in T. J. Buckland (ed.), *Dance in the Field: Theory, Methods and Issues in Dance Ethnography*, New York: Palgrave Macmillan, pp. 13–25.
Knight, D. M. and C. Stewart (2016) 'Ethnographies of austerity: Temporality, crisis and affect in Southern Europe', *History and Anthropology*, 27 (1): 1–18.
Korteweg, L. and A. Bissell (2015) 'The complexities of researching youth civic engagement in Canada with/by indigenous youth: Settler-colonial challenges for Tikkun Olam-Pedagogies of repair and reconciliation', *Citizenship Education Research Journal*, 5 (1): 14–26.
Le Breton, D. (1995) *Antropología del cuerpo y modernidad*, Buenos Aires: Nueva Visión.
Machado, F. L. (2001) 'Contextos e percepções de racismo no quotidiano', *Sociologia: Problemas e Práticas*, 36: 1–28.
Machado, F. L. and M. Abranches (2005) 'Caminhos limitados de integração social. Trajectórias socioprofissionais de cabo-verdianos e hindus em Portugal', *Sociologia*, 48: 69–91.
Malinowski, B. (1948) *Magic, Science and Religion and Other Essays*, Glencoe, IL: Free Press.
Martínez, F. (2015) 'Hopeless, helpless and holy youth', in F. Martínez and P. Runnel (eds), *Hopeless Youth!*, Tartu: Estonian National Museum, pp. 15–39.
Mauritti, R. and S. da Cruz Martins (2014) 'Consumos da classe média num Portugal em crise: cultura, lazer e tecnologias da informação', *Sociologias*, 16 (37): 144–75.
McMains, J. (2016) '"Hot" Latin dance: Ethnic identity and stereotype', in A. Shay and B. Sellers-Young (eds), *The Oxford Handbook of Dance and Ethnicity*, Oxford: Oxford University Press, pp. 480–500.
Miller, K. C. (2008) 'A community of sentiment: Indo-Fijian music and identity discourse in Fiji and its diaspora', PhD thesis, University of California.
Narotzky, S. (2016) 'Between inequality and injustice: Dignity as a motive for mobilization during the crisis', *History and Anthropology*, 27 (1): 74–92.
Nunes, C. A. (2005) 'O Baile Popular na Cabeça Gorda. A construção social de uma aldeia alentejana', unedited MA thesis, New University of Lisbon.
Nunes, P. (2003) '"É portugués? Não gosto". Ideologias e Práticas dos jornalistas de Música face à Música Portuguesa', *Forum Sociologico*, 7/8: 145–68.
Pussetti, C. (2013) '"Woundscapes": Suffering, creativity and bare life-practices and processes of an ethnography-based art exhibition', *Critical Arts*, 27 (5): 569–86.

Quintero, A. (2009) *Cuerpo y cultura. Las músicas 'mulatas' y la subversión del baile*, Madrid: Iberoamericana.
Rausch, M. (2000) *Bodies, Boundaries and Spirit Possession: Moroccan Women and the Revision of Tradition*, Bielefeld: Transcript.
Ribeiro, R., C. Frade, L. Coelho and A. Ferreira-Valente (2015) 'Crise económica em Portugal. Alterações nas Práticas Quotidianas e nas Relações Familiares', in I. C. Silva, M. Pignatelli and S. M. Viegas (eds), *Proceedings of the 1º Congresso Nacional da Associação Nacional de Ciências Sociais e Humanas em Língua Portuguesa*, Lisbon: Congresso da Associação Internacional de Ciências Sociais e Humanas em Língua Portuguesa, pp. 5155–71.
Sakellarides, C., L. Castelo-Branco, P. Barbosa and H. Azevedo (2014) *The Impact of the Financial Crisis on the Health System and Health in Portugal*, Copenhagen: World Health Organization, European Observatory on the Health Systems and Policies.
Schafer, R. M. (1993) *The Soundscape: Our Sonic Environment and the Tuning of the World*, Rochester: Destiny.
Segalen, M. (2005) *Ritos y rituales contemporáneos*, Madrid: Alianza.
Stern, D. (1996) *El mundo interpersonal del infante*, Buenos Aires: Paidós.
Travassos, E. (2004) 'Por uma cartografia ampliada das danças de umbigada', in J. M. Pais, J. P. de Brito and M. V. de Carvalho (eds), *Sonoridades luso-afro-brasileiras*. Lisbon: Imprensa de Ciências Sociais, pp. 227–53.
Velasco, H. (2007) *Cuerpo y espacio. Símbolos y metáforas, representación y expresividad de las culturas*, Madrid: Ramón Areces.
Wolffram, P. (2006) '"He's not a white man, he's a small bird like you and me": Learning to dance and becoming human in southern New Ireland', *Yearbook for Traditional Music*, 38: 109–32.
Woolford, A. (2013) 'Nodal repair and networks of destruction: Residential schools, colonial genocide and redress in Canada', *Settler Colonial Studies*, 3 (1): 65–81.

Conclusion

Repair as repopulating the devastated desert of our political and social imaginations

Tomás Sánchez Criado

Southern Europe in/as Crisis?

This volume deals in different ways with how people confront the stark aftermath of smashed cultural and economic dreams and their modes of livelihood. In assessing experiences of recuperation, it focuses in particular on the ways in which, as a consequence, different people articulate in thought or practice a series of distinct responses: responses through which we can witness 'how societies rebuild themselves' (as the Introduction here beautifully puts it). However, this begs the question, responses to what exactly? And what does it mean for a society to rebuild itself?

The collection foregrounds a particular set of issues affecting a place in a given temporal framing: the many and various crises unfolding across Portugal after the 2008 subprime mortgage financial

FIGURE CONC.1 *Graffiti found in the Feira da Ladra, Lisbon, paraphrasing Antoine Lavoisier's dictum: 'In nature, nothing is lost and nothing is created, everything is transformed'. Tomás Sánchez Criado, 2018.*

crisis, its ramifications ranging from increased unemployment to a growth in poverty, and a series of public administration spending cuts enforced by different, yet intermeshed, international economic bodies (described in the Introduction here, using the Troika epithet). As such, the volume widely contributes to a recent strand of anthropological work addressing the manifold crises of Southern Europe, whose similarities are usually addressed in terms of the implementation of austerity and spending cuts. But there are also specificities, which these chapters delve into, signalling the peculiarity of the Portuguese case with regards to, say, Greece and Spain (where the issues of a lack of democratic legitimacy of political decision-making and institutions were also brought to the fore to a larger extent).

These series of crises have rekindled the fear of 'going backwards', still very vivid in migration tropes from the 1960s–70s (like Armando Rodrigues de Sá, an icon in the history of German immigration),[1] as many had to leave the country, yet again. However, this assessment of 'backwardness' takes in a wider European genre of telling 'what the problem is': a particularly old Southern European one to be more specific, where 'modernity' and its alleged univocal drive towards 'progress' comes centre stage. In fact, for the most part of the last centuries, the European South has been a critical site, where different concerns over 'what Europe is' have been debated. In a similar vein to the European East, Southern Europe has, indeed, been a commonplace trope of inward-looking and miniaturised forms of a slightly orientalising gaze: signalling what Europe should be leaving behind, whilst at the same time being a crucial hotspot for many emotional responses regarding what Europeans should always despise or melancholically remember.

In fact, the south of Europe was romanticised throughout the nineteenth century by different travellers – like Eugène Delacroix, in his trips across the Iberian Peninsula – as a site of manageable mystery, sensory pleasure and eroticism; a place of 'recalcitrant modernity' (cf. Delgado, Mendelson and Vázquez, 2007), populated by subjects with peculiarly quixotic and baroque manners, 'joyful' gypsies or plainly miserable peasants. Subjects whose darker skin tones – be it because of their role in trade routes, the more-or-less enforced imperial hybridisation, and the strong Muslim and Jew presence – became the object of late nineteenth- and early-twentieth-century evolutionary and eugenic sciences (not only imported from abroad but also having many local expressions), suggesting race as an explanation for their kinship-based and corrupt forms of government or, in a context of colonial warfare, of the fall and weakness of their empires.

Besides, at a moment when a fast-spreading liberalism was trying to instill the clean straight line of progress in the continent and its colonies (also in many Southern European metropolises), governmental unruliness became not just an issue of the 'far away' but also of the 'near'. Indeed, the developmentalist drive of the 1960s and 1970s exploited this 'slight orientalism' in the ways in which tourism was branded and marketed, searching to attract Northern and Central European masses of workers to the newly designed resorts (Pack, 2006). Interestingly, this slight orientalism has also served later on to underpin the 'exceptionality of Europe' trope and its violent incarnation in the perceived threats of non-European migration: fierce – when not most of the time overly brutal – border and sea control, detention and containment or racialised police checks. Southern Europe as both leisure resort and boundary-maker of 'Fortress Europe'.

Southern Europe, hence, has been cast as a nearby place, conjuring images of the far away or, more precisely, a slightly far away nearby place. This has also led to interesting experimentations with closeness: notably, many have seen a first expression of 'humanitarianism' in the famous reactions of leading humanists – like Voltaire or Kant – to the disastrous effects of Lisbon's earthquake in 1755, generating a particular technology of concernment (cosmopolitanism) addressing 'those humans who are like us' (Redfield, 2013: 42–5). It was also in the European South where, in the aftermath of the Second World War, and after the upsurge of different decolonising movements all over Asia and Africa, a series of British scholars, featuring Julian Pitt-Rivers, invented what might be considered the first 'anthropology at home' research programme, with a particular focus on peasant and pastoral Mediterranean societies.[2] In doing so, the European South became a kind of 'near North', used as a pivotal point to generate differentiations between and from different forms of Europeans. In the eyes of many, the modernising dream of the Common Market as an alleged fraternal and peaceful union, together with its infrastructural and joint economic aspirations, was a way to provide a modernising closure: one in which markets and social states would be mutually engineered to redistribute wealth and conditions of equality, in line with the fundamental redefinition of the continental post-war welfare arrangements. This, together with the hope inspired by Portuguese, Greek and Spanish democratic transitions after several decades of fascist rule, was seen to end their 'backwardness' and their perpetual status of being on the verge of 'going south'.[3]

However, in this process, the European South also became not just one of the many places where a profound re-foundation of global capitalism was taking shape, but also one searching to provide a rationale as to what it was bringing. For instance, the Italian filmmaker and public intellectual Pier Paolo Pasolini (1975), argued how 'consumerism' had developed from the 1960s into a force provoking 'anthropological mutations', that is, generating a new set of aspirations and actions with devastating consequences. They were, to his mind, the hallmark of a newer type of covert fascism. And, somewhat in connection with this, the Italian autonomous and post-Marxist thinkers have been engaging in the production of timely descriptions of the sources of our contemporary predicaments. A good summary of this might be found in Maurizio Lazzarato (2004, 2015), who has been addressing the 'cognitive' capitalism arising since the 1970s as a revolutionary force capturing social creativity, as well as paying special attention to the newer forms of 'neoliberal' domination brought about by financialisation of life and the expansion of indebtedness.

Indeed, to many, the Common Market, and later the European Union, have been quintessential mechanisms for that economic transformation. One in which the developmental issue of Southern and Eastern Europe was addressed beyond explicitly racialised terms, yet forcefully reinstating a particularly modernist ontology of the social: a scalar one, which not only classifies actors in terms of a grid of the big and the small (macro and micro; the state and the people; society/group and the individual), but also creates concomitant orders of worth and causality with regards to what it might mean to take political action.[4] In the case of the EU, this particular ontology has been operating through the compilation of comparative statistics and the configuration of different socioeconomic tools and indicators, addressing the descriptive 'strata' deemed important in the implementation of heavily standardised 'technological zones' and quintessential 'infrastructures' (Barry, 2001), such as enforced border controls, cohesion funds, free internal mobility and good exchange programmes to better articulate the internal market. Europe as a particular 'infrastructural poetics' (cf. Larkin, 2013).

Both this assessment of causal and linear economic progress, and this scalar understanding of the social, already frame what a crisis is and what response, then, might mean. Indeed, to some, it is this European aspiration to be 'advanced' and 'developed' that would need to be repaired in order to go beyond the alleged 'deficiencies' or 'lacks' of Southern European countries: a particular understanding of 'recuperation' as a univocal path towards 'neoliberal economic growth'. In this argument, austerity measures have been seen by some of these actors as generating 'incentives of regeneration'. However, and as all the contributors to this volume foreground, this particular dream and its particular ontology of the social is now going through a profound crisis (as the dispute with regards to the ways in which austerity measures were enforced and how this affected the EU project clearly show). In a critical review of some of the anthropological works around austerity in Southern Europe, Andrea Muehlebach states that: 'austerity policies have thus not only broken stable work regimes, pensions, infrastructures, and the lives of impoverished Europeans, but the very idea of welfare as such' (2016: 363), now in crisis because of debt-repayment stress, and opening up Pandora's box for many neoreactionary and ethnicist movements to redevelop.

Crises, in fact, have a strange potential to unsettle our imaginaries of what we believe the issues under discussion are, and what addressing them might mean (as Mendes and Carmo in this volume well show, when addressing the particularly neoliberal specificities of the 'new urban lease regime' being implemented in Lisbon, and its contestation by social movements). Crises are difficult things to 'know' and 'react to' in themselves, as they most of the time appear to us in the form of a 'crack'. Cracks in buildings, as architect Eyal Weizman (2014) has very nicely described them, are phenomena displaying an extremely ambivalent ontology: when one sees a crack, it might mean both that structural damage is already complete or that it is just starting. Cracks are 'both a sensor and an agent' (ibid.: 16), both a potential probe into the causes or an effect of a particular structural failure, disputing or generating interesting puzzlements as to what causes them and what its effects might be. To put it in more poetic terms, and as F. Scott Fitzgerald discussed in his autobiographical account of life in the aftermath of the 1929 'crack', most of the time cracks are something 'that you don't feel until it's too late to do anything about it, until you realize with finality that in some regard you will never be as good a man [sic] again' (Fitzgerald, 2009: 69).

Repair as a repopulation of the devastated desert of our social and political imaginations

As Gilles Deleuze and Claire Parnet noted: 'Questions are invented, like anything else. If you aren't allowed to invent your questions, with elements from all over the place, from never mind where, if people "pose" them to you, you haven't much to say. *The art of constructing a problem is very important*: you invent a problem, a problem-position, before finding a solution' (2007: 1, emphasis added). What is thus the invented question and constructed problem by this research? Interestingly, this volume seeks to foreground 'repair' as a fundamental analytic to understand the different 'recuperation' strategies to these multiple cracks in Portuguese society. And there is, indeed, a wonderfully interesting conceptual potential engrained in this very term, and in the way it unfolds in the different articles: from the economic emphasis on 'resistance' and 'reciprocity' in the face of adversity – described in Pires' (this volume) chapter on Monte da Pedra – to the joyful and interstitial register that the reinvigoration of the *kizomba* dance (Jiménez, this volume) in different venues might be opening up new potential relations between people across racial, colonial and class divides.

Notably, the Portuguese verb *reparar* has a nuance that the English 'to repair' does not have: one that goes beyond 'to fix something that is broken or damaged' and 'to take action in order to improve a bad situation' (the two main definitions found in the *Macmillan English Dictionary*). *Reparar* also means 'to observe', 'to pay attention'. As I take it, paying attention to the different forms of repair brings forward an especially fertile repertoire for ethnographic descriptions. One that makes us pay close attention to what is being understood as the problem and the issues at stake, as well as the ways in which different responses are executed: the definitions of those 'bad situations' or 'what is broken and damaged' entailing different forms of 'taking action' – to return to the framing proposed in the introduction of this chapter.

In fact, in the Science Technology and Society Studies literature around maintenance and repair (see, Denis, Mongili and Pontille, 2016), focusing mostly on different types of urban infrastructures, several scholars have also pointed out that 'repair' cannot happen without extended sensory explorations in order to ascertain what the problem might be. This also involves a detailed attention to the ways in which different human and more-than-human actors and their complex joint ecologies behave to take care of broken worlds: an issue Nóvoa's contribution to this volume interestingly deals with when paying attention to the different ways in which discarded 'ugly fruit' are managed 'through the cracks in the system' by a series of zero-waste cooperatives. The descriptive repertoire around *reparar* that this anthology brings forward would thus help us shed light on the distinct nuances that different groups, people and collectives might be bringing about, unsettling unified narratives around what might have happened and what to do with it.

Observing, paying attention to the forms of repair, hence, might be the best antidote to ready-made explanations of the 'what' and 'why', and any ready-made concepts or frameworks suggesting what should be done and how: an unsettled response to an unsettling condition, perhaps? Much in the same vein, although infrastructures are often said to become visible on breakdown – *pace* Susan L. Star (1999) – sometimes, to enunciate what this breakdown is about requires finding ways of 'exhibiting the accident, exposing what usually exposes us' (Virilio, 2000: 58). Good examples of this are the public art projects (always on the verge of being co-opted by institutional discourses) around urban regeneration described by Pussetti and Barros (this volume). I find this gesture particularly difficult to make, yet a very timely one, since it is precisely in a moment of crisis when what we think about the world is also thrown into a profound crisis. And moments of crises are also full of reflections regarding the appropriate 'speed' of thought to capture unsettling events that are very difficult to grasp (Duclos, Criado and Nguyen, 2017): ranging from suggestions to 'keep calm and X' or 'slow down' to appeals to plunge into the frenzy of 'urgent' matters and situations to fully understand what things are about.

In the Spanish case, with which I am more personally and ethnographically familiar, the modes of response to 'the crisis' usually took the shape of heterogeneous groups of variegated and sometimes unclear shapes: volatile forms of the social trying to understand what was happening to them and how to respond through digital activism, massive occupations of streets and squares, together with urban interventions and events. That is, most of these actions were about creating conditions for a collective articulation around different types of cracks, and therefore generating forms of reaction, be it 'resistance', 'coping', 'reacting' or 'forging new imaginaries'. I have been addressing these situations as forms of 'joint problem-making' (Criado and Estalella, 2018): that is, situations where people feel the need to collaboratively create new problematisations about a situation, through the craft and management of shared infrastructures, platforms and devices to learn by doing.

What is more, these forms of joint problem-making led to a vast number of concrete and disparate political struggles with variegated non-coherent topologies operating beyond a scalar ontology of the social (Law, 2004). Some were wishing to 'open it up', developing 'newer' and 'more horizontal' political platforms to run for municipal, regional and state elections; while others who were not assuming that it should be the state from which they should be seeking answers (for instance a collective like 'La PAH' (*La Plataforma de Afectados por la Hipoteca*, the Platform of those Affected by Mortgages, which mobilised thousands of people in the country because of an issue affecting millions),[5] managed to generate a state-wide form of intervention against evictions, legal counselling and psychological support by establishing a network topology (cf. Riles, 2001), with each node carrying as much information as the whole through the circulation of information, minutes, formats, etc. In sum, whilst some of these modes of joint problem-making ended up having at their core the idea of defending or 'healing' the 'sick' Spanish state (Kehr, 2014) – that is, recuperation as restoring the previously existing infrastructure and its ontology of the social – others sought to undertake an experimentation around alternative infrastructures to the welfare state and its failed promises of centralised wealth redistribution, social protection and futurity through pensions, that is, understanding recuperation as re-instauration, giving an eventful meaning to those acts whereby societies rebuild themselves.

In the opening introduction, Francisco Martínez lucidly concludes by issuing a warning: recuperation can, indeed, happen without repair, in 'relationships and narratives that can be systemically co-opted' (this volume). Can this ethnographic repertoire around *reparar* help us not just to pay attention but also 'to repair' and hence transform and give further nuances to what 'recuperation' might mean? I believe that herein lies the fundamental contribution of this collection: in the juxtaposition of different modes of recuperation and variegated versions of repair practices, whereby an unsettlement of ready-made of scales is operated. The book, hence, opens up the plurality of ways in which 'societies could rebuild themselves', sometimes radically challenging their previous form.

In all these matters and struggles, maybe repair is acquiring a more hopeful meaning than just putting back to work or caring for broken materials and relations: repair as a mode of reinventing what lives should be led, how we could be situating ourselves in the world, re-crafting what responsibility and agency or our capability to do with others might mean in the face of changing circumstances. Some years ago, in Lisbon, I was wondering out loud whether we could try to find a way out of the particular reading of 'the crisis' as displaying the problems of 'incomplete' or 'not fully developed' social states of the European South. In such a conversation, a Portuguese colleague, the geographer Eduardo Ascensão, suggested that I check a contribution by the renowned sociologist Boaventura de Sousa Santos (1995), introducing a special issue on Portugal's welfare system. This little piece was very refreshing. Not only was it written shortly after the Portuguese integration into the EU (and hence it addressed the new intra-European comparative dimension these events provoked), but it also put forward an intriguing conceptual distinction that went way further than the classic social-democratic readings that idealise the post-war UK, French, German and Scandinavian welfare models.

Social-democratic readings tend to foreground centralised state-market infrastructures of protection, whereby it is the role of the state to sustain citizens, even at the expense of kinship or other forms of caring sociality (e.g. religious organisations). Interestingly, and beyond a reading of 'lack' or 'incompleteness' in the Portuguese case (a particularly dramatic one according to others, in line with the broader tendency of other Southern European countries), de Sousa Santos distinguished the 'welfare-state' from what he called a 'welfare-society' (Sociedade-Providência):

> I call welfare-society the networks of relationships of mutual knowledge, recognition and help based on kinship and neighborhood ties, through which small social groups exchange goods and services in a non-commoditized manner and with a logic of reciprocity similar to the gift relations studied by Marcel Mauss.
>
> de SOUSA SANTOS, 1995: i, my translation

The importance attributed by de Sousa Santos to 'welfare-society' stands out with regards to the centrality attributed in Central and Northern European countries to the 'welfare-state', given that many forms of the social link are either erased, or decomposed and recomposed by different institutions managing 'the social' (Rose, 1999) in an empowering quest beyond limiting and dependence-based ways, in which kinship and other forms of sociality operate. However, this centralised incarnation of the welfare state also has the subject of strong criticism by some who see this as a very violent system, either because of its expert-based centralisation, 'meeting infinite needs by fine means' (Foucault, 1990), or because of the ways in which it might be engineering in some of its citizens a 'shame of being dependent' on the state (Sennett, 2003). In fact, some have seen in the marketisation and outsourcing of care services a way to 'personalise' these caring needs.

However, and this is where de Sousa Santos' contribution became more interesting, he also stated: 'If it is necessary to reinvent the Welfare state, isn't it equally necessary to reinvent welfare-society?' (de Sousa Santos, 1995: v, my translation). A reinvention that, in his eyes, should try to go beyond 'social authoritarianism' practices lingering in the back of many of these countries with decades-long fascist dictatorships, like Portugal (or Spain, Italy and Greece, for that matter), where the traditional caring roles of women as angelic beings, and the filial obligations to care according to dated understandings of kinship, were enforced by the very state in partnership with Catholic organisations for decades. This particular concern around how to 'fabricate new ties', sometimes drawing innovatively from 'legacies', is particularly well described in the chapters by Lourenço, and Ferreira and Martínez in this volume.

In fact, maybe that is what is at stake in the particularly reparative practices and relations beyond scale, assembled in this anthology (dances, moneylending, the retrieval of ancient legacies, caring for discarded goods or engaging in different forms of urban activism), to dispute the actual definition of 'welfare'. In other words, to propose a reinvention of 'welfare society' that does not bear the mark of disaster, but of hope: a hope that in these particularly disastrous times of ours – when crises do not seem to have an end[6] – they might be 'repopulating the devastated desert of our [social and political] imaginations' (Stengers, 2015: 132). Could this be, then, what Southern European responses to the crisis, and in particular Portuguese ones, might be bringing to the fore to tackle the challenges the European project is now facing? As I see it, the allegedly small has never been more important to recasting our hopes, to repopulating our imaginations of the greater good, devastated by austerity and the path-dependency of neoliberal rule. Especially when everything seems lost, these modes repair show the hopeful character of how things might be created anew: not going back to 'what we were', but experimenting with modes of togetherness yet to be defined.

Notes

1 Rodrigues de Sá was a specialised worker of Vale de Madeiros (in the Aveiro region), who inadvertently became the 1-millionth guest worker (Gastarbeiter) in Germany in September 1964. For this, and much to his dismay, a committee of Portuguese and Spanish industrials threw a reception on his arrival in Cologne. In 2004, an exhibition showing his reception and his trajectory later on was inaugurated in Cologne; available at: https://www.iberer.angekommen.com/Mio/millionster.html (accessed 3 June 2019).
2 For an account of the reception of the work of Pitt Rivers in Spain, and the polemics on its proto- or slightly colonial nuances of his accounts or the lack of interest in fostering debate with the local anthropologists, see, Narotzky (2005).
3 Amongst the many contributions to this debate, Gramsci's essay on *la questione meridionale* (the southern question) remains a case in point, precisely because of how it addresses the enforced and structural conditions of poverty concerning both the poor urban and countryside workers brought about by both feudalism and liberalism.
4 For an anthropological examination of this, please check Lebner (2017).
5 An in-depth account of it can be found in, *Sí se puede: Seven Days at PAH Barcelona*, a documentary directed by Pau Fus (2014), and featuring the current mayor of Barcelona, Ada Colau; available with English subtitles at: https://www.youtube.com/watch?v=caD17RKJfbc (accessed 3 June 2019).
6 Even though recent public debate has tended to focus primarily on issues of public and private debt, the alleged forms of 'recuperation' after 'the crisis' have also gone together with (when not provoking) a series of hidden negative effects. Perhaps one of the most important being the impact of massive touristification, taken as the new engine of the Portuguese economy: an issue notably affecting Lisbon and Porto (in a very similar vein as other European cities like Barcelona, Madrid, Venice, Rome and Berlin), and having an impact because of

the polluting effects of cruise ships and other transportation means, the decay of other economic activities, or the rise in rents and real estate prices generating an alarming housing crisis. The 2017 documentary, *Terramotourism* (Earthquake Tourism), and a series of accompanying events, produced by the Left Hand Rotation collective, feature a series of interesting reflections on the case of Lisbon; available at: https://vimeo.com/195599779 (accessed 3 June 2019).

References

Barry, A. (2001) *Political Machines: Governing a Technological Society*, London: Athlone Press.

Corsín, A. (2013) *An Anthropological Trompe l'Oeil for a Common World: An Essay on the Economy of Knowledge*, Oxford: Berghahn.

Criado, T. S. and A. Estalella (2018) 'Introduction: Experimental collaborations', in A. Estalella and T. S. Criado (eds), *Experimental Collaborations: Ethnography through Fieldwork Devices*, Oxford: Berghahn, pp. 1–30.

de Sousa Santos, B. (1995) 'Sociedade-providência ou autoritarismo social?', *Revista Crítica de Ciências Sociais*, 42: i–vii.

Deleuze, G. and C. Parnet (2007) *Dialogues II*, New York: Columbia University Press.

Delgado, L. E., J. Mendelson and O. Vázquez (2007) 'Introduction: Recalcitrant modernities – Spain, cultural difference and the location of modernism', *Journal of Iberian and Latin American Studies*, 13 (2–3): 105–19.

Denis, J., A. Mongili and D. Pontille (2016) 'Maintenance & repair in science and technology studies', *Tecnoscienza: Italian Journal of Science & Technology Studies*, 6 (2): 5–16.

Duclos, V., T. S. Criado and V. K. Nguyen (2017) 'Speed: An introduction', *Cultural Anthropology*, 32 (1): 1–11.

Fitzgerald, F. S. (2009) *The Crack-Up*, New York: New Directions.

Foucault, M. (1990) 'Social security', in L. Kritzman (ed.), *Politics, Philosophy, Culture: Interviews and Other Writings, 1977–1984*, New York: Routledge, pp. 159–77.

Kehr, J. (2014) 'Against sick states: Ebola protests in austerity Spain', *Somatosphere*, 22 October 22. Available at: http://somatosphere.net/2014/10/against-sick-states.html (accessed 3 June 2019).

Larkin, B. (2013) 'The politics and poetics of infrastructure', *Annual Review of Anthropology*, 42 (1): 327–43.

Law, J. (2004) 'And if the global were small and noncoherent? Method, complexity, and the baroque', *Environment and Planning D: Society and Space*, 22 (1): 13–26.

Lazzarato, M. (2004) *Les Révolutions du Capitalisme*, Paris: Les Empêcheurs de Penser en Rond.
Lazzarato, M. (2015) *Governing by Debt*, Cambridge: MIT Press.
Lebner, A. (2017) 'Strathern's redescription of anthropology', in A. Lebner (ed.), *Redescribing Relations: Strathernian Conversations on Ethnography, Knowledge and Politics*, Oxford: Berghahn, pp. 1–37.
Muehlebach, A. (2016) 'Anthropologies of austerity', *History and Anthropology*, 27 (3): 359–72.
Narotzky, S. (2005) 'The production of knowledge and the production of hegemony: Anthropological theory and political struggles in Spain', *Journal of the World Anthropology Network*, 1: 35–54.
Pack, S. D. (2006) *Tourism and Dictatorship: Europe's Peaceful Invasion of Franco's Spain*, New York: Palgrave Macmillan.
Pasolini, P. P. (1975) *Scritti Corsari*, Milan: Garzanti.
Redfield, P. (2013) *Life in Crisis: The Ethical Journey of Doctors Without Borders*, Berkeley, CA: University of California Press.
Riles, A. (2001) *The Network Inside Out*. Ann Arbor, MI: University of Michigan Press.
Rose, N. (1999) *Powers of Freedom*, Cambridge: Cambridge University Press.
Sennett, R. (2003) *Respect in a World of Inequality*, New York: W.W. Norton.
Star, S. L. (1999) 'The ethnography of infrastructure', *American Behavioral Scientist*, 43 (3): 377–91.
Stengers, I. (2015) *In Catastrophic Times: Resisting the Coming Barbarism*, Lüneburg: Meson Press.
Virilio, P. (2000) *A Landscape of Events*, Cambridge: MIT Press.
Weizman, E. (2014) 'Introduction: Forensis', in Forensic Architecture, *Forensis: The Architecture of Public Truth*, Berlin: Sternberg, pp. 9–32.

Afterword

Micro-spaces of resilience and resistance

Coping with the multiple crises in Portugal

Isabel David

Portugal was one of the hardest hit EU countries by the crisis of the sovereign debts. In 2011, the Portuguese government signed a three year Memorandum of Understanding with the so-called 'Troika' of the ECB, the EC and the IMF for financial assistance worth €70 billion. In return, the country had to implement harsh austerity measures, designed to reduce public debt (111.4 per cent of gross domestic product, GDP) and the budget deficit (7.4 per cent of GDP). As a result of harsh cuts in public expenditure and higher taxes, in 2013 unemployment peaked at 17.8 per cent (youth unemployment reached 42.5 per cent) (SIC Notícias, 2013) and 27.5 per cent of the population was at risk of poverty (Rede Europeia Anti-pobreza, 2015). The income gap between the 10 per cent richest and the 10 per cent poorest increased from 9.2 to 10.6, according to the S90/S10 ratio. The income of the bottom 10 per cent fell by 25 per cent, whereas the incomes of the top and intermediate tiers diminished by 10 per cent (see Guapo Costa, 2018). Many people lost their houses, as they were unable to pay their mortgages or rents: in 2016, 140,000 families did not have enough income to pay their mortgages (Mendes, 2017). As a consequence, over 485,000 people emigrated (Observatório da Emigração, 2015).

However, we are not talking just of a financial crisis, but also about the clash between different notions of value and definitions of life (Martínez, 2017). Furthermore, the upheaval brought about by austerity has promoted a general climate of ontological insecurity. Anthony Giddens anchored 'ontological security', referring to the continuity, stability and certainty of everyday activities and of the self. In this logic, trust is the underlying mechanism, operating on an emotional and cognitive frame, in which the reliability of persons and, as I argue here, the reliability of the state institutions provide for the 'coherence of everyday life' (Giddens, 1991: 38). Trust, hope, courage, habit and routine thus form an integral part of ontological security, which is responsible for 'carry[ing] the individual through transitions, crises and risks' (ibid.). In this context, austerity policies have destroyed the mechanisms on which this ontological security is based, namely jobs, incomes and housing. As the state was the very actor responsible for implementing the cuts that led to the destruction of these mechanisms, austerity has therefore broken the link of trust between citizens and state. This process can be considered as having eroded democracy, as it has impinged on the social contract that makes the state and its institutions responsible for the well-being and common good of its citizens, in exchange for their taxes and loyalty.

Forms of ontological insecurity produced by the crisis and austerity have taken many shapes: changes in lifestyle; distrust in public institutions; lack of hope; a threat to the living conditions of people; a crisis of generational belonging; discourses of resentment; changes in social relations, including patterns of friendship and kinship; precarious employment; fundamental freedoms; and an inability to grasp the sense of past, present and future.

The set of contributions in this volume addresses the multiple crises experienced in Portugal since 2011, how large-scale events collide with biographical trajectories and the intersections where people practice their recuperation. Organised resistance to austerity has become an important focus of scholarship (e.g. Della Porta, 2015). However, much less attention has been paid to mechanisms developed by ordinary and unorganised citizens in order to deal with imminent scarcity and diminished democracy. This volume fills in the gap, since those mechanisms constitute micro-spaces of both resistance and resilience that operate in the private sphere, yet filter up to the macro. Here, I use the term 'micro-spaces of resilience' conceptualise non-confrontational forms of dealing with neoliberalism that are not the product of well-planned and organised resistance, but rather the result of quotidian attempts at dealing with growing ontological insecurity through different social intersections.

These mechanisms are used not only by isolated individuals but also by small groups (e.g. families, networks of friends and neighbours). These acts are mainly the result of reactive behaviour and learned experience to and of daily and banal acts of scarcity, and thus are not programmed beforehand. Further, they reach for cultural resources from the past – recuperation – in order to make sense of the present and relocate the future. Although not all contributions conform exclusively to the private sphere and the importance of households as units of recuperation and social systems of care (also affected, yet strongly resilient), nonetheless all touch various domains (material, relational, spatial, embodied) of recuperation and self-worth initiatives as a way of negotiating the effects of austerity.

The mechanisms of resilience observed in the essays can be summarised as:

- dancing and reconnection (Livia Jiménez Sedano)
- reciprocal practices like the exchange of money and food, clientelism/patronage, communal solidarity (Ema Pires)
- informal makeshift housing (Giacomo Pozzi)
- religious rituals and objects (Inês Lourenço)
- advice, solidarity networks in the shape of urban social movement Habita (Luís Mendes and André Carmo)
- Fruta Feia food cooperative, aiming at reducing waste and fomenting new consumption practices (André Nóvoa)

- retrieval and reparation of everyday things (Francisco Martínez)
- artistic intervention (Chiara Pussetti and Vítor Barros)
- time bank, people's assembly, public debate and deliberating, demonetised transactions, intergenerational transmission of skills (Marcos Farias Ferreira and Francisco Martínez)
- standards and aims of folk art (Maria Manuela Restivo, Luciano Moreira and Nuno Marques)

However high the potential for recuperation and repair stemming from these micro-spaces of resistance and resilience may be, their use discloses a very important dimension of Portuguese democracy: an incomplete/deficient citizenship. In fact, what can be extracted from this volume, in conjunction with other literature on the Portuguese case (David, 2018a–b), is that resorting to inner domains of conscience has helped the Portuguese cope informally with the effects of austerity but has also deflected the majority of its population from active forms of citizenship that potentially involve major changes in the organisation of its political fabric. In comparison with other austerity-hit countries in the Eurozone periphery, where core political parties (the Greek Panhellenic Socialist Movement PASOK, or the Spanish Socialist Workers' Party, for example) have been sidelined by young and dynamic anti-austerity parties (like the Greek Syriza or Spanish Podemos), the Portuguese party system remained intact (Parker and Tsarouhas, 2018). This evidence is in line with previous literature on the apathy of the Portuguese population, which depicts its declining levels of voting turnout since the implementation of democracy in 1974 (Freire and Magalhães, 2002: 47–50). As Pedro Magalhães (2005) states, there has been no correlation between feeble support for the political class and the political parties and more adherence to alternative forms of political participation (other than representative democracy mechanisms like voting). The Portuguese have traditionally demonstrated their dissatisfaction by not voting for the incumbent party (ibid.). Intense social movement mobilisation in 2011–13 by Geração à Rasca (Desperate Generation) and Que se Lixe a Troika (Screw the Troika) remains an exception in a traditionally weak civil society, strongly dependent on political parties and institutional resources for the transformation of their demands into concrete policies (Accornero and Ramos Pinto, 2014; Lisi, 2013).

As shown by a wide range of contributions, recuperation is part of, but also goes beyond, the coping strategies displayed by people to locate and access increasingly elusive resources. This volume thus provides a much needed approach to the recuperative modes of overcoming the effects of multiple crises in Portugal, from which future literature could extract inspiration at the micro- and macro-levels – for instance, by asking in which way the European project can be recuperated, in relation to the defence of collective interest and drawing from past skills, social bonds and visions of the future.

References

Accornero, G. and P. Ramos Pinto (2014) '"Mild mannered"? Protest and mobilization in Portugal under austerity, 2010–2013', *West European Politics*, 38 (3): 491–515.
David, I. (ed.) (2018a) *Crisis, Austerity and Transformation: How Disciplinary Neoliberalism is Transforming Portugal*, Lanham, MD: Lexington.
David, I. (2018b) 'Portuguese democracy under austerity: Politics in exceptional times', in O. Parker and D. Tsarouhas (eds), *Crisis in the Eurozone Periphery – The Political Economies of Greece, Spain, Ireland and Portugal*. London: Palgrave McMillan, pp. 161–80.
Della Porta, D. (2015) *Social Movements in Times of Austerity*, Cambridge: Polity.
Freire, A. and P. Magalhães (2002) 'A abstenção portuguesa em perspectiva comparativa', *Eleições*, 7: 7–36.
Giddens, A. (1991) *Modernity and Self-Identity: Self and Society in the Late Modern Age*, Cambridge: Polity.
Guapo Costa, C. (2018) 'Portuguese economy: How (not) to get away with financial crises and economic adjustment programs', in I. David (ed.), *Crisis, Austerity and Transformation: How Disciplinary Neoliberalism is Transforming Portugal*, Lanham, MD: Lexington, pp. 3–24.
Lisi, M. (2013) 'Rediscovering civil society? Renewal and continuity in the Portuguese radical left', *South European Society and Politics*, 18 (1): 21–39.
Magalhães, P. (2005) 'Disaffected democrats: Political attitudes and political action in Portugal', *West European Politics*, 28 (5): 973–91.

Martínez, F. (2017) 'Waste is not the end: For an anthropology of care, maintenance and repair', *Social Anthropology*, 25 (3): 346–50.

Mendes, L. (2017) 'Gentrificação turística em Lisboa: neoliberalismo, financeirização e urbanismo austeritário em tempos de pós-crise capitalista 2008–2009', *Cadernos Metrópole*, 19 (39): 479–512.

Observatório da Emigração (2015) 'Estimativas globais'. Available at: http://observatorioemigracao.pt/np4/1315/ (accessed 27 April 2018).

Parker, O. and D. Tsarouhas (eds) (2018) *Crisis in the Eurozone Periphery: The Political Economies of Greece, Spain, Ireland and Portugal*, London: Palgrave McMillan.

Rede Europeia Anti-pobreza (2015) 'Indicadores sobre pobreza: dados europeus e nacionais, 29 October. Available at: http://www.eapn.pt/documento/468/indicadores-sobre-pobreza-dados-europeus-e-nacionais (accessed 27 April 2018).

SIC Notícias (2013) 'Taxa de desemprego em Portugal atingiu novo recorde de 17,8% em Abril', 31 May. Available at: http://sicnoticias.sapo.pt/economia/2013-05-31-taxa-de-desemprego-em-portugal-atingiu-novo-recorde-de-178-em-abril (accessed 27 April 2018).

Index

acceleration (social),10, 16, 95, 146–7, 181–3, 186–8, 193, 197, 201
   archaeology, 19
aesthetics 27, 57, 66, 68, 76, 107, 164
affect 4, 11–12, 19–21, 27, 65, 133, 164, 193–4, 197
art 68, 71, 101, 104, 107–9, 156, 174–9
   contemporary 6–7
   folk 171–3
   street 40, 102, 105, 114
   public 103
assemblage 5, 63, 70
austerity (policy, measures, conditions) 1–2, 11, 24–5, 29, 37–40, 47–9, 51, 65, 67, 81, 119, 126, 141, 144, 147, 150, 181, 190, 201, 208, 211–12, 218, 221–2
   chic 66
   neoliberal 183
   post 103, 105, 139
authenticity 165–7

bailarico 182–3, 196, 201
Berlin 10
biography 11, 18–19, 79, 222
   auto 212
   building 90–3
body 18, 20–1, 64, 78–9, 172, 181–2, 191–5
bonds 5, 25, 27, 29, 44, 48, 52, 133, 167, 195–6, 225

bricolage 84–6
   method 134
   social 120–3, 129, 132

care 4, 6–7, 18–19, 21–7, 39–40, 45–6, 78–9, 121, 140, 149, 167, 217
China (Chinese) 14
colonial (post) 3, 7, 27, 105, 156, 183, 193, 201, 209, 213
community 6–19, 25, 27–8, 38, 44, 52, 59, 79, 81, 84, 86, 89, 103–5, 108, 112–15, 120, 129–30, 150, 155–68, 182–4, 191, 194–7, 201

decay 23
dependence 42, 44, 50–2, 217
design 2, 25, 42, 80, 103–4, 111, 114, 119, 123, 126, 128, 133, 156, 172, 209, 221, 223
destruction 22, 61, 70, 76, 91, 93, 107, 143, 222
DIY (do-it-yourself) 28
Douglas, Mary 62, 67, 70

Estonia 8
Europe (southern, eastern) 14, 24, 28, 38–9, 49, 62, 82, 102, 107, 119, 141–3, 146, 156, 183, 191, 198, 200, 207–11, 216, 218, 225
   capital of culture 115
   EU 37, 46, 55, 177

INDEX

everyday 3, 5, 8, 22–3, 26–7, 59, 78, 103, 105, 107, 140, 181, 184, 191, 194, 199, 222
experimentation 21, 23, 80, 121, 126, 210, 215

feeling (collective, together) 4, 184
Food 38, 43–5, 51, 55, 60, 64, 67, 92, 130, 159, 164
   communal 25
   dumpster-diving 59
   fast 165
   healthy 63
   reaping 130
   waste 25–6, 56, 58–9, 70
frugality 2, 42, 66
future 3, 13, 15, 25–6, 47, 51–2, 77, 79, 156, 159, 161, 165, 168, 188, 222, 225

Gell, Alfred 156, 168
Georgia 8
gift 48, 216
globalisation 18, 115, 141

heritage 8, 109, 112–15, 164–7, 172–7
household 8, 16, 29, 59, 142, 223
hybrid 126, 131, 209

Indignados (15-M) 120, 184
infrastructure 1, 4, 25, 28, 77, 82, 87–9, 121, 128, 133, 211–16
   para 8
interstice 5, 81, 94, 120, 126, 131–3, 150, 213
intravention 121

Japan(ese) 61

kinship 3, 10, 16, 26, 28, 78, 92, 209, 216–17, 222

makeshift 42, 76, 84, 91, 123, 126, 133
   urbanism 78, 86, 93–4
making-do 8, 121
material culture 8, 26–7, 40, 155, 164–5
micro (politics, power) 5, 26, 79
modernity 183, 194, 197, 208–11
   modernisation 131
   modernism 64, 68, 71
museum 18, 107, 172, 177

patchwork 1–2, 61, 84, 133–4
peripherality 82, 105, 142, 149
photography 10, 105, 115
   camera 121
plastic 40–2
poverty 2, 41, 47, 108, 221
precarity 24, 27, 38, 41, 47, 50, 80

quality 28, 76, 86, 144, 147, 184

reciprocity 4–5, 26–8, 37, 42–52, 125, 213, 216
recycling 19, 52, 59, 128, 130
resilience 1, 23, 26, 127, 150, 223
resistance 40, 50–2, 81, 90, 104, 120 126, 132, 134, 150, 179, 213–14, 222
risk 41, 88, 107–9, 141, 185, 221
ritual 4, 14, 79, 123, 155, 161–5, 181, 190–3
rupture 5

sharing 27, 77, 109, 120, 123, 150, 165, 189
skills 5, 13, 18–22, 27, 37, 52, 80, 85, 129, 172, 225
Spain 126, 149, 184, 198, 200, 217
standard 24, 26, 47, 55–9, 62, 71, 115, 179, 211
sustainability (social, environmental, self) 2, 11,

22, 60, 63, 129, 132, 143, 168

technology 60, 66, 210–11
tinkering 126, 134
tourism 101, 104, 112–14, 135, 146, 171, 179, 209, 219
transgress 81, 86, 93, 130, 133
Troika 24, 37, 40, 46, 56, 144, 147, 184, 221

UK 156, 159, 216
uncertainty 26, 42, 47, 50–2, 187, 195

utopia 135

values 3, 10, 22, 27, 44, 63, 70, 79, 85, 144–6, 156, 165, 172, 183
vulnerability 4, 23, 27, 41, 50, 75, 79–82, 86, 123, 142, 148, 160

waste 16, 25, 55–64, 70, 75–6, 213
welfare 24, 28, 41, 51, 119, 142, 183, 210–12, 215–17